Catharina Day

SOUTHWEST

IRELAND

D0188371

Cadogan Books plc
London House, Parkgate Road, London SW11 4NQ, UK

Distributed in North America by
The Globe Pequot Press
6 Business Park Road, PO Box 833, Old Saybrook,
Connecticut 06475–0833

Book and cover design by Animage
Cover illustrations by Povl Webb
Maps © Cadogan Guides, drawn by Map Creation Ltd

Series Editors: Rachel Fielding and Vicki Ingle

Editing: Polly Phillimore
Updating: Jennifer Keegan
Proofreading: Linda McQueen
Indexing: Judith Wardman
Production: Rupert Wheeler Book Production Services

**A catalogue record for this book is available from the British Library
ISBN 0–94–7754–96–2**

Output by Bookworm Ltd, Manchester
Printed and bound in the UK by Redwood
Books Ltd on Grosvenor Woodfree

About the Author

Catharina Day comes from a long-established Irish family. She was born in Kenya but moved to County Donegal as a small child. She attended Derry High School before travelling to a convent boarding school, and then University in England. She was married in County Donegal and visits frequently with her husband and four children from her home in Scotland. She has compiled an anthology of Irish literature.

Acknowledgements

Numerous people have helped me compile this book, and to them I wish to say many thanks. It would take many pages to mention all but a few by name for through my researches on the guide I have met lots of delightful people who have given me an insight into their locality. In particular I would like to thank Bord Fáilte who have always been extremely generous with information, advice and goodwill. My family have over the years been very supportive and a great help. My mother has been an enthusiastic gatherer of information and her wide general knowledge has been invaluable. My sister Angelique has been a great help, as has my sister Georgina. My husband Simon has helped me in countless ways. I am indebted to the late Araminta Swiney who advised me on what to leave out, Emily Sheard for her work on the maps, John Colclough who recommended eating out and places to stay, Victoria Ingle who helped reshape the 2nd edition of Ireland and edited it, Rochelle Guillard and Dawn Harvey who coped with my infant twins and my three-year-old. Many thanks to Polly Phillimore who has edited this latest edition, and to Jennifer Keegan who has been a great help updating the practical information. Finally thanks to Paula Levy who first gave me the opportunity to explore and write about this lovely country.

About the Updater

Jennifer Keegan was born in Dublin of a French mother and Irish father. She studied languages at Trinity College and, after spending a year in Madrid, went to work for *Vogue* in London. In addition to writing film and travel pieces, she was responsible for the revision of the Cadogan Guide to New York. She currently lives in Ireland and is a presenter on a fashion programme for Irish television.

Updater's Acknowledgements

Many thanks to my parents for their tolerance and all those who helped with my travels and research—especially Justine Keane, Hilary Finlay, Gary Coyle, Kenneth Deale, Colm McGee, Norma and Brien Boyd—and also to project editor Polly Phillimore for all her patience and her cheerfulness.

Contents

History   67–98

Religion   99–108

County Limerick   109–22

County Kerry   123–48

To My Mother

You have chosen well if the southwest of Ireland is your destination. Ireland is the perfect place to take a holiday, and Cork, Kerry, Limerick and Clare make up a most beautiful and fascinating region. These counties, which comprise most of the province of Munster, are easily accessible from Shannon, Cork and Kerry airports, and they have all the attractions of this lovely island in abundance. The landscape is varied and unspoilt, the pace of life is relaxing, and the local people know how to make a stranger feel at home.

Introduction

Munster (*Cuige Mumhan*) is the largest province in Ireland and a mixture of everything you consider Irish: the purples of the mountains melt into chessboards of cornfields in which the stooks stand like golden pieces. Houses are whitewashed, glens are deep and the coastline made ragged by the force of the Atlantic, with sandy bays and rocky cliffs.

It is a land of extremes: a large, placid, fertile plain, brooding mountain scenery, luxurious vegetation, and harsh barren land. The stately River Shannon flows out to sea between County Clare and Country Limerick. The extreme southwest coast is swept by westerly gales, and trees have been distorted into bent and twisted shapes. The moonscape of the

Burren contrasts with the softness of Killarney; the dairy-land of the inland valleys contrasts with the thrashing sea around Dingle and the Iveragh Peninsula.

The Burren is the youngest landscape in Europe and its carboniferous limestone hills have been shaped by intense glaciation. Spring gentian, mountain avens, hoary primrose, milkwort and orchids are amongst the wonderful variety of plants that flourish here. A great collection of southern and northern plants grow together: the bog violet and arbutus in Kerry, and the alpine/arctic plants of the Burren. Wild goats still range the Burren and keep at bay the ever-invasive hazel scrub. The best time for the flowers is May.

This is the land of the Mumonians; the 'ster' suffix of Munster is a Scandinavian addition to the more ancient name of Muma. The people in the southwest are warm, relaxed and musical; they are also backward-looking and quarrelsome. The province as a whole has been described as a little England. The Anglo-Normans certainly had a part in moulding the towns, as did some of the adventurers of Elizabethan times, but Cork city is the creation of lively Irish minds; whether Celts or later arrivals, Cork people think their city ought to be the capital rather than Dublin!

There's a sense of separateness about the southwest and this has helped to develop a great mythological tradition, with mother-goddesses figuring prominently in legend and place-names. There is Aire of Knockaney in County Limerick, and Aoibhill of Crag Liath, who reappears in the 18th century to preside over the judgement in Brian Merriman's famous vision poem 'Midnight Court'. Anu is mother of the Gods, whose breasts are represented in the Pap Mountains on the Kerry border. Most primitive of all is the ancient Hag of Beare, who spans many centuries and to whose activities many megalithic monuments are attributed. She is variously known as Digde, Dige or Duinech, and we are told that she passed through seven periods of youth. She is also supposed to have written the marvellous 9th century poem 'The Hag of Beare', which is a lament for lost beauty, and the struggle between bodily pleasure and salvation through the Christian way of repentence:

> *Yet may this cup of whey*
> *O! Lord, serve as my ale-feast*
> *Fathoming its bitterness*
> *I'll learn that you know best.*

Also strong in the mythological tradition is Donn Forinne, the ancestor-God to whom all the Irish will journey after death. His house is believed to be on the summit of Knockfierna Hill, Co. Limerick.

The history of Ireland has been turbulent, and its telling fraught with prejudice and misunderstandings. But a fascinating thing to do is to approach it through its excellent literary tradition. Ireland had its Golden Age of learning roughly between the 6th and 11th centuries. Frank O'Connor described it as the civilization of 'the little monasteries'. The monks wrote down the Celtic oral culture, wrote poetry and honoured God during the Dark Ages, when the rest of the Continent was in the hands of the Barbarians. Ireland also had a strict bardic tradition in which members of the poets' guild studied for up to 12 years before they were qualified. From that disciplined environment came mature poetry as evocative and delicate as a Chinese poem: stirring epics such as 'The Tain', which chronicles the wars of a heroic race, and moving love laments. Most of us can only read these poems in translation from the Gaelic; luckily the translations by present-day Irish poets bring them close to us. The voice of the Gaelic poet comments and bemoans the destruction of the Gaelic ways from the 16th century onwards. From the 18th century, the ability of the Irish to express themselves in the language of the Saxon is apparent from the works of Jonathan Swift through to W. B. Yeats and the marvellous poets of today, such as Seamus Heaney. Poetry, the novel and theatre have continued to thrive since the heady days of cultural renaissance and the uprising against the British in 1916.

With your head full of myths, legends and literature, forget the sun culture and all its paraphernalia: travel with stout shoes, a warm jersey, and an eye tuned into beauty and history. There is no such thing as a tiresome, hot journey in the southwest. The climate is good and damp, the rainfall varies between 30in in parts to as much as 87in in Killarney, but the sunshine, when it comes, intensifies the already beautiful colours of the landscape. The roads are usually empty and traffic jams are still an exception. Do not rush, for if you do the charm of the countryside and its people will pass you by. The largest concentration of houses and cars is in the energetic and attractive city of Cork; its population is well over 150,000. It is built along the river Lee and the sheltered waters of Cork Harbour, and it stretches up the little hills around. It is a place of exuberant culture and business, and its natives have a great sense of humour about life and the ridiculous. At the other extreme are the wild and beautiful headlands of West Cork, Kerry and Clare, where you can lose yourself in the mountains and on the long white strands.

Wherever you go in the southwest, it is possible to stay in friendly, hospitable B&Bs or tranquil country houses where the proportions and the furnishings of the rooms are redolent of a more gracious age. Not only is the food delicious, and made from the freshest seafood, local meat, game and vegetables, you will also often find well-chosen wines and, of course, decent whiskey and beer. The owners and staff of these places are keen to help with any request you have, whether it's finding the origins of your great-granny or directing you to the best fishing, golf, beaches, crafts, and sites of historical interest.

It is so easy to travel in a country where you can explain your needs in English, and find yourself understood. Those dry archaeological and historical facts suddenly become much more fascinating when you can ask for the local version of events, and hear for yourself the wonderful stories which make up history. The way that the Irish speak is another pleasure in store for you. You will find a race who can express themselves with great character, humour and exactness.

When you are in Ireland, it is certain that the irritations and annoyances which accompany one through everyday life will disappear, and the desire for a good day's tramp in the mountains, a spot of fishing or a good read before a warm fire will become realities. However, it is important not to stick rigidly to a scheme and become irritated when it has to be delayed for a while, for nothing in Ireland can be planned right down to the last detail. Information can sometimes only be found out on the spot; and opening times, timetables and other schedules are more subject to change than in many other countries.

Guide to the Guide

After the following selection of the best of southwest Ireland, there is a comprehensive **Travel** section, followed by the **Practical A–Z** packed with information that will help you get the best from your visit, including advice on where to stay and eat, sports and leisure activities. The next section, **Topics**, gives brief insights into notable features of Ireland and Irish life which includes some fascinating pieces on the Fairy People, historic houses, gardens of the southwest, potatoes and the famine and the Burren, and even on how to trace your ancestors. The short and simple section on **History** from pagan times to the present day outlines the main events and problems that constitute the complex Ireland of today; this is followed by a brief résumé of the religious background and a selection of the country's most famous saints.

The southwest of Ireland is made up of the four counties Cork, Kerry, Limerick and Clare. Each chapter constitutes a gazetteer of the whole county with lots of local history and anecdotal knowledge together with descriptions and details of the places of interest. Full, practical lists of transport facilities, tourist information centres and festivals are given at the beginnings of each county section, with shopping and leisure activities, places to stay and eat and entertainment possibilities at the end of each county.

At the end of the book there are features on the **Old Gods and Heroes**, ancient sites and early architecture (with a glossary of terms); an essay on **Language**; a **Chronology**; a recommended **Further Reading** list; and a comprehensive index.

Ruined Friaries and Churches

Killaloe, Co. Clare
Dysert O Dea, Co. Clare
Ardfert, Co. Kerry
Oratory of Gallarus, Co. Kerry
Adare, Co. Limerick

Castles

Blarney Castle, Co. Cork
Bunratty Castle, Co. Clare
King John's Castle, Co. Limerick

Fine Houses

Bantry Bay House, Co. Cork
Muckross House and Abbey, Co. Kerry
Glin Castle, Co. Limerick
Derrynane House, Co. Kerry

Gardens

Inacullin (Garinish Island), Co. Cork
Creagh, Co. Cork
Derreen Woodland, Co. Kerry
Annes Grove, Co. Cork
Glens of Clare, Co. Limerick

Beaches

Ventry Beach, Co. Kerry
Inch Strand, Co. Kerry
Derrynane Strand, Co. Kerry
White Strand, Co. Kerry

Golf Courses

Lahinch, Co. Clare
Ballybunion, Co. Kerry
Adare, Co. Limerick
Tralee, Co. Kerry
Fota Island, Co. Cork

Views

Gap of Dunloe, Co. Kerry
View from Mount Gabriel, near Schull, Co. Cork
View from Cathedral top in Killaloe, Co. Clare

Cliffs of Moher, Co. Clare
Moll's Gap, Co. Kerry
Bantry Bay, Co. Cork

Restaurants

Sheen Falls Lodge, Kenmare
Arbutus Lodge, Cork
Cliffords, Co. Cork
Shiro Japanese Dinner House, Ahakista, Nr Bantry
Lettercollum House, Timoleague
Ballymaloe House, Shanagarry
Aherne's Pub and Seafood Bar, Youghal
The Park Hotel, Kenmare

Places to Stay

Ballyvolane House, Castlelyons, Co. Cork
Old Presbytery, Kinsale; John and Anne Sims, Lisdoonvarna
Ballymaloe House, Shanagarry
Bantry House, Bantry Bay
Adare Manor, Adare
Doyle's Townhouse, Dingle
Assolas Country House, Kanturk, Co. Cork

Please Note

The reader will find that there are occasions when place names vary in spelling from those in this guide book. This is because different translations from the Gaelic exist; there is no completely standardized map to follow. Bartholomews, Ordnance Survey, the RAC and the AA produce very good and detailed maps.

Travel

From Europe

British Airways, British Midland, Crossair, Air France, Ryanair, Intermanx, City Jet, TAP Air Portugal, Sabena, Swiss Air, SAS (Scandinavian Airlines), **Lufthansa** and **Iberia** run regular scheduled flights from European capitals and major cities. The Irish national airline, **Aer Lingus**, also handles an enormous number of flights from European destinations, and, if you are going to immerse yourself in all things Irish, you might as well start with this airline, with its air hostesses dressed in green. For flight reservations and information in London, call ✆ (0181) 569 5555.

There are direct flights to Cork, Shannon and Dublin from the four main **London** airports (Heathrow, Gatwick, Luton and Stansted). But there are additional flights to certain cities from British regional airports. **Ryanair**, for example, has regular flights from Liverpool, Manchester and Birmingham to Dublin. For Ryanair in London, call ✆ (0171) 435 7101.

Prices are always in a state of flux but are reasonable by European standards. There is a bewildering array of price structures. As a guideline, SuperApex prices for return flights from London to Cork cost around £80, to Shannon £80 and to Dublin around £60 to £90.

The major airlines also offer a wide variety of holiday-break fares, where the price of the flight depends on how long you stay and when you travel. You can save a lot of money on these, so it is worth checking out the possibilities.

From the USA and Canada

The main airports for transatlantic flights are **Shannon** and **Dublin** which are served by direct scheduled flights from Atlanta, Boston, Chicago, Montreal and New York. The main transatlantic carriers flying direct to Ireland are **Delta Air Lines**, **Aer Lingus** and **Tower Air** who now fly two scheduled flights per week via Newark, but of course many others fly to European destinations, where you can pick up connecting flights.

Since **prices** are constantly changing and there are numerous kinds of deals on offer, the first thing to do is find yourself a travel agent who is capable of laying the current options before you. The time of year you choose can make a great difference to the price and availability of tickets. Expect to pay more and to have to book earlier if you want to travel between June and August. Apex and SuperApex are the most reliable and flexible of the cheap fares. New York to Shannon or Dublin return on an Apex fare ranges from about US$480 in the winter, to US$580 in the shoulder seasons, and US$695 in mid-summer. A number of companies offer cheaper charter flights to Ireland—look in the Sunday travel section of *The New York Times*. Remember to read all the small print as there are often catches, such as big cancellation penalties, restrictions about changing the dates of your flights; and sometimes charter contracts include provisions that allow charter companies to cancel your flight, change the dates of travel and add fuel surcharges after you have paid your fare. If you are considering travelling to Cork or Shannon via Dublin, it is cheaper to buy a ticket which includes the additional flight with the transatlantic flight, rather than pay for the second stage of the journey separately.

Shannon Airport is a free-port offering a huge variety of duty-free goods plus a selection of Irish specialities: cut crystal glass, Connemara rugs and marble, Donegal tweed, smoked salmon etcetera. If you do not want to get burdened with lots of presents and packages during your stay in Ireland, you can get everything here at the last minute. Goods bought in the duty-free area just before take-off will be taken on the plane without any extra weight charges. Information on transport and accommodation is available at the **tourist offices** at all the major airports, open all the year round.

transport from the airports

Buses and trains run between the main airports and city centres. They are comfortable, frequent and economic; taxi drivers, by contrast, tend to ask a dramatically high price for a ride into the city. Irish Bus runs a service between Cork Airport and Cork City every 20 minutes; the fare is IR£1.75 one way, and from Shannon Airport to Limerick, the nearest city, 15 miles (25km) away (IR£3.30). Dublin Bus runs a similar service between Dublin Airport and the Central Bus Station (IR£2.50).

By Boat

Gone are the days when you could cross the Atlantic by **liner**. The only regular, scheduled sea-crossings to Ireland these days come from Great Britain and continental Europe. The one exception is Cunard Line's *QE2*, which occasionally stops off to pick up travellers at Cork (Cobh) on its way from Southampton to New York, but not on its way back. This has style, but at a price: Cork to New York costs a minimum of £1095 per passenger.

The only way to get directly to the southwest of Ireland by ferry is from Swansea in South Wales to Cork. Cork also has ferry services to Le Havre and Roscoff in northern France, and there is a service between Rosslare and Le Havre. The **ferries** from the British west coast tend to cross the Irish Sea in the shortest distance possible: from the points along the coasts of Wales and Scotland which stretch out furthest towards the east coast of Ireland. Which port and crossing you choose will depend on where you are starting from, and where you wish to go in Ireland – which is not quite such an obvious statement as it may seem. The main crossings are as follows: Fishguard and Pembroke in South Wales serve Rosslare Harbour (near Wexford) and southeast Ireland. Holyhead, off Anglesey in North Wales, takes passengers to Dublin and the neighbouring port of Dun Laoghaire, in the centre of the east coast. Since early 1994 this route is also served by a high-speed **catamaran** which crosses the Irish Sea in one hour and 50 minutes. Northern Ireland has two main ports: Belfast and nearby Larne, which are served by ferries and the sea cat taking the short crossing from Cairnryan and neighbouring Stranraer in southwest Scotland, and by ferries taking the much longer journey from Liverpool. There is also a seasonal service to the Isle of Man from Dublin.

All the ferry ports are well connected to bus and rail transport (*see* pp.5–6), and all the ferry services have drive-on/drive-off facilities for car drivers.

Prices depend very much on the time of year and the length of the crossing. Price structures also relate to how long you intend to stay in Ireland and, if you are taking your car, the number of passengers in the car, the length of the car, and so forth. To give you some idea of costs, here are a few examples. Figures quoted are for 1 adult, 2 adults and a car or 4 adults and a car. The upper and lower estimates are for high and low season respectively. On the Swansea/Cork ferry prices vary between £80 and £159; with P&O, crossing from Cairnryan to Larne in Northern Ireland, passengers pay £20 to £22 each way; cars cost from £137 to £170 each way including 2 adults; but there are also special 60hr and 120hr excursion fares. On Sealink's service between Fishguard and Rosslare in the Republic, passengers pay £17 to £23 each way; cars cost £74 to £175 each way, but this price includes up to four people travelling with the car. The Sealink Catamaran costs approximately £5 more for passengers and £18 more for a car. Passenger fares for children are approximately half the adult fare.

Crossings from France are rather more expensive. Le Havre to Rosslare with Irish Ferries costs IR£57–IR£82 for one adult, IR£215–£490 for two adults and a car, and IR£266–£375 for four adults and a car. These prices are one-way.

ferry services

From Great Britain

Swansea Cork Ferries, Swansea, ✆ (01792) 456116; Cork ✆ (021) 271166:

> **Swansea–Cork**, 1 sailing every other day in each direction 10hrs (overnight crossing from Swansea).

Irish Ferries, Dublin, ✆ (01) 661 0511; London, ✆ (0171) 499 5744; Liverpool, ✆ (0151) 2273131):

> **Holyhead–Dublin**, 2 sailings daily, all year, 3¼hrs, ✆ (0171) 734 4681.

> **Pembroke–Rosslare**, 2 sailings daily, 21 May–1 Oct; 1 sailing daily rest of year, 4¼hrs.

Sealink British Ferries Ashford, Kent, ✆ (01233) 647022; Dublin, ✆ (01) 280 0338/ 280 8844:

> **Holyhead–Dun Laoghaire**, 4 sailings daily, all year (excluding 25–26 Dec), 3½hrs, plus 2 catamaran sailings.

> **Fishguard–Rosslare**, 2 sailings daily, 3½hrs (excluding 25–26 Dec).

Isle of Man Steam Packet Company, Douglas, ✆ (0624) 661661:

> **Isle of Man–Dublin**, mid-May–mid-Sept, 4½hrs (contact operators for schedule); Sea Cat, 2hrs 40mins.

> **Isle of Man–Belfast**, mid-May–mid-Sept, 5hrs; Sea Cat, 2hrs 40mins.

To Northern Ireland from Great Britain

Sealink British Ferries, Ashford, Kent, ℗ (01233) 647022):

> **Stranraer–Larne**, 9–10 sailings daily, all year (excluding 25–26 Dec and 1 Jan), 2hrs 20mins.

P & O European Ferries, Cairnryan, ℗ (01581) 200276; London, ℗ (0181) 575 8555; Larne (01574) 274321:

> **Cairnryan–Larne**, 6 sailings daily, all year, 2¼hrs.

Norse Irish Ferries, Belfast, ℗ (01232) 779090:

> **Liverpool–Belfast**, 1 sailing every other evening, all year, 11hrs.

Seacat, Dublin, ℗ (01) 661 1731 (from mid-Feb '95):

> **Belfast–Stranraer**, 4 sailings daily, all year, 1½hrs.

From France

Irish Ferries, Dublin, ℗ (01) 661 0511; Le Havre, ℗ (35) 22 50 28; Cherbourg, ℗ (33) 44 28 96:

> **Le Havre–Cork**, 1 sailing per week, summer only, 21½hrs.
>
> **Roscoff–Cork**, 1 to 3 sailings per week during summer months, 16hrs.
>
> **Roscoff–Rosslare**, 1 to 3 sailings per week during summer months, 16hrs.
>
> **Le Havre–Rosslare**, 2 to 3 sailings per week, all year, 21hrs.
>
> **Cherbourg–Rosslare**, 1 to 2 sailings per week, all year, 18hrs.

Britanny Ferries, Cork ℗ (021) 277801; Roscoff ℗ (98) 29 28 00:

> **Roscoff–Cork**, 1 sailing per week, Mar–Oct only, 14hrs.

By Train

All the car ferries crossing back and forth between England and Ireland are scheduled to link up with the **British Rail InterCity trains** which go frequently and speedily from London to Fishguard, Liverpool, Holyhead and Stranraer. You can buy your **ticket** at any British Rail station or booking office; credit card bookings can be made on the telephone, on London ℗ (0171) 387 7070. There are free **seat reservations** on all direct train services to and from the ports. You can get couchettes on the night trains, but when it is not crowded it is possible to have a comfortable snooze by stretching out along the seats.

London (Paddington) to Cork via Swansea takes 13 hrs, London (Euston) to Dublin via Liverpool/Dublin and Holyhead/Dun Laoghaire Port takes 11hrs. Adult single **fares** for London to Cork are around IR£70 each way, and between London and Dublin £39–£49.

Travelling by bus/ferry to the southwest of Ireland is quite an endurance test because the journey seems endless, with lots of stops through England and Ireland to pick up other travellers. The main advantage is that it is cheap and gets you straight to destinations in the provinces, so that you do not have to get other buses, trains and taxis on arrival in Ireland. The small coaches to-ing and fro-ing across the Irish Sea are very flourishing private enterprises in the hands of local individuals. They leave all parts of Ireland for the chief cities of England, Scotland and Wales, full to the brim with Irish returning to work or coming home on leave. You will not find details of the smaller companies at your travel agent; look instead at the back of Irish newspapers which you can buy fairly easily in Britain.

Of the major bus companies, **Irish Bus** and **National Express** (Supabus) run regular services between all parts of Ireland and Great Britain. National Express buses leave London from the Victoria Coach Station, ✆ (0171) 730 0202. Bus Eireann can be contacted at the headquarters in Dublin, ✆ (01) 830 2222. **Slattery's**, a major private bus company based in Tralee, can be contacted in Dublin, ✆ (01) 661 1366; and also at their coach terminal in London, ✆ (0171) 730 0202.

London to Cork via Swansea takes about 14 hours and costs around £54 return. London to Dublin via Holyhead takes about 12 hours and costs around £16 single, £29 return at off-peak times for day sailings; £36 single, £55 return at peak periods.

Student and Youth Fares

If you can produce an **International Student Identity Card**, you can expect to get discounts of at least 25% on standard passenger rates for travel. For air travellers, there are student/youth rates for flights between Britain and Ireland, and similar concessions for transatlantic flights. In London, contact Campus Travel, ✆ (0171) 730 3402; or STA Travel Ltd, ✆ (0171) 581 1022.

With an ISIC, you can also buy a **Travelsave Stamp** for £7, which gets you some big savings: 50% off single adult tickets on Irish Ferries crossings between Britain and Ireland, a discount off mainline rail fares in Ireland, and 50% off single adult CIE provincial bus journeys The Stamp is available from **Campus Travel** (*see* above) and also from the **USIT** (The Union of Students International Travel) in Limerick at Central Buildings, O'Connell St, ✆ (661) 415064, or from any student travel offices at Irish universities.

Tour Operators

There are literally hundreds of tour companies offering all manner of enticing holidays in Ireland. Both Bord Fáilte and the Northern Ireland Tourist Board have lists of the main operators, which are published in their brochures. Alternatively, contact your travel agent.

Special-interest Holidays

Travellers who want holidays with a special focus—ancestor-hunting, angling, bird-watching, farm and country, gastronomy, gardens, golf, horse-riding, sailing, a mixture of these or none of them—are particularly well catered for in Ireland. The main specialist holiday companies are listed in the tourist board brochures. Bord Fáilte also has a *Learning for Leisure* brochure which gives details of organizations offering holidays 'designed to enable participants to acquire new leisure skills—sports, gardening, cookery, arts and crafts, etc. in a relaxed and green environment'. We can also recommend the following specialist organizations, based in Ireland:

Irish **Cycling** Safaris Ltd (7 Dartry Park, Dublin 6, or UCD Belfield Campus, *℗* (01) 260 0749) offer leisurely one-week cycling holidays covering Cork and Kerry.

Irish **Country** Holidays is a grouping of local communities which offer the visitor a chance to live as part of a rural community. You can spend your week in Ballyhoura, County Limerick, the Barrow/Nore area, Lough Corrib country, and West Cork. Each community has something special to offer in the way of landscape, customs and amenities. Contact the Ballyhoura Fáilte Society, Kilfinane, Co. Limerick, *℗* (063) 91300; Bord Fáilte, PO Box 273, Dublin 8; or Plunkett House, 84 Merrion Square, Dublin 2, *℗* (01) 676 5796.

Celtic Nature Expeditions, Michael & Becky O'Connor, The Old Stone House, Dingle, Co. Kerry, *℗* (066) 59882. **Sailing and walking** holidays.

Lastly, John Nicholas Colclough runs fascinating, informative **tours** anywhere in Ireland. He will tailor an itinerary to suit you, organize a car with a guide/driver, and superb accommodation ranging from the traditional farmhouse to the grandest castle. His tours can take in gardens, genealogy, ghosts, gourmet meals, and sites of historical importance. He will act as guide himself—and you cannot find anyone more engaging and informative. He is prepared to investigate any obscure angle on Ireland that you may wish to pursue. Contact Colclough Tours, 71 Waterloo Road, Dublin 4, *℗* (01) 668 6463.

See also the 'Summer Schools' section in **Practical A–Z**, p.37.

Entry Formalities

Passports and Visas

British citizens travelling from Britain do not require a **passport** to enter the **Republic**. All the same, it can be useful to take a passport or some form of identification with you for completing formalities, such as hiring a car. **Citizens of the USA and Canada** must have a valid passport to enter the Republic, but no visa is required.

Citizens of **European Union** (EU) countries need a full passport for entry.

Passports and visas may be required for visitors of countries not included in the above. Check with your nearest Bord Fáilte office or with the visa departments of the Irish or British embassies. In any case, entry regulations are liable to change, so if you are in any doubt, check before you leave.

Customs

As usual, there are restrictions on the quantities of certain goods you are allowed to bring into the Republic.These apply to cigarettes and other tobacco products, alcoholic drinks, perfume and gifts and other new goods. The regulations are labyrinthine, since they differ according to whether or not you are resident in the EU, and whether or not the goods were bought in EU countries. Furthermore, EU residents have to take into account two separate structures, one for goods bought in duty-free shops in the EU, and another for goods bought, tax-paid, in an EU country.

To ensure that you have up-to-date information, it is better that you refer to to the tourist offices, airlines and ferry services. However, the **customs regulations** are standard, and, provided that you are seventeen years old or more, you can be sure of being allowed to import at least two hundred cigarettes, 50 cigars, one litre of spirits or two litres of wine and 50 grams of perfume; depending on where you live and where you bought your goods, you may be able to import rather more than this. Note also that in the Republic you are only meant to import other dutiable goods (such as watches and cameras) to a value of IR£34 (goods bought in EU countries, tax-paid, IR£302). If you are carrying used goods that look brand new, it is as well to bring receipts.

Dog- and cat-owners may like to know that they can bring their pet to Ireland, provided that it comes directly from Britain, the Channel Islands or the Isle of Man, and it has lived there for at least six months.

For residents of Britain and other EU countries, the usual EU regulations apply regarding what you can bring into your home country. Again, this depends on whether the goods have been bought in Ireland itself, tax-paid, or in a duty-free shop. Note that you cannot bring fresh meat, vegetables or plants into the UK.

Residents of the USA may each take home US$400 worth of foreign goods without attracting duty, including the tobacco and alcohol allowance. Canadians can bring home $300-worth of goods in a year, plus their tobacco and alcohol allowances.

You can claim back the **Value Added Tax** (VAT) on goods purchased in Ireland and exported by you, provided that you export them within two months of purchase and that their total value exceeds IR£50 (or IR£102 if you are resident in another EU country). The VAT rate is approx 21% since March 1993. You will need a **Cashback voucher** stamped by the shop; this must be stamped by customs before you leave Ireland. You can present the stamped vouchers at the Cashback desk at Shannon or Dublin airports and obtain a refund there and then, or you can claim the refund by post after your return.

Getting Around

By Air

It is quite possible to fly from one city to another in Ireland; but this is a small island and the main destinations are adequately covered by rail and bus, so internal air travel is mainly for the traveller under pressure. **Aer Lingus** and **Ryanair** run flights from Cork and Shannon to Dublin.

By Train

In the Republic, domestic train routes are operated by the Irish Rail arm of **CIE** (*Coras Iopair Eireann*), the national transport company which also runs a bus network to most parts of the Republic. The system is rather like the British system of 40 years ago, with the old signal boxes which still need humans to operate them and keep an eye on things. People are always friendly on trains and the ticket inspectors are far from officious. Services are reliable, and the fares are reasonable. It is generally much cheaper to buy a return ticket than two singles. Best value of all, however, are the special rail cards, allowing unlimited travel over a given period of time (*see* below).

For **information about Irish Rail services**, ✆ Dublin (01) 836 6222. There is a CIE office in Croydon, UK, ✆ (0181) 680 3226; and also in New Jersey, USA, ✆ (201) 292 3899.

Special Rail Tickets

There are a number of ways to make good advantage of Ireland's public transport systems through specially priced rail cards. For student fares, *see* p.6.

Irish Explorer for Rail and Bus:	Allows you to travel 8 days out of 15. This ticket costs £90.
Irish Explorer for Rail Only:	5 days' travel over 15 days. This ticket costs £60.
Irish Rover:	An all-Ireland ticket which allows you up to 5 days' travel over 15 days costing £75.
Emerald Card:	15 days' travel over 30 days on Bus/Rail for IR£180. There is also an 8-day version which allows 8 days' travel out of 15. This costs IR£105. Children's tickets are all half-price.

Ireland is now part of the **Eurail Pass** network which allows unlimited rail travel on European railways including the Republic of Ireland, but excluding the UK and Northern Ireland. To obtain a pass you must be a resident of a non-European country and buy your pass outside Europe. Prices in Irish punts for under 26/over 26 are as follows: 15 days' travel IR£321–IR£402, 21 days IR£522, 1 month IR£466–IR£643, 2 months IR£619–IR£885. There are also special youth rates for anyone up to 26 years old. With a Eurail Pass you can also go from France to Ireland free on the ferry, provided you do not pass through Britain.

By Bus

The **bus service** throughout Ireland is efficient and goes to the most remote places. The main companies are **Irish Bus** (or *Bus Eireann*), run by CIE, in the Republic. Freelance operators also run many tours. Prices are reasonable. For example, Cork to Limerick £9, Killarney to Tralee £4.40.

In the Republic the main routes are covered by **Expressway** bus services. For details get in touch with Bus Eireann, Dublin, ✆ (01) 836 6111.

You can pick up a Provincial Bus and Expressway Timetable at CIE or tourist offices and at some newspaper stands. Note that, in the Republic, bus destinations posted on the front of the bus are often given in Irish. If in doubt, ask.

Special Bus Tickets

For concessionary tickets applying to both bus and rail, *see* the 'Special Rail Tickets' section, above.

Travelsave Stamps can also be used for certain bus services (*see* p.6).

By Car

To explore the southwest of Ireland with minimum effort and maximum freedom, bring a car. If you fill it up with people who share the ferry and petrol costs, it won't be too expensive. Buy a detailed **road map** and, if you have time, choose the minor roads and just meander. It is along these little lanes that the secret life of the southwest of Ireland continues undisturbed. The black and red cows still chew by the wayside whilst the herdsman, usually an old man or a child, salutes you with an upward nod. Nearby is the farmstead cluttered with bits of old machinery and a cheerful sense of makeshift, where everything is kept to be used again: an old front door will stop a gap in the hedge; old baths serve as cattle troughs; clucking hens roost on the old haycart—next year it might be bought by the tinkers, who will varnish it up to adorn some suburban garden. You will come upon castles, and the ruins of the small, circular buildings called *clochans*, still breathing with memories, tumbled even further by the local farmer in search of stone; and there are views of those many hills which have never reached the pages of any guidebook. One of the best things about driving in Ireland is the lack of other cars and the absence of ugly, if efficient motorways with their obligatory motor inns and petrol stations.

Beware of the country driver who tends to drive right in the middle of the road, never looks in his mirror to see if anyone is behind, and is unlikely to indicate if he suddenly decides to turn left or right. Beware of drivers wearing an old tweed cap—they are usually the worst offenders. Then you get the other extreme with crazy speeds on narrow roads. Cars frequently pull out of a side-road in front of you and, just as you are getting up enough steam to pass, suddenly decide to turn off down another side-road again. Don't be alarmed by the sheepdogs which appear from every cottage door to chase your car—they are well skilled at avoiding you.

If your car **breaks down** you will always be able to find a mechanic to give you a hand; whether it's late at night or on a Sunday, just ask someone. He or she will sweep you up in a wave of sympathy and send messengers off in all directions to find you someone with a reputation for mechanical genius. If it is some small and common part that has let you down, he will either have it or do something that will get you by until you come to a proper garage. One thing you will notice is that the Irish have a completely different attitude to machinery from most nationalities. In England, if you break down, it is an occasion for embarrassment; everybody rushes by hardly noticing you or pretending not to. In Ireland, if your car has broken down the next passing car will probably stop, and the problem will be readily taken on and discussed with great enjoyment. The Irish can laugh at the occasional failure of material affairs.

Facts and Formalities for Car Drivers

You **drive on the left** (when you are not driving in the middle of the road). **Petrol stations** stay open until around eight in the evenings, and the village ones are open after Mass on Sundays. If you are desperate for petrol and every station seems closed, you can usually knock on the door and ask somebody to start the pumps for you. Petrol is around 60p per litre. The **speed limit** is 62mph (99kph) on all roads and 30mph or 40mph (48kph or 64kph) through the villages and towns.

Drivers and front-seat passengers must always wear a **seat belt**—it is illegal not to. Children under 12 should travel in the back. There are strict drink-driving laws and the police will use a breathalyzer test if they suspect that you are driving under the influence of alcohol.

There are some excellent **motoring maps**: Bartholomew's ¼-inch, obtainable from the AA and Bord Fáilte, gives good details of minor roads. The old system of T (trunk) and L (link) routes is currently being altered to N (national) and R (regional), and you are liable to encounter both systems for a while yet. Scenic routes are signposted and marked on the Bord Fáilte map. Place names on signposts in the Republic are usually given in English and in Irish; in the places where Irish only is used a good map will be useful. The old white signposts give distances in miles; the new green ones give distances in kilometres. All other traffic signs are more or less the same as the standard European ones.

Car parking in Cork city centre is controlled by a disc system. Parking discs can be bought, usually in books of ten, at shops and garages near the car parks. Unexpired time on a parking disc can be used at another parking place.

Car Hire Operators

These are only some of the big ones who will meet you at the airports and the ferry ports.

Avis Rent-A-Car Ltd, Shannon ✆ (061) 471 094; Cork ✆ (021) 281 166; Dublin ✆ (01) 677 4010.

Budget Rent-A-Car, Shannon ✆ (061) 471 361; Cork ✆ (021) 314 000; Dublin ✆ (01) 844 5919.

Hertz Rent-A-Car, Shannon ✆ (061) 471 369; Cork ✆ (021) 965 849; Dublin ✆ (01) 844 5466.

Murray's Europcar, Shannon ✆ (061) 471 165; Cork ✆ (021) 966 198; Dublin ✆ (01) 668 1777.

For further details contact the **Car Rental Council**, 5 Upper Pembroke St, Dublin 2, ✆ (01) 676 1690.

Local firms (consult the phone book) can offer even better deals. That said, renting a car in Ireland is never cheap. You might be able to bargain slightly if business is slack. Prices start at around IR£185 per week. Look out also for fly-drive, or rail-sail-drive packages offered by some of the airlines and ferry companies: these usually represent major savings. Note that to hire a car you should normally be over 23, and should in possession of a licence which you have held for at least two years without endorsement. The car hire company will organize insurance, but do check this. If you do not take extra collision-damage waiver insurance you can be liable for damage up to IR£1350.

By Bicycle

The southwest of Ireland is one of the pleasantest places to cycle in. The roads are uncrowded, there are still lots of birds and animals that live around the hedgerows, and there is no pollution to spoil the illusion of rural Ireland. In between the delicious whiffs of gorse or honeysuckle will come strong manure smells! You can bring your bicycle free on the ferry, or you can rent one. There is a **Raleigh Rent-A-Bike** network, with centres throughout the southwest. Prices begin at about IR£7 per day, IR£30 per week, with a deposit of at least IR£40. Tandems, racing bikes and ordinary touring bikes are available. For full details get the *Cycling Ireland* leaflet from the nearest Bord Fáilte office; this gives details of the main hire companies, lists Irish cycling holiday specialists, and also suggests a number of routes.

On Foot

From all accounts hitch-hiking seems to be a safe but rather slow method of transport. You will see more cows and sheep wandering along the minor roads than cars. On major roads, write your destination on a bit of cardboard and hold it up. You will find you have to compete with local people who hitch regularly from town to town.

Practical A–Z

Children

If you are travelling with children you will find that bed and breakfast establishments will welcome them. Many have family rooms with four or five beds, and charge a reduced price for children. Most supply cots and high chairs, and offer a baby-sitting service, but always check beforehand. Some farm and country houses keep a donkey or pony, and have swings and a play area set up for children.

Irish people love children, and are very tolerant of seeing and hearing them in bars and eating places during the daytime. They will offer children's menus at a cheaper price and generally be helpful, but they will not be so tolerant if you turn up with them for dinner at night. If you are contemplating staying in some of the smart country-house hotels which are full of precious antiques, etcetera, please check that it is a suitable place for children in advance. The many national monuments, heritage centres, gardens and parks usually charge much less for children or offer a family ticket which is cheaper.

Climate

Ireland lies on the path of the North Atlantic cyclones, which makes the climate mild, equable and moist. In the southwest, rainfall is heaviest in the coastal areas, where it averages over 80 inches (203cm) a year. Rain is the country's blessing, yet from the reputation it has in its own country and abroad you might imagine it was a curse. It keeps the fields and trees that famous lush green, and the high level of water vapour in the air gives it a sleepy quality and softens the colours of the landscape. The winds from the east increase the haziness and mute the colours, but these are nearly always followed by winds from the northwest which bring clearer air and sunshine. So the clouds begin to drift and shafts of changing light touch the land. Nearly every drizzly day has this gleam of sunshine, which is why the Irish are always very optimistic about the weather. The Gulf Stream in the Atlantic means that there are never extremes of cold or hot.

Snow is not common, and is seldom severe. The spring tends to be relatively dry, especially after the blustery winds of March, and the crisp colours and freshness of autumn only degenerates into the cold and damp of winter in late December. You can hope for at least six hours of sunshine a day over most of the country during May, June, July and August.

Average Temperatures

January	4°C (39°F)	–	7°C (45°F)
July/August	14°C (57°F)	–	24°C (75°F)

Disabled Travellers

A considerable effort has been made to help handicapped travellers and Bord Fáilte has produced useful booklets containing advice. One of these publications, *Accommodations for the Disabled*, is updated annually. In Britain, RADAR (Royal Association for Disability and Rehabilitation), Unit 12 City Forum, 250 City Road, London EC1V 8AF, © (0171)

250 3222, is an excellent source of advice, and publishes its own fact sheets on holiday planning, accommodation and so forth, and fuller guides for the disabled traveller for the UK and abroad. The Holiday Care Service, 2 Old Bank Chambers, Station Road, Horley, Surrey RH6 9HW, ✆ (01293) 774535 offers advice for all travellers with special needs, and publishes a short information sheet on the Irish Republic.

Electricity

The current is 220 volts AC, so you should bring an adaptor if you have any American appliances. Wall sockets take the standard British-style three-pin (flat) fused plugs, or two-pin (round) plugs. If you are worried, there are good travellers' adaptors on the market which can usually cope with most socket-and-plug combinations that you are liable to encounter abroad.

Embassies and Consulates

British Embassy, 31 Merrion Road, Dublin 4, ✆ (01) 269 5211.

US Embassy (Dublin), 43 Elgin Road, Dublin 4, ✆ (01) 668 8777.

US Consulate (Belfast), 14 Queen's Street, Belfast BT1 6EG, ✆ (01232) 328239.

USTAA, American Embassy, Grosvenor Square, London W1A 1AE, ✆ (0891) 616000.

Canadian Embassy, 65 St Stephen's Green, Dublin 2, ✆ (01) 4781988.

Canadian High Commission, 38 Grosvenor Street, London W1, ✆ (0171) 629 9492.

Australian Embassy, Fitzwilton House, Wilton Terrace, Dublin 2, ✆ (01) 676 1517.

Australian High Commission, Australia House, Strand, London WC2 B4L, ✆ (0171) 379 4334.

New Zealand High Commission, New Zealand House, 80 Haymarket, London SW1Y 4TQ, ✆ (0171) 930 8422.

Fishing

We are grateful to Antony Luke for the following personal account. Antony has been returning on holiday to Ireland since 1963. He acts as a consultant on fishing matters to the corporate entertainment company Country & Highland, gives fly-fishing instruction,  *and organises salmon-fishing parties. He has a cottage on one of the northern isles of Orkney where he keeps a lobster boat, and from where he runs a successful business exporting fish and shellfish. Thanks also to Peter O'Reilly for his help with the updating of this section.*

Whatever the catch, one always returns from Ireland with a story and happy memories. The sport is excellent, and all visitors are treated with great hospitality and charm. Tackle shops are very helpful, and The Irish Tourist Board issues a wealth of information, including dates of angling competitions, and an excellent brochure entitled *Angling in Ireland*.

Fishing in the southwest is readily available to the general public. You can fish on any day including Sundays. Unlike the UK, there is no closed season for coarse fishing. Seasons for other types of fishing vary and some rivers have their own seasons. Costs are also comparatively low. With few exceptions, a day's permit is unlikely to cost more than IR£25. Government licences, which are not hefty, are required for salmon and sea trout fishing.

For the purposes of licensing, fishing in the Republic can be divided into four categories: game, for salmon and sea trout (migratory); trout (non-migratory); coarse, for perch, roach, rudd, bream, tench, etc., and pike; and sea-fishing. Visitors require a licence for the first. A general licence covering all salmon and sea trout costs IR£10 for 21 days, or IR£25 for a season, or IR£3 a day. It is possible to purchase individual or composite licences from Bord Fáilte offices in your country of residence. They can be bought from any Tourist or Fisheries Board office in the southwest, from all government-run fisheries, and many tackle shops.

One of the finest aspects of the sport in Ireland is the variety of different fishing techniques that are to be found in quite small areas. It is possible to fish a lake system—either dapping or wet-fly—and a river, on the same day. In the UK, this is only possible in a few places on the west coast of Scotland, and to some extent in the Hebrides. A ghillied boat is often necessary if you wish to fish on the lakes. Irish ghillies have a great knowledge of the shoals and bays where fish lie. They are also highly entertaining.

Coarse fishing is immensely popular, particularly with visitors from the UK, where there is a closed season from mid-March to mid-June, and pike-fishing here is amongst the best in Europe.

It would take a book longer than this one to list all the rivers and loughs for visiting game-fishers. On the whole, salmon-fishing is privately owned, but good association water is available for the general public. In the southwest the River Blackwater has early runs of salmon and grilse later and there are a number of rivers and lake systems, notably Lough Currane at Waterville, and the Maine and Laune including the Killarney Lakes. Fishing on the mighty Shannon was adversely affected by the introduction of the hydro-electric scheme in 1929, but the Castleconnell beats are still worth a visit.

Sea trout have been in sad decline over the past five years, especially and a number of well-known sea-trout fisheries have suffered badly due to 'Sea Lice' (which many claim is due to salmon farming). Considerable research is now being done by the Salmon Research Trust at Newport and things have shown a slight improvement. By contrast, runs of salmon and grilse have held up well in recent years.

Sea-angling is becoming increasingly popular with the more hardy fisherman. The Central Fisheries Board issues a comprehensive booklet. More boats are available for hire than ever before, although they can be expensive for the individual; it is best to organise a group of four or more. Kinsale is one of the main centres for sea-angling. Here, when the sea warms a degree or so, odd species of tropical fish arrive. Out of Kinsale there is also good shark-fishing, and many other species such as conger, skate and, for the less selective, huge bags of large pollack can be caught. Other main sea-fishing stations are Youghal, Ballycotton, and Baltimore in Co. Cork, and Cahirciveen and the Dingle Peninsula in Co. Kerry. As a rule, all stations will be able to supply boats for hire, rods, tackle, etc.

Food and Drink

Eating Out

Eating out in the southwest of Ireland can be a memorable experience, if the the chef gets it right. The basic ingredients are the best in the world: succulent beef, lamb, salmon, seafood, ham, butter, cream, eggs and wonderful **bread**—which is often homemade, and varies from crumbly nutty-tasting wheaten bread to moist white soda bread, crispy scones, potato bread and barm brack, a rich fruity loaf which is traditionally eaten at Hallowe'en. Irish **potatoes** are light and floury and best when just off the stalk, and crispy carrots and cabbages are sold in every grocery shop, often bought in from the local farms. If you stay in a country-house hotel, the walled garden will probably produce rare and exotic vegetables and fruit.

The history of Ireland has quite a lot to do with the down-side of cooking: overcooked food, few vegetables, and too many synthetic cakes. The landless peasants had little to survive off except potatoes, milk and the occasional bit of bacon, so there is little traditional 'cuisine'. **Fish** was until recently regarded as 'penance food', to be eaten only on Fridays. Local people talk with amusement of those who eat oysters or mussels, and most of the fine seafood harvested from the seaweed-fringed loughs and the open sea goes straight to France, where it appears on the starched linen table-cloths of the best restaurants. But do not despair if you love fat oysters or fresh salmon, because they can always be got, either in the bars, the new-style restaurants which are really excellent, or straight from the fisherman. Remember, everything in Ireland works on a personal basis. Start your enquiries for any sort of local delicacy at the local post office, grocer or butcher, or in the pub.

Having got over the trauma of the famine, and since the relative prosperity of the 1960s, many people in Ireland like to eat **meat**: you cannot fail to notice the number of butchers or 'fleshers' in every town. Steak appears on every menu, and if you are staying in a simple farmhouse, huge lamb chops with a minty sauce, Irish stew made from the best end of mutton neck, onions and potatoes, and bacon and cabbage casserole baked in the oven are delicious possibilities; fish, however, is becoming more and more readily available.

The standard of **restaurants** is getting much better. This is especially true of those that are run by people from the Continent, many of whom set up here because of the beauty of the country and the raw ingredients. There are Irish cooks, too, who combine the local specialities and traditional recipes with ingredients and cooking methods from other cultures. Ballymaloe Restaurant in Co. Cork springs immediately to mind. Still, eating out can be a massive disappointment, and it is wise to go to only those establishments which have been recommended. Too many restaurants still serve up musty and watery vegetables, overcooked meat, frozen fish, and salads of the limp lettuce and coleslaw variety. Also, eating out is not cheap, unless you have a pub lunch. Some restaurants offer a tourist menu, but on the whole these establishments offer good value rather than good cooking.

To get around the serious problem of eating cheaply, fill up on the huge breakfasts provided by the bed and breakfast places. If the lady of the house also cooks high tea or supper for her guests, take advantage of that as well. The food she produces is usually delicious and very good value. Irish people love their food, and are generous with it: huge portions are normal in the home and often in restaurants. It is a sign of inhospitality to give a poor meal. (They say, 'It was but a daisy in a bull's mouth.') Bakeries usually sell tea, coffee and soft drinks along with fresh apple pie, doughnuts, cakes and sausage rolls. Roadside cafés serve the usual menu of hamburgers, chicken 'n' chips, etc. The bigger towns and cities have Chinese restaurants, pizza places and fish and chips. Vegetarians will find an increasing number of restaurants cater specifically for their needs. Certainly, vegetarians will find that even where no special menu exists, people are generally keen to provide suitable fare. If you are staying in a country house, you should telephone in advance to let them know you are vegetarian. You can sample the many delicious Irish cheeses by finding a good deli or wholefood shop, buying some bread and salad and taking yourself off to eat a picnic in some wonderfully scenic place. If it is drizzling, warm yourself up afterwards with a glass of Irish coffee in the local pub.

You will normally find the service friendly and helpful. A variety of good eating places are listed at the end of each county chapter. In the various culinary deserts which exist, those listed are the best of an indifferent lot! The establishments are categorized in the following cost brackets. Do bear in mind that proprietors and places change, so it is always best to telephone before you arrive.

luxury

Cost no object. These restaurants include creative and delicious cooking from fine ingredients. They are often in the dining-rooms of rather stately country houses or castles, where the silver and crystal sparkle and you are surrounded by fine pictures and furniture. Or they may be smart, fashionable places in the cities.

expensive

Over IR£20 a head, excluding wine. Restaurants in this category are similar to those in the luxury bracket, with an emphasis on well-cooked vegetables and traditional ingredients. Again, many country-house hotels come under this category, as do seafood restaurants around the coast and city establishments. Lunch in expensive places is often a very reasonably priced set meal, so ask about it if you do not want to fork out for dinner.

moderate

IR£10–20 a head excluding wine. The quality of the food may be as good as the more expensive places, but the atmosphere is informal and, perhaps, a little less stylish.

inexpensive

Under IR£10 a head excluding wine. This category includes bar food, lunchtime places and cafés. You can usually be sure of good homemade soup and one, simple course.

Most restaurants do lunch and dinner but do check before you go. A few do only dinner and Sunday lunches. Some country places only open for the weekend during the winter months. Cafés and snack places are not usually open in the evening for meals. Service is usually included in the bill at all restaurants. Quite a number of places don't accept credit cards so check this out before you order your meal! If there is no liquor licence of any sort, the manager is usually quite happy to let you bring in your own wine or beer, if you ask. (The publicans have a monopoly on licences and many restaurants cannot get them without having to fulfil ludicrous requirements for space-planning).

Literature

The Irish Country Houses and Restaurants Association issues a booklet every year which includes some of the best restaurants in the southwest, and they are not necessarily all that expensive. It is called *The Blue Book*, and can be found in tourist offices throughout the country. Possibly the best publication is Bridgestones *Irish Food Guide*, which lists a directory of sources—smoked salmon, cheese, organic vegetables and good restaurants. Compiled by Sally and John McKenna, price IR£12.95.

Drink

'The only cure for drinking is to drink more', so goes the Irish proverb. Organizations such as the Pioneers exist to wean the masses off 'the drink'—alcohol costs an arm and a leg, what with the taxes and the publican's cut; yet, nevertheless, an Irish bar can be one of the most convivial places in the world. The delicious liquor, the cosy snugs and the general hubbub of excited conversation, which in the evening might easily spark into a piece of impromptu singing, makes the business of taking a drink very pleasant. Pubs can also be as quiet as a grave, especially in the late afternoon when a few men nod over their pint, and an air of contemplation pervades. Murphy's, Smithwick's ale and Harp lager are three very good legal brews made in Ireland.

Guinness

You are bound to have been lured into trying Guinness by the persuasive advertisements you see all over Europe, for the export trade is thriving; but the place to get a real taste of the creamy dark liquor is in an Irish bar. The quality of taste once it has left the brewery in Dublin depends on how well the publican looks after it and cleans the pipe from the barrel, so it varies greatly from bar to bar.

If it's obvious that you are a tourist, your Guinness will be decorated with a shamrock drawn on its frothy head! They've finally managed to get Guinness into a can—by all accounts it's very good but it's apparently important that it's drunk chilled (bottled draught no longer exists). If you are feeling adventurous, try something called black velvet—a mixture of Guinness and champagne.

bars

The old-fashioned serious drinking bar with high counter and engraved glass window, frosted so that the outside world couldn't intrude, is gradually disappearing. It used to be a male preserve. Farmers on a trip into town can be heard bewailing the weather or recounting the latest in cattle, land prices or gossip. What the inns have lost in character they compensate for, to a degree, with comfort. The bar of the local hotel is the place to find the priest when he is off-duty. My favourite drinking establishment is the grocery shop which is also a bar, where you ask for a taxi/plumber/undertaker, only to find that the publican or his brother combine all these talents with great panache!

whiskey

Whiskey has been drunk in Ireland for more than five hundred years and the word itself is derived from *uisge beatha*, the Irish for water of life. It is made from malted barley with a small proportion of wheat, oats and occasionally a pinch of rye. There are several brands, but Jameson's and Paddy are the best made in the south, and Bushmills in the North.

Irish coffee

Irish coffee is a wonderful combination of contrasts: hot and cold, black and white, and very intoxicating. It was first dreamed up in County Limerick earlier this century. It's made with a double measure of Irish whiskey, one tablespoon of double cream, one cup of strong, hot black coffee, and a heaped tablespoon of sugar. To make it, first warm a stemmed whiskey glass. Put in the sugar and enough hot coffee to dissolve the sugar. Stir well. Add the Irish whiskey and fill the glass and pour the cream slowly over a spoon. Do not stir the cream into the coffee; it should float on top. The hot whiskey-laced coffee is drunk through the cold cream.

poteen

Poteen (pronounced 'pot-cheen') is illicit whiskey, traditionally made from potatoes, although nowadays it is often made from grain. Tucked away in the countryside are stills which no longer bubble away over a turf fire, but on a Calor gas stove. Poteen is pretty disgusting stuff unless you get a very good brew, and it probably kills off a lot of braincells, so it's much better to stick to the legal liquid.

wine

If you happen to stay in that wonderful country house, Longueville, near Mallow, you must order a bottle of dry fruity white wine from Ireland's only vineyard. It is delicious, and rare because of the fierceness of the frost and uncertainty of the sunshine.

licensing hours

Public houses are open Mon–Sat 10am–11.30pm (unofficially, they may stay open into the early hours of the morning). In winter they close half an hour earlier. On Sundays and St Patrick's Day they open from 12.30am–10pm. There is no service on Christmas Day or Good Friday. Children are often allowed to sit in the lounge bar with packets of crisps and fizzy orange to keep them happy.

If you do get into a conversation in a bar, a certain etiquette is followed: men always buy everybody in your group a drink, taking it in turn to buy a round; women will find they are seldom allowed to! Both sexes offer cigarettes around when having one. If there are ten in your group you will find yourself drunk from social necessity and out of pocket as well! The price of wine, whiskey and beer is much higher than in the UK. A bottle of whiskey is about IR£14. If you are bringing a car from France or the UK, it might be as well to bring some booze in with you. The customs allowance is 1½ litres of distilled beverages or spirits, 12 litres of beer and (if the alcohol is bought duty-paid) 4 litres of wine per person. If you are a resident, you have to have been out of the Republic for 48 hours; this is to stop local people from nipping across the border to buy drink! At the time of writing, the European Court has ruled against this restriction, but the judicial process may not be over.

Golf

We are grateful to Bruce Critchley for this expert guide to Ireland's golf courses. Bruce is one of television's golf commentators, following a successful amateur international career in the 1960s. Now a consultant to golf-course developers, he also, in association with his wife's company, Critchley Pursuits, arranges tours of British, Irish and Continental courses for both English and American enthusiasts.

With the possible exception of Scotland, Ireland can boast more courses per head of population than any other country in the world. As with Scotland, quality is in no way diminished by quantity and, in common with the rest of the British Isles, the greatest courses are situated at the seaside.

Should the visitor be anxious to get going after flying into Shannon, he could almost walk to the **Shannon Golf Club** from the airport terminal building. A modern course, inland in character, there is good use of water and lovely views down to the River Shannon. But the real treasures lie on the other side. **Ballybunion** has long stood beside the very best, and recently a second 18 has been added of almost equal quality. Some 20 miles (32km) to the south, Arnold Palmer has laid out an outstanding course on Kerry's coastline at **Tralee**.

The Ring of Kerry offers two widely differing courses, the **Dooks at Glenbeigh** and the mighty links of **Waterville**. Glenbeigh, only 5750 yards (5260m) in length, is supposedly the third-oldest course in the country and follows the naturally undulating dunes, as courses only could in the last century. Waterville is of much more recent construction and, with the ocean on three sides, the wind is an ever-present factor.

Just inland are a pair of courses on the shores of **Killarney**. Can there be any more beautiful setting for golf anywhere in the world? Perhaps the courses don't quite match up to the view, but then very few would. Nevertheless, it is a joy to play here.

Finally, and even though a little off the beaten track, no trip to this neck of the woods should miss the little nine-hole gem at **Bantry**, overlooking the famous bay with its stunning views. To the north, **Lahinch**, traditionally the home of the South of Ireland Championships, is another course with nothing but the Atlantic between it and Boston.

Away from the pounding of the Atlantic Ocean, the courses don't have the sand dunes out of which links courses are traditionally carved. Nonetheless, the natural beauty of the countryside lends a great backdrop wherever courses are constructed. And on the scenic front, the little nine-holer at **Doneraile** should not be passed up.

Cork has a couple of courses of which **Little Island** is the most spectacular. Holes alternate between the edge of a massive quarry on one side and views over the estuary on the other. Southwest of the city, **Bandon Golf Course**, set in the grounds of Castle Bernard Castle, is well worth a visit, as is **Midleton** to the east.

So wherever you go in the southwest, golf courses abound, and whatever your standard you'll find something to enjoy. With facilities getting ever more crowded around the major cities of the world, here golf as it used to be—the ability to get on a course in the hours of daylight, and green fees that are not going to break the bank.

A couple of words of advice. If you are thinking of a golfing holiday, some of the courses do get busy in summer and it is always advisable to check with clubs in advance and, where necessary, get a confirmed tee time. Also, every travelling golfer should carry a handicap certificate as proof of competence. Trolleys will be for hire at most clubs and quite a few will be able to lay on caddies if ordered in advance. Golf carts are not yet a feature of Irish golf and are not encouraged. One or two courses will permit their use with a medical certificate, but you will have to provide the cart!

For further information contact Bord Fáilte which publishes a couple of good guides on golfing. Clubs and courses in the southwest are listed below:

Bandon Golf Club, Castle Bernard, Bandon, Co. Cork, ✆ (023) 41111.

Bantry Golf Club, Cahir, Bantry, Co. Cork, ✆ (027) 50579.

Beaufort Golf Club, Beaufort, Killarney, Co. Kerry, ✆ (064) 44440.

Cobh Golf Club, Ballywilliam, Cobh, Co. Cork, ✆ (021) 812399.

Cork Golf Club, Little Island, Co. Cork, ✆ (021) 353451.

Douglas Golf Club, Douglas, Co. Cork, ✆ (021) 891086.

Dromoland Castle Hotel Golf Club, Newmarket-on-Fergus, Co. Clare, ✆ (061) 368144.

East Cork Golf Club, Gurtacrue, Midleton, Co. Cork, ✆ (021) 631687.

Fermoy Golf Club, Fermoy, Co. Cork, ✆ (025) 31472.

Fernhill Golf Club, Carrigaline, Co. Cork, ✆ (021) 373103.

Fota Island Golf Club, Fota Island, Carrigtwohill, Co. Cork, ✆ (021) 883700.

Harbour Point Golf Complex, Clash Road, Little Island, Co. Cork, ✆ (021) 353094.

Kanturk Golf Club, Fairy Hills, Kanturk, Co. Cork, ✆ (029) 50534.

Kenmare Golf Club, Killowen, Kenmare, Co. Kerry, ✆ (064) 41291.

Kilkee Golf Club, Kilkee, Co. Clare, ✆ (065) 56048.

Killarney Golf Club, Mahony's Point, Killarney, Co. Kerry, ✆ (064) 31034.

Killorglin Golf Club, Stealroe, Killorglin, Co. Kerry, ✆ (066) 61979.

Kilrush Golf Club, Ballykett, Kilrush, Co. Clare, ✆ (065) 51138.

Kinsale Golf Club, Kinsale, Co. Cork, ✆ (021) 772197.

Lahinch Golf Club, Lahinch, Co. Clare, ✆ (065) 81003.

Lee Valley Golf & Country Club, Clashenure, Ovens, Co. Cork, ✆ (021) 331721.

Limerick County Golf & Country Club, Ballyneety, Co. Limerick, ✆ (061) 351881.

Listowel Golf Club, Feale View, Listowel, Co. Kerry, ✆ (068) 21592.

Ted McCarthy Municipal Golf Course, Mahon, Co. Cork, ✆ (021) 294280.

Macroom Golf Club, Lackduv, Macroom, Co. Cork, ✆ (026) 41072.

Mallow Golf Club, Ballyellis, Mallow, Co. Cork, ✆ (022) 21145.

Mitchelstown Golf Club, Mitchelstown, Co. Cork, ✆ (025) 24072.

Monkstown Golf Club, Monkstown, Co. Cork, ✆ (021) 841376/841686/841225.

Morgan Donal, Coosheen Golf Links, Coosheen, Schull, Co. Cork, ✆ (028) 28182.

Muskerry Golf Club, Carrigrohane, Co. Cork, ✆ (021) 385297.

Rafeen Creek Golf Club, Ringaskiddy, Co. Cork, ✆ (021) 378430.

Shannon Golf Club, Shannon Airport, Co. Clare, ✆ (061) 471020.

Skibbereen & West Carberry Golf Club, Skibbereen, Co. Cork, ✆ (028) 21227.

Tralee Golf Club, West Barrow, Ardfert, Co. Kerry, ✆ (066) 36379.

Water Rock Golf Course, Water Rock, Midleton, Co. Cork, ✆ (021) 613499.

Waterville Golf Links, Waterville, Co. Kerry, ✆ (066) 74102.

Woodstock Golf & Country Club, Woodstock House, Ennis, Co. Clare, ✆ (065) 29463.

Youghal Golf Club, Knockaverry, Youghal, Co. Cork, ✆ (024) 92787.

Guides

In most areas of the southwest you can obtain the services of a guide. They love their country and their famous facility with words can make touring with a guide an unforgettable pleasure. The local tourist office (*see* pp.52–5) should be able to put you in touch with a guide. Expect to pay around IR£60 a day, or IR£10 per hour. Contact Beatrice Healy, a well-respected freelance guide, at ✆ (01) 454 5943.

Hazards and Emergencies

midges

Toads and adders are said to have fled from Ireland at the sound of St Patrick's bell tolling from the top of Croagh Patrick mountain in Mayo; unfortunately, the voracious midges of the west coast did not take their cue! They are very persistent on warm summer evenings, so remember to arm yourself with some sort of insect repellent. There is plenty of choice in the chemists. Wasps, hornets and horseflies also emerge in summer to irritate.

beasts

If you decide to have a picnic in some inviting green field, just check that there is not a bull in it first. High-spirited bullocks can be just as alarming; they come rushing up to have a good look and playfully knock you over in the process!

sea

A major hazard can be strong currents in the sea. One beach may be perfectly safe for bathing, and the one beside it positively dangerous. Always check with locals before you swim. There are lifeguards on most of the resort beaches.

walkers

Walkers who intend to go through bog and mountainous country be warned that, even though it looks dry enough on the road, once into the heather and moss you will soon sink into waterlogged ground. Wear stout boots (brogues) and bring at least an extra jersey. Sudden mists and rain can descend, and you can get very cold. Experienced mountain rescue teams are non-existent here, so if you do disappear into a mountain range, leave word locally as to where you plan to go, or a put a note on your car. During the shooting season (grouse and snipe from August to 3 January, duck from September to 31 January, and pheasant from 1 November to 1 January), be careful of wandering into stray shot on the hilly slopes or in marshy places.

motorists

Although it hardly seems necessary in some of the more isolated spots in the southwest, it is always safer to lock your car, or if you're in a city leave it in an authorised car parks. Cars are stolen so take sensible precautions. Do not leave luggage or valuables in the car.

the fairies

There is just one last possible hazard which you might only have dreamt about: the mischievous fairies might put a spell on you so that you never want to return to your own country. It's not a joke, for Ireland is an enchanting country and difficult to leave. As a rule it is no use enquiring about charms against this enchantment, or any other; the answer is always the same: 'There used to be a lot of them in the old days but the priests put them down.' You get that answer about poteen too! Underneath, there is a sort of sneaking belief in fairies; for why, in a perfectly modern housing estate outside Sligo, is there a ragged mound which escaped the bulldozer and cement? Perhaps because it is a fairy rath? One last word on fairies: have you ever heard how they came about? Padraic Colum found out from a blind man whom he met in the west, who believed in them as firmly as in the Gospels. When the Angel Lucifer rebelled against God, Hell was made in a minute, and down to it God swept Lucifer and thousands of his followers, until the Angel Gabriel said, 'O God Almighty, Heaven will be swept clean.' God agreed and compromised, saying, 'Them that are in Heaven let them remain so, them that are in Hell, let them remain in Hell; and them that are between Heaven and Hell, let them remain in the air.' And the angels that remained between Heaven and Hell are the fairies.

emergencies

As mentioned above, if you do find yourself in trouble in, you will find no shortage of sympathetic help. If you fall ill, have an accident, or are the victim of some crime, people will rush to your aid. Whether they bring quite the help you need is another matter. If in doubt, get the advice of your hotel, the local tourist office, or the police. In serious cases (medical or legal), contact your embassy or consulate (*see* p.15). Try to keep your head: in the case of medical treatment, take your insurance documents, inform the people treating you of your insurance cover, and make sure you keep all receipts (or at least get someone reliable to do this for you).

The emergency telephone number (to call any of the emergency services) is 999.

Heritage and Interpretative Centres

In the last ten years there has been a huge growth in these centres all over Ireland. The larger ones incorporate local history, flora and fauna, using audio visual aids or lifesize models and actors dressed in period costume, producing 'an experience to remember'. The Office of Public Works have purpose-built a few Interpretative Centres in places of great natural beauty and fragile ecology. Controversy has been provoked by the siting of one such centre in the middle of the Burren. Inevitably such places destroy some of the beauty and peace with huge carparks, WCs, craft centres etc., however sympathetic the architecture and landscaping may be. Many of the small heritage centres double as genealogical centres and are situated in fine old buildings (mainly in towns), which have been restored by the efforts and enthusiasm of the local people.

Insurance

general

The best advice is, always insure your holiday, and do so as soon as you book your ticket. Standard travel insurance packages issued by the major insurance companies cover a broad range of risks, including cancellation due to unforeseen circumstances, transport delays caused by strikes or foul weather, loss or theft of baggage, medical insurance and compensation for injury or death. The cost of insurance may seem substantial, but it is negligible when compared to almost any claim, should misfortune befall you.

That said, it is worth checking to see whether any of your existing insurance schemes cover travel risks: certain British household insurance schemes, for example, include limited travel cover.

medical

Remember that if you need medical or dental treatment you will be expected to pay for it yourself, and then claim back the costs from your insurance company. This, of course, may not be something you can discuss on the operating table. *In extremis* the international emergency services offered by companies such as Europ Assistance or Travel Assistance International, which are often incorporated into travel insurance packages, demonstrate their blessings. For all kinds of medical care, citizens of EU countries can benefit from the mutual agreements that exist between EU member countries. British citizens travelling to Ireland can make use of any GP who has an agreement with the Health Board, but to benefit from this you should take Form E111 with you, obtainable from a Social Security Office in the UK in advance of your departure (you need to allow several weeks for your application to be processed). The same scheme also applies to dentists and to hospitals.

claims

Remember that to make a claim for loss or theft of baggage, you will need evidence that you have reported the loss to the police. Check your insurance details for the documentation required of you by the insurance company in such circumstances. It is, by the way, useful to have more than one copy of your insurance policy—if your baggage is stolen, the document may go with it.

currency

Since the Republic joined the European Monetary System, the Irish pound (IR£) and the English pound (UK£) are no longer worth the same. The difference fluctuates, usually to the detriment of the Irish pound or punt (pronounced 'poont'), although at the time of writing the two currencies stand at about the same level give or take 3 or 4p.

Shopkeepers generally accept sterling. Both currencies use the pound as the basic unit, divided into 100 pence. There are coins for the pence in both currencies; and £1 and IR£1 coins. There are notes of £5, £10, £20, £50 in both currencies, and a IR£100 note.

You may bring any amount of foreign or Irish currency into Ireland, but you must not leave with more than IR£100 cash, in denominations of IR£20 or less, although any uncashed traveller's cheques may be taken out. There are various *bureaux de change* where you can change money, and most major hotels also provide this service, but these are unlikely to offer as good a rate of exchange as the banks. There are exchange counters at some airports for international flights: Shannon, open to service all flights; Cork, 10am–3pm (Mon–Fri); Dublin, summer 6.45am–10pm, winter 7.30am–8.30pm.

traveller's cheques

Traveller's cheques and Eurocheques are accepted throughout the southwest. Leading credit and charge cards (MasterCard/Access, Visa, American Express and Diner's Club) are widely accepted in major hotels and restaurants, but do check this beforehand. If the banks are closed, hotels and many large shops will take traveller's cheques.

banks

Small towns have at least one bank. The banks are open Mon–Friday, 10–12.30 and 1.30–4 and open until 5.30pm on Thursday. Banks in the larger towns will usually have one day each week—normally market day—when they will stay open until 5pm.

The bank usually occupies the grandest house in town—the various banking groups seem to have some sort of conscience about historical buildings, which is very rare in Ireland. The moving of money is accompanied by massive security, which looks very out of keeping with the happy-go-lucky attitude in Ireland, but is necessary because bank raids have become so common.

the cost of living

Prices in are generally on a par with other European countries. What will influence the visitor's view of the general level of costs is more likely to be the current rate of exchange than the local price structure.

Here are a few guidelines for the visitor. An expensive hotel will cost about IR£120 per night for two people in a double room; bed-and-breakfast accommodation (guesthouses), around IR£20 for two. A meal in a restaurant will cost anything from IR£15 to IR£25 and more per head, although tourist menus at hotels can often offer a set meal at around IR£6. A pint of beer costs around IR£2.00; a litre of milk 62p; a pack of 20 cigarettes IR£2.50; a loaf of bread 86p; butter per lb IR£1.40; a kilo of potatoes 30p.

Tipping is not really a general habit except in taxis and in eating places where there is table service. Taxi-drivers will expect to be tipped at a rate of about 10 per cent of the fare; porters and doormen 50p or so. There is no tipping in pubs, but in hotel bars where you are served by a waiter it is usual to leave a small tip.

A service charge of 12 (sometimes 15) per cent is usually raised automatically on hotel and restaurant bills. Where this is not the case, a tip of this magnitude would be in order, if the service merits it.

Newspapers

The best newspaper to read is the *Irish Times*, followed closely by the *Irish Independent* and the *Cork Examiner*. The *Irish Times* on Saturdays lists 'What is on'—exhibitions, festivals, concerts, etc. around the country. *Image* is a glossy magazine on the lines of *Harpers & Queen*, and has information on fashion, interior decoration and restaurants. *Phoenix* is the Irish equivalent of *Private Eye*.

Packing

Whatever you do, come expecting rain—gumboots, umbrellas, raincoats, etcetera are essential, unless you want to stay inside reading a book all day. Once you get out into the rain it is never as bad as it looks, and the clouds begin to clear as you appear. Bring warm jerseys, trousers, woollen socks, and gloves for autumn, winter and early spring. The best thing to do is to expect the cold and wet and then get a pleasant surprise when it's sunny and hot—so do not forget to sneak in a few T-shirts just in case. Sometimes the sun shines furiously in March and April and you end up with a very convincing tan.

If you like walking, bring a pair of fairly stout shoes—trainers end up bedraggled and let the water in. Fishing rods and swimsuits are worth packing, if you think you may have cause to regret leaving them behind. Bring a sleeping bag if you plan to stay at youth hostels. If you plan to stay in bed-and-breakfast accommodation, take your own towels, as those traditionally supplied tend to be on the mean side.

You will be amazed at what the village shop sells, from pots and pans to fine wines, and maybe some fresh salmon trout if you are lucky. In the Republic you can be sure of finding a shop open until 10 o'clock in the evening and on Sundays as well. Chemists are also well stocked so that headache pills, camera films, contraceptives etc. are easily obtainable.

Post Offices

Letterboxes are green. If you do not have a fixed address in Ireland, letters can be sent Poste Restante to any post office and picked up when you produce proof of your identity. If after three months they are gathering dust in the corner of the post office, they will be sent back to the sender. There is a post office in every village which is usually the telephone exchange as well and a hive of activity. You can send telemessages from the post office but you need to book in advance.

The post office should be open 9–5 in weekdays, 9–1 on Saturdays, and closed on Sundays and public holidays. Sub-post offices close on one day a week at 1.

Public Holidays

New Year's Day	1 January
St Patrick's Day	17 March
Good Friday	(widely observed as a holiday, but not an official one)
Easter Monday	
May Day	1 May
June Holiday	First Monday in June
August Holiday	First Monday in August
October Holiday	Last Monday in October
Christmas Day	25 December
Boxing Day/St Stephen's Day	26 December

Sailing

The coastline is uniquely beautiful, with diverse conditions and landscapes. The waters are never crowded, and the shoreline is completely unspoilt. On one of those sublimely beautiful evenings when the light touches each hill and field with an exquisite clarity, you will think yourself amongst the most privileged in the world. And if you want a bit of a 'crack', there are splendid bars and restaurants to be visited in the sheltered harbours. But the peace and calm of the sky, land and sea in the many inlets is deceptive, for the open seas in the northwest can be rough and treacherous, exposed as they are to the North Atlantic. So a journey around the whole coastline should only be attempted by experienced sailors. If you do not have your own yacht, it is possible to charter a variety of craft; whilst if it is your ambition to learn to sail, there are several small and friendly schools.

Ireland has a long sailing tradition, with many yacht and sailing clubs on the southwest coast The Royal Cork Yacht Club at Crosshaven is the oldest in the world, and was founded in 1720 as the Water Club of the Harbour of Cork. Cork Harbour is a very large and sheltered expanse of water with several pleasant marinas, notably East Ferry. Many of these clubs preserve their original clubhouses, and emanate a feeling of tradition and comfort. Visitors are made very welcome, and are encouraged to use the club facilities. Those who wish to eat on board can buy wonderful bread, cheese and other high-quality groceries from the local shops. Seafood can be brought from the trawlers fishing the waters around you. And it is possible to find good food and entertainment in local bars and restaurants, especially in the Cork and Kerry area.

Where to Sail

The coastline bordering the counties of Cork and Kerry is a favourite with sailors, and it has a good selection of charter companies, sailing schools and boardsailing (wind-surfing) facilities. The harbours are charming, and the peninsulas and islands around which you can sail are magnificent. You will also find many sites of historical interest close to the harbours of Crosshaven, Kinsale, Rosscarbery, Glendore, Schull, Rosbrin, Castletownbere, Kenmare, Caherdaniel, Dingle, Kilrush and Tralee.

If you want to circumvent Ireland, further west, in County Galway and County Mayo, there is exciting sailing around the Aran Islands, Clifden, Renville and Clew Bay, and the many deserted islands with hauntingly beautiful names such as Inishgloria and Inishkea.

Just north of Dublin there are several excellent sailing centres which still retain the charm of fishing villages. Inland is the huge freshwater expanse of Lough Derg in the River Shannon system, where you can anchor in a sheltered bay or in one of the charming canal harbours.

Galway Hookers

The most traditional form of sailing boat is the Galway hooker, with its black sails. Galway hookers used to be a familiar sight, transporting turf and other goods between the islands, but by the 1970s they had almost disappeared. Happily, a few sailors discovered what great sport can be had with hooker-racing—you can see these races at summer regattas in the west of Ireland—and the craft of making the hooker is slowly reviving. (Contact address below.)

Bringing Your Own Yacht

There is no tax or duty if you bring in your own yacht for a holiday; a special sticker is issued by customs officials on arrival. Mariners should apply to the harbour master of all ports in which they wish to anchor. On arrival at the first port of entry, the flag 'Q' should be shown. Contact should then be made with the local customs official or with a *garda* (civil guard) who will be pleased to assist. Fees are very reasonable in marinas and harbours. It is illegal to land any animals without a special licence from the Department of Agriculture, but this does not apply to pet dogs which come from Great Britain.

Yacht Charter

The main centres for charter are the southwest coastline. Private charter can be arranged at leading sailing centres elsewhere. Bare-boat and crewed charters are available on boats ranging from four- to seven-berth. The average cost of chartering a four-berth yacht ranges from IR£100 per person per week in the low season to IR£130 per person per week in the high season.

For a complete list of yacht charter companies, contact Bord Fáilte, PO Box 273, Dublin 8, ℂ (01) 284 4768. One of the biggest charter companies in the Cork area is Sail Ireland Charters, ℂ (021) 772927.

Sailing Holidays

The Celtic Nature Sailing Holidays, Michael & Becky O'Connor, the Old Stone House, Cliddaun, Dingle, ℂ/🖂 (066) 59882. Expeditions off Dingle and Iveragh Peninsulas on a 13-metre cutter sail boat, with emphasis on the natural and cultural history of the area.

Sailing Schools

Most of the schools are residential and located in areas of scenic beauty. Many offer other outdoor sports such as boardsailing (wind-surfing), canoeing and sub-aqua. A full list of schools is available from Bord Fáilte in Dublin and from the Irish Association for Sail Training, Confederation House, 84–86 Lower Baggot Street, Dublin 2, © (01) 660 1011.

Sailing Organisations

Irish Sailing Association, 3 Park Road, Dun Laoghaire, County Dublin, © (01) 280 0239. Cormac P. McHenry, the Hon. Secretary, Irish Cruising Club (ICC), 8 Heidelberg, Ardilea, Dublin 14, © (01) 288 4733.

Useful Media

The Irish Cruising Club (address above) publishes *Sailing Directions* which covers the entire coast of Ireland, and includes details of the coast, sketch plans of harbours, tidal information and information about port facilities. The *Directions* come in two volumes— one for the south and west at IR£30, and one for the north and east, price IR£27. Available from most Irish booksellers, and from Mrs Fox-Mills, The Tansey, Baily, County Dublin, © (01) 832 2823. Also recommended: *Sailing Around Ireland* by Wallace Clark (Batsford), and *Islands of Ireland* by D. McCormick (Osprey, 1977). The BBC issues gale warnings and shipping forecasts on Radio 4.

Shopping

Shopping in Ireland is the most relaxing pastime because nobody ever makes you feel that you have to buy anything, so you can browse to your heart's content. Good design and high-quality craftsmanship make for goods which will last you for a lifetime, and delight the senses. I would choose to take home Irish linen, handloomed tweed, Aran sweaters, pottery, glass and modern Irish silver. These you can find easily in the craft centres which have been set up all over the country. The Craft Council of Ireland, Powerscourt Townhouse, South William St, Dublin 2, © (01) 679 7383, a relatively new body, has given a great boost to the many talented craft workers, and helped them to market their wares and join forces in studios and workshops, usually in IDA (Industrial Development Authority) parks, © (01) 668 6633. If you see something you like at any of the craft shops and centres, buy it then and there because you are not likely to see it again in another shop. Craft items are not cheap because of the artistry and labour involved, but you can find bargains at china, crystal and linen factory shops if you are prepared to seek them out.

The main goodies to take home with you are described in detail below. More fleeting pleasures, which you can share with your friends back home, are smoked salmon, cheese, wheaten bread, home-cured bacon, and whiskey. These are available at Shannon and Dublin Airport shops. Grinning leprechauns, colleen dolls, Guinness slogan T-shirts and shamrock mugs are stacked high in most gift shops if you want something cheerful and cheap, but do not ignore the real products from Ireland.

Shops are open 9.30–5.30, Mon–Sat. Craft shops in scenic areas are usually open on Sundays as well, especially if they combine as tea shops. In some towns there is an early-closing day when businesses close at one. This is normally a Wednesday, although it may be a different day in some areas. You can be sure that if one town has shut down, its neighbour will be busy, and open for business. Large shopping centres which operate on the outskirts of town are unaffected by early closing. Dunnes Stores can usually be found in these shopping centres. It is the equivalent of the British Marks & Spencer, and sells cheap clothing.

Irish specialities

Irish lace, one of the lightest and most precious of all the specialities you can pack in your suitcase, can be found in Kenmare, County Kerry (Kenmare Lace and Design Centre, Kenmare, ✆ (064) 41679; shop open Mon–Fri), and in Limerick City (the Good Shepherd Convent, Clare Street, Limerick, ✆ (061) 45183/45178; available Mon–Fri in the shop attached). In Limerick the lace is worked completely in thread on the finest Brussels net.

Tweed is a wonderful fabric. Not only does it keep you warm in winter, but it also lets your skin 'breathe' and it is useful most of the year round if you live in northern climes and are not addicted to central heating. It is hand-woven from sheep's wool, and the Irish have got not only the texture and tension of the cloth right, but also the speckled, natural colours of the countryside. Donegal tweed is particularly attractive, in all its subtle shades.

Hand-knitted sweaters: make sure you buy one which has the hand-knitted label on it; it makes the whole difference when you are buying an Aran. These are made out of tough wool, lightly coated in animal oils, so they are water-resistant and keep you as warm as toast. You can get them in natural white or various colours, and the pattern differs quite a bit. In the past the wives of the fishermen used to have a family pattern so that they could identify anyone who had drowned. These knits come in a variety of styles; they stretch after being worn a while and last for years. It is possible to buy original and attractive hand-knitted clothing in craft shops all over the southwest. Elegant stoles and generous shawls, woven bedspreads and car rugs are other excellent buys.

Linen: Irish linen is another item to look out for, tea cloths, sheets and hand-embroidered tablecloths and handkerchiefs.

Glass: Waterford Crystal is world-famous for its quality and design. You can buy it in good quality stores all over the southwest, but remember it can also be purchased as you leave the country at Shannon Airport's duty-free shop, although the selection is small. All the stores will pack and mail glass overseas for you. It is still possible to buy old Waterford glass, which has a blackish tint to it, in antique shops—but it is very costly. Attractive crystal glass can be bought in Cork, at the factory there. As you travel through the southwest you may well discover other original glass-blowers, as small craft industries are flourishing all over the country.

Pottery and china: talented potters work in rural communities all over Ireland, and one of the best places to find their work for sale is at IDA centres. Craft shops also usually carry the local potters' work.

Jewellery, silver and antiques: amongst all the other trinkets and souvenirs available, *claddagh rings* still remain the nicest of all love tokens and are very evocative of the south-west of Ireland.

Woven baskets: all over Ireland you can buy baskets made of willow or rush in different shapes and sizes: bread baskets, turfholders, place mats and St Brigid Crosses—charms against evil.

Traditional musical instruments: a wonderful present for a musical friend. For *uillean* pipes, contact Eugene Lambe, Fanore, Co. Clare, ✆ (065) 76122. For fiddles/violins, contact Peadar O'Loughlin, Clare Business Centre, Ennis, Co. Clare, ✆ (065) 88083.

Food and drink: soda, wheaten and potato bread are found all over the southwest. When you are leaving the country, McCambridge's brown bread is available at the airport shops. Smoked salmon is sold all over the southwest, and at the airport shops. Farmhouse cheese in every shape, size and texture is available from the producer and from wholefood shops and delicatessens. Irish whiskey (note the 'e', which is the Irish way of spelling it), is slightly sweeter than Scotch. Try Bushmills, Paddy's, Powers and Jamesons. All these brands are available in off-licences throughout the southwest. Cork gin is considered to have a delicious tang of juniper, far superior to the English brand of Gordon's. Popular liqueurs are Irish Mist, which contains whiskey and honey; Tullamore Dew; and Bailey's Irish Cream. Definitely worth trying if you like sweet and tasty things, Black Bush is a liqueur whiskey.

weights and measures

1 kilogram	=	2.205 lb		
1 litre	=	1.76 Imperial pints	=	2.11 US pints
1 centimetre	=	0.39 inches		
1 metre	=	39.37 inches	=	3.28 feet
1 kilometre	=	0.621 miles		
1 hectare	=	2.47 acres		
1 lb	=	0.45 kilograms		
1 Imperial pint	=	0.56 litres		
1 US pint	=	0.47 litres		
1 Imperial gallon	=	4.54 litres		
1 US gallon	=	3.78 litres		
1 foot	=	0.305 metres		
1 mile	=	1.609 kilometres		
1 acre	=	0.404 hectares		

adventure sports

The Association for Adventure Sports (AFAS) can give you information and contact telephone numbers and addresses for hand-gliding, mountaineering, canoeing, sub-aqua, board-sailing, surfing—in fact, almost any sport that you can think of! Contact the Association for Adventure Sport (AFAS), House of Sport, Longmile Road, Dublin 12, ℰ (01) 450 9845 to obtain a list of what is available in the southwest.

bird-watching

Bird sanctuaries abound in the southwest and if you walk along rocky shores there are some spectacular cliffs dripping with hundreds of birds. For details write to the Wildlife Service, Office of Public Works, 51 St Stephen's Green, Dublin 2, ℰ (01) 661 3111. Field trips are organized by local branches of the Irish Wild Bird Conservancy, and there are details in the quarterly newsletter. Write to the Irish Wild Bird Conservancy, Ruttledge House, 8 Longford Place, Monkstown, Co. Dublin, ℰ (01) 2804322.

the bowl game

Pronounced to rhyme with owl, traditionally this is only played in Co. Cork and Co. Armagh, along country lanes. The ball is made of very heavy iron, and the object of the game is to cover the greatest possible distance with a given number of bowls. The best players are strong and skilful, and the ball, a dangerous missile. It is illegal to play on public roads, but this did not stop it happening in the past; small children were stationed along the roads to warn competitors of oncoming traffic and the police. Today, the game has been saved from extinction and accommodated into the tourist calendar.

canoeing

This is an exciting and compelling sport with smooth-flowing stretches of beautiful rivers, rapids and weirs. The principal rivers are the Shannon, Suir and Blackwater. You can always camp by the waterside as long as you get permission from the owner. For details of the many rivers and waterways, sea canoeing and tuition, write to: AFAS, House of Sport, Longmile Road, Dublin 12, ℰ (01) 450 9845.

caving

This activity has become more organised recently with the establishment of the Speleological Union of Ireland. For information, contact: AFAS (address above) or Dave Miller of the Irish Speleological Association, 22 Abbey Park, Blackrock, Co Dublin.

cruising the inland waterways

This is an unforgettable and exciting way to travel around. The River Shannon is the main area in the southwest, and it is navigable from Lough Key to Killaloe. Along the waterways you pass tumbledown castles, abbeys, beautiful flowers, birds and peaceful, lush scenery. In the evening you can moor up your boat for a meal and a jar and listen to some good traditional music. There are festivals and boat rallies, but they only happen for a couple of days a year, so if it's peace and quiet you want, don't worry.

On the **Shannon** there are several companies offering luxury cabin cruisers for self-drive hire, ranging from two to eight berths. All are fitted with fridges, gas cookers, hot water and showers; most have central heating. A dinghy, charts, binoculars and safety equipment are included on the river and lough routes. Groceries and stores can be ordered in advance and collected when you arrive. You have to be over 21 to be skipper, and the controls must be understood by at least two people, but no licence is necessary. You get an hour of tuition, or more if you need it. The average price for a six-berth cruiser for one week ranges from IR£550 in April to about IR£1000 in July/August. Ask for details from your travel agent, or the nearest Irish tourist office, or contact the following companies direct:

Emerald Star Line Ltd, ✆ (01) 679 8166 (Dublin office), or ✆ (01509) 41120 (Portumna), or ✆ (078) 20234 (Carrick-on-Shannon).

Derg Line Cruisers, Killaloe, Co. Clare, ✆ (061) 376364.

Day trips and pleasure cruises are also available on the Shannon. Some of the companies listed above also operate river cruises. It is possible to take the **Killarney Waterbus** through the famous lakes for a trip of 1½ hours, ✆ (064) 32806.

Useful reading: *The Shell Guide to the Shannon.*

hang-gliding

Ireland is a hang-glider's paradise: shaped like a saucer with a mountainous rim. The wind blows from the sea or from the flat central plains. Most of the hills are bare of power-lines and trees, and the famous turf provides soft landings. Flying is controlled by the Irish Hang-Gliding Association. Contact: AFAS House of Sport, Longmile Rd, Dublin 12, ✆ (01) 450 9845.

horse-racing

Irish people are wild about horses; they breed very good ones, and they race them brilliantly. Limerick and Mallow are well known provincial courses in the southwest and holiday meetings are held at Killarney (mid-July), Tralee (end of August), and Listowel (late September).

Course admission charges vary between IR£5 and IR£10 per adult. A good-value annual badge is available at about IR£75. Most hunts organise Point-to-point meetings—3-mile (4.8km) chases over fences for amateur riders—between January and May. Car park charges are approximately IR£5. Point-to-points are usually freezing cold but great fun; the background and form of each horse is known and discussed with great enthusiasm.

A speciality of Irish National Hunt racing are 'Bumpers' which are 2-mile (3.2km) flat races confined to amateur riders, riding novice jumpers. The weekly *Irish Field* and daily *Racing Post* and *Sporting Life* publish form, venues and times of all race meetings and point-to-points. The Irish Tourist Board (Bord Fáilte) *Calendar of Events* lists racing fixtures at the back.

hunting

This is another popular sport in Ireland. Any visitors are welcomed by the various hunts, and it is not very expensive. Ask the Irish Tourist Board (Bord Fáilte) for a list, or the local riding centre for details. Altogether there are 85 recognized packs, and although some are stag hounds and harriers, in the main they are foxhounds. The hunting **season** starts in October and ends in March, with meets starting in the mid-morning. Stables for the hire of a horse for the day's hunting can usually be found through the local hunt secretary, (although you must be experienced), and costs about IR£60. The cap fee varies from IR£30 to IR£70 per day.

hurley

Munster men are famed for their prowess at this game which is similar to hockey, but much more vigorous, and played with a larger, broad bladed stick (also known as a caman or a hurley) and a hide covered ball. There are fifteen to a side, and the ball may only be picked up to be tossed into the air and struck. It may also be caught on the flat of the stick and carried like this while the player runs. This is to the Irish what cricket is to the English. Hurling and Gaelic football are promoted by the **Gaelic Athletic Association** and when it is played well it can be beautiful to watch and occasionally extremely dangerous. Money earned is put back into national programmes; the GAA is still closely connected with Nationalist objectives. Look in local newspapers for details of matches.

mountaineering and hill-walking

The mountains and hill areas are not high (few peaks are over 3000ft/915m), but they are rugged, varied, beautiful and unspoilt. There are quartz peaks, ridges of sandstone, bog-covered domes, and cliff-edged limestone plateaux. Excellent walking trails have been or are in the process of being developed. General advice, information and a list of hill-walking and rock-climbing clubs can be obtained from the Mountaineering Council of Ireland, Association for Adventure Sports (AFAS), House of Sport, Long Mile Road, Dublin 12, ✆ (01) 450 9845. They can also send you a full list of guides. Bord Fáilte offices throughout the southwest also stock hill-walking information sheets for individual areas.

The Ordnance Survey ½-inch-to-1-mile maps and a compass are essentials for serious walkers. Please remember there are very few tracks on the mountains, and always let your hotel know where you are climbing or walking, or leave a note in your car, just in case you have an accident. Mountain rescue in the main mountain areas is co-ordinated by the Gardai (Police).

riding holidays

There are many new residential schools and companies offering pony-trekking holidays. The Irish are putting their natural love of horses to good use, and the areas of beauty where you can ride include empty beaches that stretch for miles, heathery valleys, forests, empty country roads and loughside tracks. Accommodation and food are arranged for you. Full details from Bord Fáilte, PO Box 273, Dublin 8, ✆ (01) 284 4768, or from the following equestrian centres:

The Clonshire Equestrian Centre, Adare, Co. Limerick, ✆ (061) 396770.

Dunraven Arms Hotel, Adare, Co. Limerick, ✆ (061) 396633.

Green Glens Horse Village, Green Glens, Millstreet Town, Co. Cork, ✆ (029) 70039/ 70707.

El Rancho Farmhouse & Riding Stables, Ballyard, Tralee, Co. Kerry, ✆ (066) 21840.

Thompson's Country Home & Horse Riding, Carhoo, Dunquin, Dingle, Co. Kerry, ✆ (066) 56144.

horse-drawn caravans

You get a trustworthy and solid horse, a barrel-shaped caravan which sleeps four, and you can travel at a relaxing pace, usually about 9 miles (15kms) a day. Cost per week is from IR£200 low-season to IR£500 in July and August. Write for the relevant Fact Sheet, No. IS16C, to Bord Fáilte, PO Box 273, Dublin 8, or contact Mr David Slattery, Slattery's Horse-drawn Caravans, 1 Russell Street, Tralee, Co. Kerry, ✆ (066) 21722.

steeplechase

In Co. Cork in 1752 a group of sporting gentlemen rode their horses hell for leather from the steeple of Buttevant Protestant church to the Spire of St Legers Church at Doneraile, about 4 miles (7km). The wager was to see who was the fastest. No obstacle was too great and they urged their horses over hedges, walls, streams. Thus the steeplechase was born.

sub-aqua

Ireland's oceans are surprisingly warm and clear because they are right in the path of the Gulf Stream, so it would be very difficult to find a better place for underwater swimming or diving. The underwater flora and fauna is vast and varied, and you are always bumping into shoals of fish. *Subsea* is the official journal of the Irish Underwater Council, which publishes information about the affiliated clubs, articles on diving, etcetera. Write to the Hon. Secretary, Irish Underwater Council, Haigh Terrace, Dun Laoghaire, ✆ (01) 284 4601 There are centres for experienced divers and equipment hire in Co. Kerry and Co. Clare. Ask for the relevant fact sheet in any tourist office.

By the way, it is illegal to take shellfish from the sea.

surfing

Due to the geographical position of Ireland great swells endlessly pound the southwest coast, producing waves comparable to those in California. Many of the beaches in Counties Kerry and Clare are considered first-rate for breakers. As hire centres are not numerous, it is best to bring your own board and wetsuit; although you can occasionally hire them from hotels and adventure sports centres.

All those interested in the huge Atlantic swell should contact Mr Roc Allan, Chairman of the Irish Surfing Association at 1, Ardeelan Dale, Rossnowlagh, Co. Donegal, ✆ (072) 52522, 🖷 (072) 52523 and Mrs M. O'Brien-Moran, Hon. Secretary, 7 Marine Terrace, Tramore, Co. Waterford, ✆ (051) 386582. They will send out details of beaches and surfing centres.

swimming and beaches

There are lovely beaches (also called strands) wherever the sea meets the land. If you wish to go sea-bathing (it can be surprisingly warm because of the Gulf Stream), bear in mind that swimming is not a regulated sport, and that there are lifeguards only on the most popular beaches, if at all. Be aware of the possibility of a strong undertow or current, and ask locally about the safety of beaches.

The phrase 'Ireland, land of saints and scholars' is delightfully apt when it comes to the tradition of learning. You can study and learn some fascinating subjects in a beautiful environment, and still feel as if you are on holiday. The Irish Tourist Board will send you a free up-to-date list of programmes and prices if you write and ask for the *Live and Learn* booklet, from the **Group and Education Department**, Bord Fáilte, PO Box 273, Dublin 8. The courses range from the seriously intellectual to activity holidays. You can study for a month, two weeks, a few days, the variety is tremendous. Some are run by Ireland's own universities which offer courses on literature, politics, history, Gaelic, and archaeology. Private companies run arts and crafts courses, landscape painting, and English language courses. There are courses in environmental studies in beautiful places such as the Burren, and classes in traditional music and dancing.

Activity holidays include wind-surfing, hill-walking, riding, canoeing, fishing, cycling, golfing and dinghy-sailing. Some cater for all ages from toddlers upwards; in particular the adventure centres which are mainly on the west coast. USIT organize adventure sports, cycling and water sports holidays. For details, contact: 19 Aston Quay, Dublin 2, ✆ (01) 679 8833.

Here is a selection of those on offer:

Music

Milltown Malbay, Co. Clare: William Clancy summer school, Co. Clare's greatest piper ✆ (065) 37955.

Art/painting

Kerry summer painting school: call Cahirciveen tourist office has details; ✆ (066) 72589.

Burren Landscape Painting Course, Lisdoonvarna, Co. Clare; ✆ (065) 74208.

Photography/painting/sculpture workshop, Burren College of Art, Ballyvaughan, Co. Clare; ✆ (065) 77200.

Crawford School of Art and Gallery, Emmett Place, Cork; ✆ (021) 966777.

Cookery

Ballymaloe Cookery School, Kinoith House, Shanagarry, ✆ (021) 646785, Darina and Tim Allen. Courses vary from three months to one day.

Crafts

Clare Craft Summer School. Courses in pottery, basket-weaving and more, July; ✆ (065) 41605.

Irish Studies

Folklore School, Lahinch, Co. Clare, April/May; ✆ (065) 84365/(065) 81079.

Irish Studies, University College, Cork; ✆ (021) 276871.

Telephones

To call the Irish Republic from the UK dial **010 353** followed by the area code minus the first 0. It is more expensive to telephone during working hours than outside them. For example, at the time of writing a call to Britain costs 36p per minute, but after 6pm and at weekends and on public holidays the charge is 28p per minute. For direct-dial transatlantic calls the standard rate is about 83p per minute with reduced rates after 6pm of 71p and economy rates of 64p a minute.

Note that if you telephone from your hotel you are liable to be charged much more than the standard rate.

Ireland shares the same time zone as Great Britain, and follows the same pattern of seasonal adjustment in the summer (i.e. Greenwich Mean Time plus one hour, from the end of March to the end of October). This is in review at the time of writing in both the UK and Ireland.

Toilets

Loos—public ones, labelled in Irish: *Fir* (men) and *Mna* (women)—are usually in a pretty bad way. Nobody minds if you slip into a lounge bar or hotel to go to the loo, though it's a good excuse to stop for a drink as well.

Tourist Boards

Ireland is served by **Bord Fáilte** (or the Irish Tourist Board).

Bord Fáilte

The people who work for Bord Fáilte would get you to the moon if they could—should you ask for it. They will do literally anything to help and organise whatever is practicable; and if they do not know the answer to something, they can always refer you to someone who does. They can supply you with a wealth of beautifully presented information; most of this is free, although they also publish fuller booklets on, for example, accommodation, for which there are modest charges. They can also book your hotel or B&B, helping you to find one which is in your price range. The Head Office in Dublin is at Baggot Street Bridge, Dublin 2, ✆ (01) 676 5871, ✆ (01) 602 4100. For general postal enquiries write to Bord Fáilte, PO Box 273, Dublin 8. The Head Office is mainly the administration centre; when in Dublin a more useful office to visit is the one at 14 Upper O'Connell Street, Dublin 1, ✆ (01) 284 4768, ✆ (01) 284 1751.

There are many tourist information offices scattered all around the southwest, most of which open only during the summer season. The following, however, are open throughout the year. (A full list of tourist information offices can be obtained from Bord Fáilte.)

Cork City, ✆ (021) 273251, ✆ (021) 273504.

Dublin Airport, ✆ (01) 284 4768, ✆ (01) 284 1751.

Ennis, ✆ (065) 28366.

Killarney, ✆ (064) 31633, 📠 (064) 34506.

Limerick City, ✆ (061) 317522, 📠 (061) 317939.

Shannon Airport, ✆ (061) 471664.

Skibbereen, ✆ (028) 21766, 📠 (028) 21351.

Tralee, ✆ (066) 21288.

Great Britain

London, 150 New Bond Street, London W1Y 0AQ, ✆ (071) 493 3201, 📠 (0171) 493 9065.

Europe

France, 33 rue de Miromesnil, 75008 Paris, ✆ (1) 47 42 03 36, (1) 47 42 01 64.

The Netherlands, Spuistraat 104, 1012VA Amsterdam, ✆ (020) 622 3101, 📠 (020) 620 8089.

West Germany, Untermainanlage 7, 60329 Frankfurt am Main, ✆ (069) 236492.

Belgium (telephone and written enquiries), Avenue de Beaulieu 25, 1160 Brussels, ✆ (02) 673 9940, 📠 (02) 672 1066.

Denmark (telephone and written enquiries), Klostergarden, Amagertorv 29/3, 1160 Copenhagen K, ✆ (33) 15 80 45, 📠 (33) 93 63 90.

Italy, Via S. Maria Segreta 6, 20123 Milan, ✆ (02) 869 0541, 📠 (02) 869 0396.

North America

USA, 345 Park Avenue, New York, NY 10017, ✆ (212) 418 0800, 📠 (212) 371 9059.

Canada (written and telephone enquiries), 160 Bloor Street East, Suite 1150, Toronto, Ontario, M4W 1BN, ✆ (416) 929 2777, 📠 (416) 929 6783.

Australia

MLC Centre, 38th Level, Martin Place, Sydney, NSW 2000, ✆ (02) 232 7177.

New Zealand

2nd Floor, Dingwall Building, 87 Queen St, PO Box 279, Auckland 1, ✆ (9) 379 3708 and 377 0374.

Where to Stay

Whether you are a traveller with plenty of loot to spend, or one who is intent on lodging as cheaply as possible, the southwest offers plenty of choice. Places to stay range from romantic castles, graceful country mansions, cosy farmhouses, smart city hotels and hostels which, although spartan, are clean and well-run. Many of these hostels have double or family rooms; are independently owned and require no membership cards. They welcome young and old!

At the end of each county chapter there is a list of recommended accommodation, divided into price categories which are explained below. With this list as a guide, it is possible to avoid the many modern and ugly hotels where bland comfort is doled out for huge prices, and to avoid the shabby motels and the musty bed-and-breakfast establishments which are very uncomfortable. Farmhouse accommodation is usually a safe bet. One thing you can be sure of is that the Irish are amongst the friendliest people in Europe, and when they open their doors to visitors they give a great welcome. The many unexpected kindnesses and the personal service that you will experience will contribute immeasurably to your visit. The countryside is beautiful, and there are many sights to see, but what adds enjoyment and richness is the pleasant conversation and humour of the people.

Prices

Bord Fáilte register and grade hotels and guest houses, and they divide the many B&B businesses into Farm, Town and Country Houses. All of this is very useful, but apart from indicating the variety of services available and the cost, you really do not get much idea of the atmosphere and style of the place. The establishments listed in this book are described and categorized according to price, and include a variety of lodgings ranging from a luxurious castle to a simple farmhouse—all have something very special to offer a visitor. This may be the architecture, the garden, the food, the atmosphere and the chat, or simply the beauty of the surrounding countryside. The most expensive offer high standards of luxury, and the cheapest ones are clean and comfortable. Most are family-owned, with a few bedrooms, and none fits into a uniform classification, but they are all welcoming and unique places to stay. The price categories are of necessity quite loosely based, and some of the more expensive establishments do weekend deals which are very good value. Please, always check prices and terms when making a booking. Rates are quoted in Irish punts—the value of which at the time of writing is more or less on a parity with sterling.

luxury

Cost no object. B&B from IR£90 per person. You can expect top-quality lodgings with style and opulence. Furnishings will include priceless antiques, whilst the facilities and service provide every modern convenience you could wish for.

expensive

From IR£60 B&B per person. All the bedrooms have their own bathroom, direct-dial telephone, central heating, TV and the other paraphernalia of modern living, but they have something else as well—charm, eccentricity, and a feeling of mellow comfort. They are places where you might sleep in a graceful four-poster hung with rich cloth, and wake up to the sort of hospitality where the smell of coffee is just a prelude to a delicious cooked breakfast, and the sharp sweet taste of homemade jam on Irish wheaten bread.

moderate

From IR£30 to IR£60 B&B per person. Although not as luxurious, most of these places have private bathrooms and an extremely high standard of cooking and service. Again, they have a wonderful atmosphere combined with attractive décor which is sometimes more atmospheric for its touch of age.

From IR£10 to IR£20 B&B per person. Pretty whitewashed farmhouses, Georgian manses, rectories, old manor houses, modern bungalows and fine town houses come under this heading. They are very good value, good 'crack', and you will get marvellous plain cooking. Only some of the bedrooms will have en suite facilities, and some will not have central heating, but there will be perfectly good bathrooms close by and washbasins in the room. And if you are travelling in the late spring/summer, you do not need heating anyway!

Reservations

Bord Fáilte can be of immense help when you are making a reservation or trying to decide where to stay. You can make a reservation direct with the premises, or use the Irish Tourist Board offices in Great Britain who operate an enquiry and booking service. Offices in other countries operate an enquiry service only. Bord Fáilte offices throughout the southwest will make you a reservation for the price of a telephone call. They will only book you into registered and approved lodgings, and a 10 per cent deposit is payable.

Make sure that you book early for the peak months of June, July and August. At other times of the year it is usually quite all right to book on the morning of the day you wish to stay; this gives you great flexibility. However, the excellent lodgings soon get known by word of mouth, so they are always more likely to be booked up in advance.

Literature

The Bord Fáilte Tourist Offices keep plenty of booklets on various types of accommodation: the most comprehensive list, covering the whole of Ireland, is the *Accommodation Guide*, price IR£4.00; others include an *Illustrated Hotels and Guesthouses Guide*, price IR£1; an *Illustrated Farmhouse Guide*, an *Illustrated Town and Country Guide*, and a *Caravan and Camping Guide*, all priced at IR£1.50. There is also the *Self-catering Guide*, *The Blue Book*, which lists Irish country houses and restaurants, *The Hidden Ireland Guide*, *Friendly Homes of Ireland*, and *Elegant Ireland*. All these are available from tourist offices (*see* pp.52–5 for addresses) or from the various associations that publish them.

Hotels

Bord Fáilte register and grade hotels into five categories: **A*** stands for the most luxuriously equipped bedrooms and public rooms with night service, a very high standard of food and plenty of choice. Most bedrooms have their own bath and suites are available— the sort of place where delicious snacks are automatically served with your cocktails. This grading includes baronial mansions set in exquisite grounds or the rather plush anonymity of some of the city and town hotels. **A** grade stands for a luxury hotel which doesn't have quite so many items on the *table d'hôte*, nor does it have night service; but the food is just as good and the atmosphere less restrained. **B*** grade stands for well-furnished and comfortable; some rooms have a bath, cooking is good and plain. **B** and **C** grades are clean, comfortable but limited, **B** offering more in the line of bathrooms and food. All Bord Fáilte graded hotels have heating and hot and cold water in the bedrooms. If you come across a hotel that is ungraded, it is because its grading is under review or because it has just opened, or does not comply with Bord Fáilte requirements. The prices of hotels vary enormously, no matter what grade they are, and the grading takes no account of atmosphere and charm. Many of the most delightful and hospitable country houses come under grades B or C, whilst some of the grade A hotels are very dull. All graded hotels are listed in the Bord Fáilte *Guest Accommodation* booklet and in the *Be Our Guest* booklet.

Guest Houses

These are usually houses which have become too large and expensive to maintain as private houses. The minimum number of bedrooms is five. The grade **A** houses are just as good as their hotel equivalent, as are those graded lower down the scale, although the atmosphere is completely different. In fact, guesthouses are some of the best places to stay

If you decide to vary your accommodation from guest house, to town and country house or farmhouse, you will discover one of the principles of Irish life: that everything in Ireland works on a personal basis. If you are on holiday to avoid people, a guest house is the last place you should book into. It is impossible not to be drawn into a friendly conversation, whether about fishing or politics. You will get a large, thoroughly uncontinental breakfast, and delicious evening meals with a choice within a set meal. Dinner is always very punctual, at eight, after everyone has sat around by the fire over very large drinks. Lunch or a packed lunch can be arranged. All grades of guest house have hot and cold water, and heating in the bedrooms. Grade **A** guest houses have some rooms with private bathrooms, but their reputation is based on scrumptious food and comfortable surroundings. You can get full details of guest houses in the Bord Fáilte booklets entitled *Be Our Guest*. As a general guide, a comfortable, even luxurious night's sleep will cost between IR£14 and IR£30, although the more basic guest houses do not cost more than a farmhouse B&B. A delicious meal ranges from between IR£11 and IR£20. Sometimes the owners provide high tea, sometimes the only meal they do is breakfast. Our selection of guesthouses is included in the list of places to stay at the end of each county section.

Farmhouses, Town and Country Houses

Often these family homes make your stay in this country, for you meet Irish people who are kind, generous and intelligent. This is also the most economical way to stay in Ireland if you don't want to stay in a tent or in a youth hostel. If you are not going to a place that is recommended, it is largely a matter of luck whether you hit an attractive or a mediocre set-up, but always watch out for the shamrock sign, the Bord Fáilte sign of approval. Wherever you go, you should get a comfortable bed (if you are tall, make sure it is long enough, as sometimes Irish beds can be on the small side), and an enormous breakfast: orange juice, cereal, two eggs, bacon, sausages, toast and marmalade, and a huge pot of tea or coffee. If you get rather tired of this fry-up, ask your hostess the night before for something different and she will be happy to oblige. Another thing—the coffee is invariably weak and tasteless; it's much safer to stick to tea! Nevertheless, breakfast is still a very satisfying meal, which means you don't feel hungry again until the evening.

Bed and breakfast per person ranges from IR£13 to IR£20 if you are sharing a bedroom (a single room is sometimes more expensive). You can get much cheaper weekly rates, with partial or full board. Very often you can eat your evening meal in the dining room of the

B&B. Again, there will be masses to eat – and piping hot—often so much better than local restaurants and cafés. Breakfast and other meal times are flexible: they happen when it suits you, but you should give notice before 12 noon if you want to eat dinner.

Some houses serve dinner at between IR£9 and IR£15, and some 'high tea', which is less costly (between IR£6 and IR£8). 'High tea' is a very sensible meal which has evolved for the working man who begins to feel hungry at about 6pm. You get a plate of something hot, perhaps chicken and chips, followed by fresh soda bread, jam and cakes and a pot of tea. Sometimes you get a salad. This leaves you with plenty of time to go out and explore in the evenings—whether to the pubs or the countryside! Some houses provide tea and biscuits as a night-cap for nibblers at around 10pm.

More and more establishments have en suite bathrooms with a loo, basin and bath or shower. You usually pay about IR£2 extra for this. If there is only a communal bathroom you will be charged a trivial amount for the hot bath—if you are even charged at all. Ask the woman of the house for a towel or, better still, carry your own, as those you are given are usually the size of a tea towel. Take your bath whenever you want; your hostess will ask you how many you had at the end of your stay. The bathroom is shared by everybody, family and guests, and it should be immaculately clean. Don't have your bath when it is obvious that everyone else is trying to use the bathroom.

For people hitching or using public transport, the town houses are the easiest to get to and find, but my favourites are farmhouses, followed closely by country houses. The farms concentrate on dairy, sheep, crop farming or beef cattle and often a mixture of everything. Tucked away in lovely countryside, they may be traditional or modern. The farmer's wife, helped by her children, makes life very comfortable and is always ready to have a chat, and advise you on the local beauty spots, and good places to hear traditional music or go for a *ceili*. Some of the town and country houses are on fairly main roads, but they are generally not too noisy as there is so little traffic about. The type of house you might stay in ranges from the Georgian to the Alpine-style bungalow, from a semi-detached to a 1950s dolls' house. There are a bewildering number of architectural styles in the new houses beginning to radiate out from small villages.

It is wise to book maybe a night or two ahead during July and August, though it is rarely necessary. This means that you do not have to be tied, and can dawdle in a place as much as you want.

Renting a House or Cottage

This is easy. Every regional office of Bord Fáilte has a list of houses and apartments to let; there is also a short list of self-catering houses at the back of the *Guest Accommodation* booklet. Places to rent range from converted stable blocks, modern bungalows to stone-built cottages.

There is a very popular Rent-an-Irish-Cottage scheme with centres in Counties Limerick, and Clare. On the outside the cottages are thatched, whitewashed and traditional; inside they are well-designed with an electric cooker, fridge and kettle—all the mod cons you could want. There are built-in cupboards, comfy beds, and linen. Simple, comfortable Irish-made furniture and fittings make it a happy blend of tradition and modern convenience. The cottages vary in size: some take eight, others five. Easter and May, June, July and August are the most expensive times with prices hovering around IR£250 to IR£400 a week, but in October, sometimes the nicest month weather-wise, a cottage for eight is very reasonable at around IR£150 per week. The local people take a great interest in you because they are all shareholders in the scheme and so do their best to make you content! Write to Bord Fáilte for details of the scheme and other self-catering cottages.

Youth Hostels

The Irish YHA is called *An Oige* and has a number of hostels in the southwest. They are often in wild and remote places, so that they are doubly attractive to the enterprising traveller. Members of the International Youth Hostel Federation can use any of these. If you haven't got a card, you can join for IR£8.50; there is no age limit! All you have to do is buy something called an International Guest Card, by purchasing six welcome stamps costing IR£2 each. The stamps may be bought one at a time at six different hostels, if you like.

The youth hostels are often the most superb houses, and they range from cottages to castles, old coastguard stations to old military barracks. They are great centres for climbers, walkers and fishers, and not too spartan; many have a comfortable laxity when it comes to the rules. You must provide your own sheet and sleeping bag. A flap or pocket to cover the pillows can be bought at the *An Oige* office, and the hostel provides blankets or sheet bags. Bring your own knives, forks, spoons, tea towels, bath towel, soap and food. All the hostels have fully equipped self-catering kitchens, and most also provide breakfast, packed lunches and an evening meal on request.

Charges vary according to age, month and location; during July and August it is slightly more expensive, and it is vital to book. This applies also to weekends. All *An Oige* hostels may be booked from one hostel to another, or centrally by contacting the head office (*see* below). Most hostels are open all year round. It's quite a good idea to combine hostelling with staying at B&Bs (*see* under 'Farmhouses, Town and Country Houses', above.)

There are several rail/cycling holidays on offer to hostel members. The average approximate cost of staying overnight ranges from IR£4.50 to IR£5.90 from July to August and from IR£2 to IR£5.50 for other months. All enquiries, an essential handbook and an excellent map can be got from the *An Oige* Office, 61 Mountjoy Street, Dublin 1, ✆ (01) 830 4555, ✉ (01) 830 1610. Independent Holiday Hostels of Ireland (IHH) is a completely separate organisation to YHA. It is a co-operative society of hostels , ranging from Georgian houses to restored mills. They are friendly, open to everyone (children are welcome in most hostels), and most have double and family rooms. All hostels will rent you sheets and all hostels provide duvets and blankets. The average price for a dormitory bed in high season is IR£6. Send off for a list of hostels to IHH Office, UCD Village, Belfield, Dublin 2, ✆ (01) 260 1634, 🖷 (01) 269 7704.

Many other organizations such as the YWCA, ISSACS, and colleges of further education offer cheap and comfortable accommodation. Some of them have excellent eating facilities attached; send for a *Discover Young Ireland* brochure from the Bord Fáilte, Baggot Street Bridge, Dublin 2, ✆ (01) 676 5871.

Camping and Caravanning

The camping and caravan parks which meet the standards set by Bord Fáilte are listed in a booklet available from the tourist offices. You can also order it direct from Ms A. Dillon, Irish Camping and Caravanning Holidays, 2 Offington Court, Sutton, Dublin 13. There is also a selection in the *Guest Accommodation Guide* republished every year by Bord Fáilte. The sites are graded according to amenities and many of them are in beautiful areas. Laundry rooms, excellent showers and loos, shops, restaurants, indoor games rooms and TV make camping easy and also more civilized, especially if you have children. It is possible to rent tents and camping equipment.

For a complete list of sites, write to the main Dublin tourist office. Here is a useful contact: in Co. Cork you could try the Tent Shop, Rutland Street, off South Terrace, Cork City, ✆ (021) 316184. It is also possible to rent caravans and motor homes. For full details check the *Caravan and Camping* booklet. Overnight charges in the camping parks vary between IR£5.50 and IR£7.00 per night, with a small charge per person at some parks and IR£1 for electrical linkup. If you are bringing your own caravan or camping equipment to Ireland, and have Calor gas appliances, the only ones on sale in Ireland which are compatible are those supplied by Gaz. Some caravan parks accept dogs if they are on a leash.

Farmers can be very tolerant of people turning up and asking if they can camp or park their caravan in a field. You must ask their permission first, and tell them how long you want to stay. Be polite, do not get in the way and you will find that they will give you drinking water, lots of chat, and even vegetables from their gardens.

Women Travellers

Irish men have an attitude towards women which is as infuriating as it is attractive. They are a grand old muddle of male chauvinism, with a dash of admiration and fear for their mothers, sisters and wives. Irish women have a sharpness and wit which makes them more than a match for 'your man' in an argument, but at the same time they work their hearts out.

If you are a lone female travelling around you will find an Irish man will always help you with your luggage, your flat tyre and stand you for a meal or a drink, without any question of you buying him a round. If one tries to chat you up in a bar, or at a dance, it is always a bit of 'crack', not to be taken seriously, and the game is abandoned at once if you get tired of it. They probably think that you ought to be travelling with somebody else, but it's only the women who will say so, saying, with a smile, that it must be a bit lonesome. If you walk into an obviously male preserve, such as a serious drinking pub, don't expect to feel welcome, because you won't be unless everybody is drunk and by that time you would need to scarper. A bit of advice, which does not apply just to women, was pithily put by an Irish politician: 'The great difference between England and Ireland is that in England you can say what you like, so long as you do the right thing. In Ireland you can do what you like, so long as you say the right thing.' If you are hitch-hiking on your own, or with another girl, you will get plenty of lifts, and offers to take you out dancing that night; your driver will never believe that you have to get on and be somewhere by a certain date, so the journey is passed in pleasant banter. You would be better off hitch-hiking with someone else if possible, although it is pretty safe on the whole.

Topics

The people are thus inclined: religious, frank, amorous, sufferable of infinite paines, verie glorious, manie sorcerers, excellent horsemen, delighted with wars, great alms-givers, passing in hospitality.

(From *Holinshed's Chronicles*, 1577)

This description so aptly fits the Irish today that I can only add a few very superficial remarks on the subject. Conditions have changed radically. For a start, almost half of the population lives in the spreading cities. Still, compared to its near-neighbour, England, and to many other European countries, Ireland is a very rural place and even city-dwellers have close links with their country background. Wherever they live, Irish people have a healthy disdain for time and the hustle and bustle of business. Remember the old Irish saying as you travel around that, 'When God made time he made plenty of it.' You will become aware of a great sense of shared identity and neighbourly feeling, particularly towards those in trouble, or the very old.

The traits peculiar to the Irish which always reassert themselves, wherever they are in the world, are numerous. Amongst them is a delight in words and wordplay (reading anything by Flann O'Brien or James Joyce will give you a taste of it); a love of parties and crack (a good time), music, dancing and witty talk; a ready kindness which never fails; great hospitality and an interest in your affairs which is never mere inquisitiveness, but a charming device to put you at your ease. They are an untidy race—in their houses and in the countryside. This, mixed in with a certain sloppiness, leads to the phenomenon of rusty cars dumped in lonely glens, litter in any old place, and general mess. Not for the Irish the freshly painted doors and gateways of the Anglo-Saxon. There is a lot of ignorance and indifference in matters aesthetic. Old buildings go to rack and ruin, and vile ribbon development chokes the towns and the countryside around.

An Irish person never forgets an insult or a wrong, and this memory will go back for generations. It might have been a quarrel over land or the meanness of the local gentry. Oliver Cromwell is still remembered with hatred for his savage campaign in the 1650s. The Irish have a quarrelsome spirit which is quickly roused in the face of bland priggishness.

Each province and county of Ireland produces more individual traits: the northerners have a reputation for directness of speech and a fighting spirit. The Munster people are held in respect for their poetry. A Dubliner might be considered a bit of a know-all. The people of Connacht are famous for their hospitality and strength.

Finally, one last word in this briefest of outlines: the Irish still have a great sense of the spiritual. The Catholic Church is very strong, but so is the faith of Church of Ireland members, and of the Presbyterians, to judge by the numbers who attend their churches on Sundays. Religion is the great anchor; it pervades all aspects of living, which perhaps partially explains the paradox that in Ireland there is little thought for the future, and life is lived for the moment.

The Fairy People

The Fairy People, or *Daoine Sidhe*, are a rich part of Irish folklore. According to peasant belief, they are fallen angels who are not good enough to be saved and not bad enough to languish in Hell. Perhaps they are the gods of the Earth, as it is written in the *Book of Armagh*; or the pagan gods of Ireland, the Tuatha Dé Danaan, who may also have been a race of invaders whose origins are lost in the mists of time. Antiquarians have different theories but, whatever they surmise, these fairy people persist in the popular imagination; they and their characteristics have been kept alive in tradition and myth.

The Fairy People are quickly offended, and must always be referred to as the 'Gentry' or the 'Good People'. They are also easily pleased, and will keep misfortune from your door if you leave them a bowl of milk on the window-sill overnight. Their evil seems to be without malice, and their chief occupations are feasting, fighting, making love and playing or listening to beautiful music. The only hardworking person amongst them is the leprechaun, who is kept busy making the shoes they wear out with their dancing. It is said that many of the beautiful tunes of Ireland are theirs, remembered by mortal eavesdroppers. The story is that Carolan, the last of the great Irish bards, slept on a rath which, like the many prehistoric standing stones in Ireland, had become a fairy place in folk tradition, and forever after the fairy music ran in his head and made him the great musician he was. Some of the individual fairy types are not very pleasant, and here are brief descriptions of a few.

The banshee, from *bean sidhe*, is a woman fairy or attendant spirit who follows the old families, and wails before a death. The keen, the funeral cry of the peasantry, is said to be an imitation of her cry. An omen which sometimes accompanies the old woman is an immense black coach, carrying a coffin and drawn by headless riders.

The leprechaun, or fairy shoemaker, is solitary, old, and bad-tempered; the practical joker amongst the 'Good People'. He is very rich because of his trade, and buries his pots of gold at the end of rainbows. He also takes many treasure crocks, buried in times of war, for his own. Many believe he is the dé Danaan god Lugh, the god of arts and crafts, who degenerated in popular lore into the leprechaun.

The leanhaun shee, or fairy mistress, longs for the love of mortal men. If they refuse, she must be their slave; if they consent, they are hers, and can only escape by finding another to take their place. The fairy lives on their life, and they waste away, but death is no escape. She has become identified in political song and verse with the Gaelic Muse, for she gives inspiration to those whom she persecutes.

The Pook seems to be an animal spirit. Some authorities have linked it with a he-goat from *púca* or *poc*, the Gaelic for goat. Others maintain it is a forefather of Shakespeare's Puck in *A Midsummer Night's Dream*. It lives in solitary mountain places and old ruins, and is of a nightmarish aspect. It is a November spirit, and often assumes the form of a stallion. The horse comes out of the water and is easy to tame if you can only keep him from the sight of water. If you cannot, he will plunge in with his rider and tear him to pieces at the bottom.

Boglands

Ireland is literally rich in boglands, formed over many hundreds of years. In the past, boglands were despised except as a source of fuel, but now we know how rich they are in flora and fauna. And a vast quantity of folklore has grown up around them, beautifully described in *Irish Folk Ways* by E. Estyn Evans. In many fairy stories the human is lured off the path into the bog by strange lights at night. Walking on bogs can be very mucky and sometimes dangerous, so keep to the few paths and try and go with a local to guide you. Many writers describe the great peace and well-being to be had from a day out on the bogs cutting turf. Even now, a Dubliner clings to his cutting rights on a piece of Wicklow hill, for there is something eminently satisfying about cutting the sods of rich blackness, and then, later, during the bitter cold winter nights, heaping it onto the open fire. Underneath the bog, well-preserved bodies, jewelled crosiers for bishops, golden cups, giant elks' antlers and brittle pots of butter have all been revealed as the turf is cut away.

About 14 per cent of Ireland's land surface is bog. The brooding immutability of the bog, the drizzling rain and winds which sweep it have surely contributed towards the Irish philosophy of fatality. There are two types of bogs—blanket and raised. The latter are mainly to be found in the midlands. In Ireland, wetness is a key factor in the formation of the peat which begins to grow on lakes and ponds as plants invade the water. Sphagnum moss is the vital plant because it holds water like a sponge and has a great capacity for trapping nutrients. Peat builds up because it releases acid which inhibits the breakdown of dead plants.

The Irish economy has been bolstered by the boglands. Bord na Mona, the Government-owned turf company, was set up in 1946 and has drained vast areas of peat, cutting it by machines and using the fuel to generate electricity. The sphagnum in the upper layers is baled as horticultural peat and sold for use in gardens all over Britain. But the draining of the bogs has consequences for rivers, and for those living near them in valleys, for the bogs

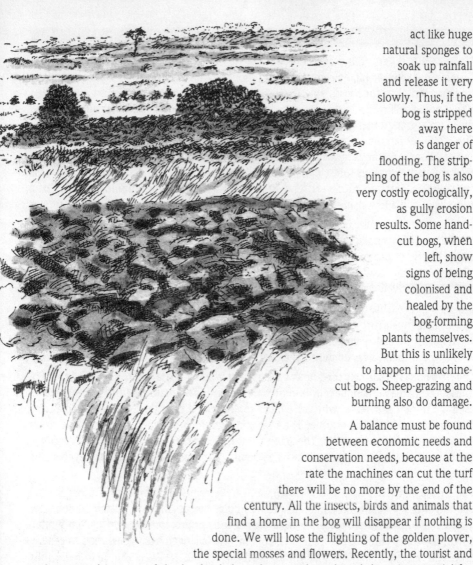

act like huge natural sponges to soak up rainfall and release it very slowly. Thus, if the bog is stripped away there is danger of flooding. The stripping of the bog is also very costly ecologically, as gully erosion results. Some hand-cut bogs, when left, show signs of being colonised and healed by the bog-forming plants themselves. But this is unlikely to happen in machine-cut bogs. Sheep-grazing and burning also do damage.

A balance must be found between economic needs and conservation needs, because at the rate the machines can cut the turf there will be no more by the end of the century. All the insects, birds and animals that find a home in the bog will disappear if nothing is done. We will lose the flighting of the golden plover, the special mosses and flowers. Recently, the tourist and environmental interest of the boglands have been evaluated, and there is potential for wildlife conservation in 'cutaway' bogs—the bogs which are exhausted of peat. If you are interested there is a bogland centre at Lullymore, Rathangan on the Bog of Allan in Co. Kildare, ✆ (0762) 851102. A fine raised bog is the Clara Bog and Mongan Bog, Co. Offaly. For more information contact the Peatland Conservation Council, 3 Lower Mount Street, Dublin 2, ✆ (01) 872 2392; also the Peatlands Park, Lough Neagh, Dungannon, Co. Armagh, ✆ (0762) 851102.

Music

Traditional Irish music is played everywhere in Ireland, in the cities and the country. Government sponsorship helped to revive it, especially through Radio an Gaeltachta (Irish-language radio) in the west. Now there is great enthusiasm for it amongst everyone: a nine-year-old will sing a lover's lament about seduction and desertion, without batting an eyelid, to a grandfather whose generation scarcely remembered the Gaelic songs at all. The 1845–49 famine silenced the music and dancing for a while, but today Ireland has one of the most vigorous music traditions in Europe. Irish ballads are sung the world over; each emigrant considers himself an exile still, and the commercial record industry churns out ballads. Most record covers tend to be decorated with the grinning features of a leprechaun and a few shamrocks for good measure.

Serious traditional music is not in this sweet folksy style. Listening to it can induce a state of exultant melancholy, or infectious merriment; whatever way, it goes straight to your heart. The lyrics deal with the ups and downs of love; failed rebellions, especially that of 1798; soldiering, dead heroes; religion and homesick love for the beauty of the country-side. Comparatively few deal with occupations or work!

The bard in pre-Christian society was held in honour and great awe, for his learning and the mischievous satire in his poetry and music. After the Cromwellian and Williamite wars, he lost his status altogether; music and poetry were kept alive by the country people who cheered themselves up during the dark winter evenings with stories and music.

The harp is, sadly, scarcely used nowadays, except when it is dragged out for the benefit of tourists at medieval banquets in Bunratty Castle, etc. The main traditional instruments used are the *uillean* pipes, which are more sophisticated than the Scottish bagpipes, the fiddle (violin) and the tin whistle. The beat and rhythm is provided by a handheld drum made from stretched goat hide. This instrument is called the *bodhran*, and the accordian, the flute, guitar and the piano are used by some groups as well. These are played singly or together.

The airs, laments, slip jigs, reels and songs all vary enormously from region to region, and you might easily hear a Cork man or a Clare fiddler discussing with heated emotion the interpretation of a certain piece. Pieces are constantly improvised on, and seldom written down; inevitably some of the traditional content gets changed from generation to genera-tion. A form of singing that had almost died out by the 1940s is the *Sean-Nós*, fully adorned, sung in Gaelic and unaccompanied by instruments. Now the *Sean-Nós* section in music festivals is overflowing with entrants.

You will have no difficulty in hearing traditional ballads or folk music in the local bars or hotels; players usually advertise in the local newspaper or by sticking up a notice in the window. The group of players seem only too happy to let you join in, and as the atmos-phere gets smokier the music really takes off. In 1951 Comhaltas Ceoltoírí Eireann was set up for the promotion of traditional music, song and dance. It now has two hundred branches all over the country, and their members have regular sessions (*seisiún*) which are open to all. Ask at the local tourist office or write to Comhaltas Ceoltoírí Eireann, 32

Belgrave Square, Monkstown, Co. Dublin, ✆ (01) 280 0295. A popular feature of the traditional music scene are the Seisuns—these are informal sessions of music, ceilidhs and traditional cabaret. For information on local musical happenings contact ✆ (066) 32323 or ✆ (066) 32134—there is bound to be a *fleadh* going on somewhere near you. The All-Ireland Fleadh is held at the end of August in a different town every year. There are smaller festivals around the southwest each year. At these you can hear music of an incredible standard brimming over the streets from every hall, bar, hotel and private house. It takes a great deal of stamina and a lot of jars to see the whole thing through. Do not expect a formal concert-hall environment, as music and 'crack' thrive best in small intimate gatherings, and are often unplanned sessions in the local bar.

In Kerry, Father Pat Ahearn has got together a National Folk Theatre, which has performances in song, mime, and the dance of ordinary life set in rural Ireland years ago. They are based in two thatched cottages, in Finuge and at Carraig on the west tip of the Dingle Peninsula. Each cottage is known as *Teach Saimsa*, the house of musical entertainment. Contact: The National Folk Theatre of Ireland, Godfrey Place, Tralee, Co. Kerry, ✆ (066) 23055, which was founded in 1974 to promote Irish Folk Culture through the medium of music and heavy emphasis on traditional Irish dancing and singing.

If you get a chance to watch the Orangemen marching with their flute bands (practising ground for the celebrated James Galway when he was a youngster), you will see how important music is to every Irishman. Boys beat the great Lambeg drums till their knuckles bleed, while the skilful throwing of the batons makes a great performance—well worth seeing, in spite of its sectarian associations.

Today Ireland is producing some good musicians of a completely different type from the folk groups. The local bands that play in the bars play jazz, blues, and a rhythmical and melodious combination of pop and traditional instruments. Look in the local newspaper of any big town or ask in a record shop; they will know what gigs are on and probably be able to sell you a ticket as well. Some of the top names on the rock and pop scene come from Ireland, for instance, Van Morrison, U2 and the Cranberries.

Tracing Your Ancestors

If you have any Irish blood in you at all, you will have a passion for genealogy; the Irish seem to like looking backwards. When they had nothing left—no land, no Brehon laws, no religious freedom—they managed to hold on to their pride and their genealogy. Waving these before the eyes of French and Spanish rulers ensured that they got posts at court or commissions in the army. There is no such thing as class envy in Ireland: the next man is as good as you, and everybody is descended from some prince or hero from the Irish past. It is the descendants of the Cromwellian parvenues who had to bolster up their images with portraits and fine furniture. Now the planter families have the Irish obsession with their ancestors too!

The best way to go about finding where your family came from is to write to the Public Record Office in Dublin. First you must have found out as much as possible from family papers, old relatives, and the records of the Church and State in your own country; your local historical or genealogical society might be able to help. Find out the full name of your emigrant ancestor, the background of his or her family, whether rich, poor, merchants or farmers, Catholic or Protestant. The family tradition of remembering the name of the parish or townland is a great help.

In America, immigrant records have been published by Baltimore Genealogical Publishing Company in seven volumes, and lists the arrival of people into New York between 1846 and 1851. In Canada, the Department of Irish Studies, St Mary's University, Halifax is very helpful. In Australia, the Civil Records are very good: try the National Library, Canberra, the Mitchell Library, Sydney, and the Society of Australian Genealogists, Richmond Villa, 120 Kent Street, Sydney.

The following addresses are important sources of information in Ireland:

The General Civil Registration of Births, Marriages and Deaths, The Registrar General, Joyce House, 8–11 Lombard Street East, Dublin 2, ✆ (01) 671 1000. Open Mon–Fri, 9.30–12.30 and 2.15–4.30. Marriages of non-Catholics were recorded from 1845. Registration of everybody began in 1864. Search fees are very reasonable.

The Genealogical Office, 2 Kildare Street, Dublin 2, ✆ (01) 661 8811. Consultations are by appointment only. This office handles enquiries into heraldry, genealogy and family history for the whole of Ireland, and will make searches for you for a small fee. It is also the contact address for a list of Research agencies in the Republic.

The Registry of Deeds, Henrietta St, Dublin 7, ✆ (01) 873 2233. Open Mon–Fri, 10–4.30. It has records of land matters from 1708 onwards. You may make your research in person for a small fee.

The National Library, Kildare St, Dublin 2, ✆ (01) 661 8811. Open Mon 10–9; Tues/Wed 2–9, Thurs/Fri, 10–5, Sat 10–1. It has many sources in its books, newspapers and manuscripts.

National Archives, Bishop Street, Dublin 8, ✆ (01) 478 3711. Open Mon–Fri, 10–5. Unfortunately, the Pubic Record Office in Dublin was burnt in 1922, and with it many of the Church of Ireland registers, but not all. It houses Griffith's Primary Valuation of Ireland, 1848–63, which records the names of those owning or occupying land and property, as well as other important genealogical sources.

The State Paper Office, Dublin Castle, Dublin 2, ✆ (01) 478 3711, ext. 2518. Rebellion reports and records relating to 1798, and convict records of those transported to Australia.

If your ancestors were Presbyterian, **the Presbyterian Historical Society,** Church House, Fisherwick Place, Belfast, may be able to assist you. **The Ulster Historical Foundation,** attached to the Northern Ireland Public Record Office, will undertake searches. The address to write to is the Secretary, UHF, 12 College Square East, Belfast, ✆ (01232) 332288. Local records are held at a county level dating from 1864. Church records vary widely in age, and are an essential primary source. The parochial registers are in the keep of parish priests and Church of Ireland rectors all over Ireland. Wherever there is an enthusiastic historical society or heritage society and the co-operation of the parish priest, the process of indexing parish records within their own counties has begun. All parish and appropriate civil records are being collected and filed and much of it is already on computer. For a list of the current Genealogical centres write to **Irish Genealogical Project,** 1 Clarinda Park North, Dun Laoghaire, Co. Dublin or the Kildare Street address above. For a listing, please enclose return postage. In the southwest the main centres of information are the City Library, Cork ✆ (021) 277110; The Granary, Limerick ✆ (061) 410777; Corrofin Heritage Centre ✆ (065) 37955; the Library, Tralee ✆ (066) 21200.

Hibernian Researchers, 24 Bainagowan, Palmerston Park, Dublin 6, (01) 496 6522, employ full-time professional genealogists with plenty of experience; they will undertake searches for you. Another genealogical research agency is **Irish Genealogical Services,** 111 South Parade, Belfast, BT7 2GN, ✆ (01232) 646489.

Historic Houses

If you want to try to understand the Anglo-Irish, who have a very muddled status amongst most shades of opinion, the best thing to do is look round one of their houses.

The expression 'Anglo-Irish' has political, social and religious connotations. It is used to describe the waves of English settlers and their descendants who became so powerful in the land after the success of the campaigns of Elizabeth I of England. An optimistic view is held by some that Anglo-Irish is a tag that should only be applied to literature, and indeed it does seem ridiculous that after three hundred years of living in a place these landowning families are not counted as truly Irish. On the one hand, it is a fact that the sons of the Ascendancy were educated in England, and served the British Empire as soldiers or civil servants, and that they beheld themselves as different from the native Irish; whilst on the other, many of these people felt a great and patriotic love for Ireland, led revolts and uprisings against British rule and, starting with the Normans, became in the very apt, anonymous and undated Latin saying 'more Irish than the Irish'.

Ireland's big houses were built by families who would be most offended if you called them English, although as far as the Gaelic Irish are concerned that is what they are! 'The Big House' is another very Irish expression; it is applied to a landowner's house regardless of its size or grandeur. In fact, if you look through Burke's *Guide to Irish Country Houses* and the rather depressing, but fascinating, *Vanishing Houses of Ireland* (published by the Irish Architectural Archive and the Irish Georgian Society) you will get a very good idea of the variety and huge number of houses that belonged to the gentry.

The English monarchs always financed their Irish wars by paying their soldiers with grants of land in Ireland, and as the country was so unruly, the settlers lived in fortified or semi-fortified houses during the 17th century. There are only a very few examples of Tudor domestic architecture, the most famous being Ormonde Castle, Carrick on Suir, County Tipperary—and if you visit Bunratty Castle, Co. Clare, look out for the early 17th-century plasterwork.

The most impressive and the first Irish building in the grand Renaissance style is the late-17th century Royal Hospital at Kilmainham in Dublin, which has been rescued from dereliction and restored. It is now the Irish Museum of Modern Art. The victory of

William of Orange over James II was complete when the Jacobites surrendered at the Treaty of Limerick in 1696. Within a few years the Penal Laws were introduced, which severely restricted the freedom of both Catholics and non-conformists. The majority of big houses were built in the hundred years following the 1690s when the Protestant landowners settled down to enjoy their gains. The civil and domestic architecture that survives from these times is both elegant and splendid, and is to be found in every county.

The 'Big House' usually consists of a square, grey stone block, sometimes with wings, set amongst gardens and parkland with stables at the back, and a walled garden. Sometimes it is called a castle, although the only attribute of a castle it may have is a deep fosse. A lingering insecurity must often have remained, for many are almost as tall as they are wide, with up to four storeys, rather like a Georgian version of the 16th-century tower house.

The buildings are completely different in atmosphere here from their counterparts in England. They have not undergone Victorian 'improvements' or gradually assumed an air of comfortable mellowness over the centuries. It was an act of bravado on the part of the Anglo-Irish to build them at all, for they had always to be on the alert against the disaffected natives, who readily formed aggressive agrarian groups such as the White Boys. They never had enough money to add on layer after layer in the newest architectural fashion; their houses remained as Palladian splendours or Gothick fantasies built during the Georgian age, when the fortified house could at last be exchanged for something a good deal more comfortable.

The big houses that remain are full of beautiful furniture, pictures, *objets d'art* and the paraphernalia of generations who appreciated beauty, good horses, hard drinking and eating, and were generous and slapdash by nature. It is against this background of grey stately houses looking onto sylvan scenes and cosseted by sweeping trees that one should read Maria Edgeworth, supplying some details yourself on the Penal Laws, the famine, the foreignness of the landlords and their loyalties. The literature on the 'Big House' is huge, and if you read Thackeray, Trollope, Charles Lever, Somerville and Ross, and more Maria Edgeworth on the subject, you will not only be entertained but well informed. The big house, courthouse, jail and military barracks were all symbols of oppression, and not surprisingly many of them got burnt out in the 1920s; but the rooms of these houses echo with the voices of talented and liberal people—the wit of Sheridan, Wilde, the conversations of Mrs Delany, the gleeful humour of Somerville and Ross—as you wander around.

In England there is a whole network of organizations and legislation to protect the historic house. In the Republic of Ireland there is no equivalent of the National Trust, the Historic Building and Monuments Commission, no National Heritage fund. This means there are no grants for repairs to buildings, and no effective legislation to protect them from dereliction or neglect. Even now the big house is persistently regarded by the powers that be as tainted with the memories of colonialism and an oppressive age. They are labelled as 'not Irish', although the craftsmen who built and carved the wonderful details of cornicing, stucco-work and dovetailing, elegant staircases and splendid decoration were as Irish as could be. There are many desolate shells to glimpse on your travels, though it is still possible to go around quite a selection of well cared-for properties.

The National Heritage Council set up by Charles Haughey has helped to change official attitudes, but it is the Irish Georgian Society which so far has done most to secure the future of the 'big house'. Founded in 1958 to work for the preservation of Ireland's architectural heritage, the society has carried out numerous rescue and restoration works on historic houses.

If these gracious buildings and their gardens and parkland interest you, book into country-house hotels such as Bantry House, Longueville House and Ballymaloe House in Co. Cork, Adare Manor or Glin Castle in Co. Limerick, and Dromoland Castle in Co. Clare For more details of country-house lodgings, *see* **Practical A–Z**, 'Where to Stay', pp.42–3, and individual entries at the end of each county chapter.

There is a growing demand to stay in or rent an Irish castle and some of them are quite reasonable in price. Elegant Ireland is a company which will organize the most specialized of requests and holiday schedules. They have a range of very exclusive and attractive country houses where you can stay as the guest of friendly, interesting hosts, and where you can be sure of good food. They will also organize rented properties from a castle to a thatched cottage. For details contact Elegant Ireland, 15 Harcourt Street, Dublin 2, ✆ (01) 475 1665/475 1632, ✉ 475 1012. If you are in the US, you may call their agent Abercrombie & Kent at their toll-free number ✆ (800) 323 7308, or in their Oakbrook (Illinois) office, ✆ (708 954) 2944. Luxurious tours can be arranged, by which you can stay as a guest in some of these splendid buildings and be entertained to dinner by the owner. 'Hidden Ireland' is the collective name for a number of privately owned historic houses offering accommodation and often dinner, ✆ (01) 668 1423.

John Colclough runs specialized tours of public and private houses and castles in Ireland. You can contact him at Irish Country House Tours, 71 Waterloo Road, Dublin 4, ✆ (01) 668 6463. If you simply want to wander around ask for a list of houses, and castles open to the public from the Irish Tourist Board.

Later Architectural Forms

Palladian

The term used to describe a pseudo-classical architectural style taken from the 16th-century Italian architect, Palladio. Sir Edward Lovett Pearce introduced the Palladian style to Ireland, and it was continued by his pupil, Richard Cassels, also known as Castle.

Neoclassical

A style of building which is similar to that of Palladio, but was more directly inspired by the civilization of Ancient Rome. It became popular in the 1750s until the Gothic Revival.

Gothick

An amusing and romantic style which was popular in the late 18th century. It is spelt with a 'k' to distinguish it from the serious, and later, Gothic Revival. Gothick Castles were built by Francis Johnston and the English Paine brothers, who came over to Ireland with John Nash during the 1780s. Towers and battlements were added to more severe classical houses.

Gothic Revival

From the 1830s onwards many houses and churches were built in a style harking back to the Tudor and perpendicular forms; the popularity of these gradually gave way to the more severe style of the Early-English and Decorated Gothic. The English church architect Augustus Pugin (1812–52) equated Gothic with Christian and Classicism with pagan. He designed some churches and cathedrals in Ireland including St Mary's Cathedral in Killarney. J. J. McCarthy (1817–82), an Irish architect, was very strongly influenced by Pugin.

Hibernio-Romanesque

A style which was popular in church architecture from the 1850s onwards. It fitted in with growing national feelings to lay claim to an 'Irish style' which existed before the Anglo-Norman invasion.

Irish Rococo Plasterwork

The great period of rococo plasterwork in Ireland began with the Swiss Italian brothers Paul and Philip Francini, who came to Ireland in 1734 to decorate the ceiling at Carton, Maynooth, for the Earl of Kildare. They were great stuccodores, and modelled plaster figures, trophies, fruit and flowers in magnificent combinations.

The Irish craftsmen quickly learned the technique, and between 1740–60 many beautiful ceilings were created. These craftsmen tended to leave out figures, concentrating instead on birds, flowers and musical instruments. The ceilings are graceful, yet full of life, with a swirling gaiety which make Adam ceilings, which later became the fashion, seem stilted.

Selected Architects

Francis Johnston (1760–1829). Originally from Armagh, where he was responsible for many fine buildings, such as the Observatory, he moved to Dublin in 1793. He did a lot of fine work in Dublin and made a huge contribution to founding the Royal Hibernian Academy of Painting, Sculpture and Architecture in 1823; he was its president for many years. He designed some 'Gothick' castles such as Charleville Forest in County Cork.

Sir Richard Morrison (1767–1849). Regency architect from West Cork who designed the neoclassical Fota House in County Cork where the estate buildings, including a huntsman's lodge, are scaled-down versions of the house.

The Paine Brothers—James and George Richard: Pupils of the famous English architect, John Nash who designed grand houses all over Ireland, the Paine brothers came to Ireland around 1818. James went to Limerick and George Richard built up his practice in Cork where he constructed many fine buildings. One example is St Patrick's Church in Lower Glanmire Road built in 1836, it has a fine corinthian portico.

Davis Ducart: A Sardinian who moved to Ireland in the 18th century, he designed two notable buildings: The Limerick Custom House between 1765–69, and the Mayoralty House in Prospect Row, Cork between 1765–1773, it is now the Mercy Hospital. He also designed Riverstown House at Glanmire.

Thomas and Kearns Deane: architects at the beginning of the 19th century, bothe brothers left their mark on Cork: Kearns Deane designed and built St Mary's Dominican Church on Pope's Quay, Cork between 1832–39, and Thomas Deane produced University College Cork in Tudor Gothic collegiate style, modelled on the Oxford colleges, between 1845 and 1849.

Gardens and Parklands of the Southwest

Gaelic Ireland does not have a long horticultural tradition. It began when the Anglo-Normans and later settlers introduced the idea of a pleasure garden, with its flowers and fruits. The unsettled state of Ireland, with its many hundreds of years of internal fighting and conquest, left little time for gardening until the 18th century. By then the country was calmer, and the new 'Ascendency' began to build themselves comfortable houses, formal gardens and parklands. They planted their estates with fine oak and beech woods, and it is usually fairly obvious today where the lands around you formed part of a demesne because of the trees. Inevitably, these parks and gardens were regarded as symbols of conquest, and were often attacked by the landless peasants. An attitude still prevails in Ireland which does not value trees, except as firewood, and very few are left to grow on the lands of the small farmer. That said, one of the most attractive features of the Irish landscape is the way your eye is drawn to the top of ancient raths or ring forts which are crowned by graceful trees. These grow undisturbed because of their association with the fairies. Many landlords planted exotic species of trees around these forts and on small hillocks in the 19th century, and they do much to beautify the landscape.

The mid 18th century saw the fashion for naturalized parkland take over from formal gardening. In the 19th century William Robertson, who started life as an Irish garden boy in County Laois, led the revolution against bedding plants and artifice and became the advocate of wild gardens—where the plant was suited to the situation and the garden to the nature of the ground Anne's Grove Gardens in County Cork is a fine example of his style. Cork and Kerry have some of the finest and most inspiring gardens in Ireland. The climate is especially favourable—mild and damp—with magnificent scenery to offset the artful designs and grand schemes of plants and trees, water and stone. The gardeners and creators of these magical places have had the benefit of the climate, but also the talent to make something very beautiful to the eye and to the spirit. Co. Clare has its own natural garden in the Burren, where you can spend hours gazing at the cracks and fissures in the limestone pavements where the varied plant life arrange themselves beautifully. Co. Limerick has one magnificent garden at Glin which is open to the public.

Cork City has many small suburban gardens, each a jewel of imagination in this city of little hills. It is possible to see quite a few by appointment, particularly if you time your visit during the Cork Garden Festival in May ✆ (021) 353119 for details. It is also instructive and fun to join a gardening seminar at Darina Allen's Cookery School at Kinoith, Shanagarry. They have also made a kitchen garden with a colourful parterre of herbs—well worth a visit. ✆ (021) 646785.

What follows is only a skeleton list of gardens to give you an idea of those you can visit. Always make an appointment first and check the opening times, as many of these gardens do not open on a regular basis:

Clanaboy, Woodleigh Park, Model Farm Road, Cork, ✆ (021) 541560.

Lakemount, Glanmire, ✆ (021) 821052.

Kaduna, Maryborough Hill, Douglas, ✆ (021) 893560.

Fota Arboretum, Fota Island, ✆ (021) 812678.

Hillside, Annemount, Glounthane, ✆ (021) 353119.

Amergen, Walshestown, Ovens, ✆ (021) 331326.

Annes Grove, Castletownroche, ✆ (022) 26145.

Lismore Castle, Lismore, ✆ (058) 54424 (just inside the Co. Waterford border).

Timoleague Gardens, ✆ (021) 831512.

Bantry House, Bantry, ✆ (027) 50047.

Creagh, Skibbereen, ✆ (028) 22121.

Ilnacullin, Garinish Island, Glengarriff, ✆ (027) 63040.

Derreen, Lauragh, Kenmare, ✆ (064) 83103.

Dunloe Castle Gardens, ✆ (064) 31900.

Muckross, Killarney, ✆ (064) 31440.

Glin Castle Gardens, ✆ (068) 36230.

Potatoes and the Famine

Potatoes were the main food of the peasant in the 19th century. The whole family would sit around a rishawn (basket) made of willows placed on the three legged iron pot in which they had been boiled. The summer months were known as the hungry months, as the old crop of potatoes was finished. The last Sunday in July, or the first Sunday in August, was the ancient feast of Lughnasa (Lammas), a celebration of the start of the new harvest.

Sometimes a delicious mixture of new potatoes, milk, chopped onion, spices and melted butter would be eaten from the first digging of the new potatoes. This is known as a Calcannon. The potato crop enabled large families to live on tiny, subdivided holdings on the poorest land. The spuds were grown in lazy beds, the farmers using spades to build up ridges of soil on these stony hillside farms. You can still see the traces of lazy beds in hillside parts of Munster. Today they are no longer cultivated; many were abandoned in the famine times.

The potato blight, a fungal disease which struck between 1845 and 1849, had fatal consequences for the peasants living on this subsistence economy, especially in the west and southwest of the country. Huge suffering, death and disease followed, and the departure of millions of folk for Britain, Australia, Canada and America.

The effects of the famine and emigration were enormous, and still affect Ireland today. The population of Irish-speaking small farmers declined dramatically by 1847; nearly a quarter of a million emigrated every year. The landscape was emptied of people, villages were deserted, and the more prosperous farmers increased their land holdings. Very often all but the eldest son in a family emigrated; he was left to carry on with the farm, and he did not marry until very late in life, usually when his parents were dead.

The wandering labourer who had an important place in society gradually died out as a class after the famine. These wandering labourers went to hiring-fairs all over the provinces to be taken on by comfortable farmers, as the better off were called. Many were poets and storytellers and helped to keep the myths and tales of an ancient oral tradition alive. The spade was the essential tool that each labourer carried with him, and every region in Ireland had its own variation of spade made by the blacksmith to suit local conditions. A Munster spade is typically a very long, narrow blade with fishtail ends.

'Clonakilt God help us' is an expression which originates from the time when that area westwards through Roscarbery and Skibbereen suffered terribly. At Knockfierna in west Co. Limerick is a very well preserved famine village. At the time of the famine, about one thousand people lived on the hill overlooking the Golden Vale. After the famine, only three hundred remained. These people lived in terrible conditions, doing back-breaking work to survive. Today there is no one left; only the derelict huts remain.

The Knockfierna Heritage and Folklore Group is in the course of developing a National Famine Commemoration Park which will include the restoration of a total of 15 famine dwellings on their original sites around which you can still see the potato ridges. The group has also compiled much local history of the time. It is a fascinating place, and provokes sombre reflection as well as admiration for the resilience of these poor people. The park is due to open in September 1995. It is possible to have tea in the Rambling House, which also becomes a place of traditional music and fun at night.

The Group also stage a Festival of Lughnasa (pronounced Lunasa) at the beginning of August (contact Pat O'Donovan, Newcastle West, ✆ 069 64526, ✉ 069 62713). Another interesting museum concerned with the famine is at Strokestown, Co. Roscommon, which not only tells the story of the Strokestown estate during the famine but also explains the significance of the famine nationally and reflects critically on contemporary global poverty and hunger.

1995 is the 150th anniversary of the start of the famine, and there are many events planned to commemorate it. Contact the local tourist offices for details. See 'Further Reading' for some of the recent publications on the famine.

Wren Boys

Ireland of past times was a place of fascinating customs which fitted around a calendar of feast days and penance days. Many of the traditions pre-dated Christianity, but were absorbed by the Christian calendar. One custom which is still alive is 'hunting the wren' on St Stephen's day, the day after Christmas. In the past, groups of young boys caught a wren (or more if they could). The tiny bird was hung on a small holly bush decorated with ribbons which was then carried triumphantly from house to house. The first group to reach a house would be given some money as their arrival signalled good luck for the coming year. Each region had slight variations of this practice, although the rhyme the boys chanted as they went on their rounds was fairly universal and went something like this:

> *The wren, the wren, the king of birds,*
> *On St Stephen's day was caught in the furze,*
> *Although he is little, his family is great,*
> *Put your hand in your pocket and give us a treat.*
> *Sing holly, sing ivy, sing ivy, sing holly,*
> *A drop just to drink it would drown melancholy.*

The money collected would be spent on drink and food. Some folk did not approve of these goings on and refused to open their doors, so the wren boys would revenge themselves by burying the wren opposite the house, which was supposed to bring bad luck.

In the Dingle Peninsula the custom has continued and, on St Stephen's Day in Dingle, groups of wren boys converge on the town, and there is much fun and entertainment. The ceremony was always more complicated in these parts and involved mock battles, the use of masks and disguises, the fife and drum and the lair Ohan ('white mare')—a hobby horse which in olden days could turn quite nasty and threaten any folk who did not pay up. Nowadays, besides the straw and tinsel decorations, all sorts of wigs, masks, and other disguises are used by the wren boys. They dance and sing and a band of fife and drum musicians march around the town. The tradition of using fife and drum in Dingle is perhaps because it used to be a garrison town in the days of English rule. The pubs are full and the streets crowded, and although Dingle is a town devoted to the tourist in summer, this is one traditional custom which does not need cultivation by the tourist board to survive. If you happen to be in Dingle on St Stephen's Day, it is a riot of colour and fun; if you are not, try and catch the Listowel Harvest Festival and Races in mid-September when there is an all Ireland wren boys competition, and plenty of traditional music and dancing. Festival Contact: Maria O'Gorman © 068 22675/21600.

The Burren

The Burren is an area of about 150 square miles (380sq km) of rock, a wild desolate place, but a fascinating place too, especially for archaeologists and plant lovers, which is best sought out on foot. The best maps to have with you are the folding landscape series by Tim Robinson, and you will need strong shoes for it is rough country. You can get some small sense of its beauty from the car if you follow some of the tiny country roads around Ballyvaughan, Kilfenora and Turlough.

This is a classic limestone karst landscape overlain in its southern parts by shale and clay which is being very gradually worn away. The processes which formed it are very complicated, but a very simplistic explanation is this: about 270 million years ago, the plateau which is now the Aran Islands and the Burren lay under a shallow sea. Movements in the earth's crust thrust it up, and subsequent movements caused the limestone to crack and fracture into blocks and rectangular slabs. That it did not fracture even more dramatically is probably due to the granite underlying it. Glaciation made further changes gouging out turloughs or hollows which now form temporary lakes, breaking off chunks of stone which were then left in the train of the glacier, where today they make striking shapes against the skyline.

The Burren has no outstanding mountains; the hills are not much more than 1000 feet (305m), weathered to a flaky silver, and the valleys are filled with hazel scrub and more stones. These stones are known as pavements, slashed as they are with fissures and holes where colonies of beautiful plants can grow. Wild feral goats roam the valleys, and you might be lucky and spot a pine marten. One of the glories of the Burren are the colonies of Bloody Cranesbill. Other plants which delight the eye are the Spring Gentian, the Hoary Rock Rose, Spring Sandwort, Mountain Avens, Orchids and many other plants. Often plants of alpine and arctic origin grow near species of Mediterranean origin. They are sheltered in the grykes (fissures) and in the clints (small hollows) in the limestone where rain and soil gather. The grykes are sometimes up to six feet or more deep and in the shadowy, wet atmosphere lots of plants flourish. Very little surface water lies on the Burren, any rainwater quickly runs into the fissures, holes and subterranean passaages which pierce the limestone. All the rivers in the Burren (except for the Caher River in the northwest) flow mostly under ground. Where streams re-emerge as springs or turloughs (lakes which rise and fall according to the water table), it is usual to find a green patch of flowering herbs and grazing.

About ten miles east of Kilfenora is the Hill of Mullaghmore, one of the wildest and most beautiful parts of the Burren. Controversially, this area has been chosen as the proposed site for an Interpretative Centre. Objections to this site have been voiced worldwide and it is currently under discussion (March '95). There is a centre here already, the Burren Display Centre at Kilfenora which was opened in 1975. It contains a lot of information on various aspects of the Burren, a scale model and a number of excellent audio-visual displays. The Burren is also threatened by modern farming methods. The small cattle farms barely bring in a living, and the obvious way to make the pastureland more profitable is to use the EU grants to spray the hillsides,which of course kills the unique flora. Some of the ancient settlements and ringforts are in danger of being destroyed, many of which have never even been listed because of lack of funds. There are excellent local guides who will show you the Burren and its wealth of plant life and prehistoric settlements. Enquire at the Burren Centre, ✆ (065) 88030.

Courting at Lisdoonvarna

This breezy spa town on the edge of the Burren has had a reputation for respectable matchmaking ever since people came to take the sulphur-tasting waters in the late 18th century. Comfortable farming families came to relax and socialise, settle deals and match their sons and daughters in advantageous marriages. Lisdoonvarna adapted itself very well to helping along these deals, traditionally with the help of a matchmaker. Most people came to the spa after the harvest in September. Nowadays it is a resort town all year round, although September is the liveliest month. The tradition of matchmaking and courting is assiduously promoted by the hoteliers, and various festivals attract those on the lookout for a romance. There are two official matchmakers now, and people do meet and end up marrying the stranger they met in Lisdoonvarna. They may meet first in the attractive pump room, drinking a glass of the healthy mineral waters. Their acquaintance will be furthered in the Ballrooms of Romance where waltzes, country music and Irish jigs melt the reserve of the mainly rather elderly bachelor boys and girls. Lisdoonvarna is an amusing place to visit and a good base from which to visit the Burren and the dramatic Clare coastline. Match Making Festival: contact James White, ✆ (065) 74042/74005 (he is one of the official matchmakers and owner of the main hotel in Lisdoonvarna).

Naomhogs

These are canoes made of tarred canvas stretched on a frame similar to the curraghs of Connacht. They are still used for fishing off the coast of Kerry, although they are now rare in comparison to motor boats. The main difference between the *naomhogs* and the curragh is that the *naomhog* is driven by bladeless oars that swivel between two thole pins, the curragh has only a single thole pin by which the oar is hinged through a hole.

J. M. Synge (1871–1909) spent some time on the Blasket Islands and he described a conversation about the canoes that he had with Maurice O'Sullivan who wrote a wonderful account of his youth on the Blaskets called *Twenty Years a Growin'*. 'They are no better than boats' said Maurice, 'but they are more useful. Before you get a heavy boat swimming you are up to your waist, and then you will be sitting the whole night like that; but a canoe will swim in a handful of water, so that you can get in dry and keep warm and dry the whole night. Then there will be seven men in a big boat and seven shares of fish, but in a canoe there will be three men only and three shares of fish, though the nets are the same in the two'.

Puck Fair (*Aonach an Phuic*—the Fair of the Goat)

This festival is held in Killorglin, Co. Kerry every year on the 10th, 11th and 12th of August and attracts thousands of people from all over the country. On the evening of the first day of the Festival, a billy goat, ribbons flowing from his horns, is hoisted onto a platform in the Market Square where, for the next two days, he presides as a pampered king over crowds of people and a busy livestock market. Much drinking and enjoyment is in order, especially on the third day, and shops and business premises stay open day and night. There are various theories as to the origins of this ritual—some believe it is a custom dating from pagan times, and the worship of the Celtic God, Lugh; this was reinforced when a stampeding of goats warned the town of the impending arrival of the British forces—it was seen as a pagan warning. It was previously held at Lughnasa (Lammas) on the first of August when many fairs were held all over Ireland.

The Munster Cloak

The Munster Cloak is a black hooded cloak that country women used to wear. Although it is an image of a 'bygone Ireland', old women wore this garment, derived from the great mantle of ancient Ireland, right up to the 1970s in Co. Cork. It is made of heavy lined wool and in the past could be scarlet, blue or grey as well as black. Today a few Irish designers have revived this romantic and warm cloak. Try Cleo, 2 Shelbourne Street, Kenmare, Co. Kerry, ✆ (064) 41410.

Michael Collins (1890–1922)—Revolutionary Leader

Michael Collins is to many the popular hero of the War of Independence, and a martyr of the Civil War. He was born at Woodfield, on a small farm north of Lisavard Pike between Clonakilty and Roscarbery. His dark good looks, daring, and formidable intelligence have become the stuff of legend. He went to London at the age of sixteen and worked as a clerk and whilst he was there he joined the IRB (Irish Republican Brotherhood). He returned to Ireland to fight in the Easter Week Rising of 1916. He was imprisoned for nine months and after his release became one of the leaders of the Sinn Fein and Volunteer movements. After the Sinn Fein victory in the 1918 General Election and the establishment of the Irish Parliament, he became Minister of Home Affairs and later Minister of Finance. War was declared on Britain (*see* **History** p.88).

During this time he escaped capture by the Black and Tans and the British Army many times through clever disguises and concealments. He also organised jail breaks for Republican prisoners, amongst them being Eamon de Valera. Collins also directed the organisation and intelligence system of the Volunteers and soon kept the Republican side well informed of British plans. By 1921 he had come to accept that negotiations with Britain must begin, and Collins was a member of the delegation which negotiated the Anglo-Irish Treaty of December 1921 which partitioned Ireland. He became Chairman of the Provisional Government which had to persuade the anti-partitioners that the Treaty was the best compromise. He was now hated by many of his former colleagues and the Civil War in Ireland began in June 1922. In Ireland this war is called 'the Uncivil War' or the 'War of Brothers', it was a terrible time and Collins knew that it was only a matter of time before the assassin's bullet would find him. He became Commander-in-Chief of the Government forces, and on August 22, 1922, the last day of his life, he returned to visit his old home only to find it in a blaze of flames; later that day he was ambushed and murdered on the road to Bandon.

History

I found in Munster, unfettered of any
Kings and queens, and poets a many–
Poets well skilled in music and measure,
Prosperous doings, mirth and pleasure.
I found in Connaught the just, redundance
Of riches, milk in lavish abundance;
Hospitality, vigour, fame,
In Cruachan's land of heroic name
I found in Ulster, from hill to glen,
Hardy warriors, resolute men;
Beauty that bloomed when youth was gone,
And strength transmitted from sire to son.
I found in Leinster the smooth and sleek,
From Dublin to Slewmargy's peak;
Flourishing pastures, valour, health,
Long-living worthies, commerce, wealth.

from 'Prince Alfrid's Itinerary'
(version by James Clarence Mangan)

If you happen to fall into conversation with an Irishman in any bar the subjects of religion and politics are bound to come up. With any luck you will have a cool glass of Guinness in front of you, for discussions on Ireland are inevitably rather emotional. The Irish are good talkers and have very long memories, so when you are in Ireland it's a good idea to have some idea of their history.

Many of Ireland's troubles have stemmed from her geographical situation—too far from Britain to be assimilated, too near to be allowed to be separate. Queen Elizabeth I poured troops into Ireland because she appreciated the strategic importance of Ireland to her enemies. Throughout the centuries Ireland has been offered help in her fight for independence, but it was never disinterested help; whoever paid for arms and fighting men in Ireland wanted to further some military, political, religious or ideological cause of their own. France in the late-18th century supplied arms to Ireland to distract England from other policies; and in Northern Ireland some of the guns were supplied by foreign powers to the IRA. Things have not changed much.

General History

Pre-Celtic Ireland

The hills and river valleys are scattered with ancient monuments dating from the Stone, the Bronze and the Iron Age. Most of them suggest some religious significance, though the myths and legends of Ireland have swathed them in romance and heroic stories. These were recounted by the Celtic story-tellers or *shanachies* in the cottages and castles. Unfortunately only a few survive today as 'memory men'.

The earliest record of man in Ireland is dated between 8700 and 8600 years ago, as deduced from fragments found at a camp in **Mount Sandel** near Coleraine. The people of this time lived a nomadic life, hunting and trapping; they could not move around very easily as the countryside was covered by forest, interrupted only by lakes and river channels. They used *curragh* boats, similar to the ones used today by fishermen in the west of Ireland. They also built lake-dwellings or *crannogs*, many of which were used until a couple of centuries ago. No one is sure where these people came from but they had the island to themselves for 3000 years. Then came **Neolithic** man, who perhaps is the Fir Bolg in Celtic mythology: at this stage everything is very vague. These people were farmers and gradually spread over the whole of Ireland, clearing the forest as best they could with their stone tools. They evidently practised burial rites, for they built chambered tombs of a very sophisticated quality, decorated with spirals and lozenge shapes. For example, the Great Burial Chamber at Newgrange in the Boyne Valley is a superb piece of construction using a tremendous variety of building stones. The chamber is large enough to contain thousands of cremated bodies. These people must have been very well organized, with the energy and wealth to spare for such an ambitious project—similar in its way to the pyramids, and a thousand years older!

Around 2000 BC yet another race appeared, who were skilled miners and metal-workers. They were called the **Beaker People**; or the Tuatha dé Danaan, as they are known in Irish legend. They opened up copper mines and started to trade with Brittany, the Baltic and the Iberian Peninsula. They had different beliefs about burial: their dead were buried singly in graves lined with stone slabs and covered with a capstone. There are a thousand chambered graves, ring-shaped cairns, standing stones, rows and circles of stones left from these times, and the Boyne Valley culture; they hint at various rituals and, it has been suggested, at observations of the stars. You will glimpse them from the road: solitary forms in a ploughed field, often used as scratching posts for cattle. They are often called 'fairy stones', and the chambered graves have been nicknamed 'Dermot and Grania's bed'.

The Celts

The next invaders arrived about 500 BC. These people had iron weapons and defeated the Beakers, whose legendary magical powers were no defence against the new metal. Known as the **Celts** or **Gaels**, the new invaders had spread from south Germany, across France, and as far south as Spain. Today everybody in Ireland has pride in the 'Celtic' past: epic tales sing the praises of men and women who were capable of heroic and superhuman deeds, and the beautiful gold jewellery is carefully preserved as proof of their achievements. The Celts brought to Ireland a highly organized social structure, and the La Tène style of decoration (its predominant motif is a spiral or a whorl). Ireland was divided into different clans with three classes: the **free**, who were warriors and owned land and cattle; the **professionals**, such as the jurists, Druids, musicians, story-tellers and poets, who could move freely between the petty kingdoms; and, finally, the **slaves**. Every clan had a petty king, who in his turn was ruled over by the high king at Tara, County Meath.

The Gaels made use of the customs and mythology that had existed before their arrival, so their 'Celtic civilization' is unique. They were also very fortunate, for although they were probably displaced themselves by the expanding **Roman Empire**, once they got to Ireland they were isolated, and protected to some extent by England which acted as a buffer state. The Romans never extended their ambitions to conquering Ireland, so the Gaels were able to develop their traditions, unlike Celts elsewhere in Europe. They spent most of their time raiding their neighbours for cattle and women, who were used as live currency. They also had their religion. The stone images and pillars which have survived from those days have a strange and powerful aura. Most are head idols. The human head was all-important as a symbol of divinity and supernatural power—even when it was severed from the body it still retained its powers. The warriors used to take the heads of their slain enemies and display them in front of their houses. The Gaels also believed firmly in an afterlife of the soul: they would lend each other money to be repaid in the next world!

The Arrival of Christianity

Christianity was brought to Ireland in the 5th century AD by **St Patrick**, and quickly became accepted by the kings. One of them, **Cormac MacArt**, who ruled in Tara about a century and a half before St Patrick arrived, saw the light and told his court of Druids and nobles that the gods they worshipped were only craven wood! The Druids put a curse on him and soon afterwards he choked to death on a salmon bone; but before he died he ordered that he was not to be buried in the tomb of Brugh (Newgrange) but on the sunny east point by the River Rosnaree. When St Patrick lit a fire which signalled the end of Druid worship, legend has it that he was looking down from the Hill of Slane on to Rosnaree.

The Christians displayed great skill in reconciling their practices and beliefs with those of the pagans; a famous saying of St Columba was, 'Christ is my Druid'. The early Christians seem to have been very ascetic, preferring to build their monasteries in the most wild and inaccessible places. Today you can still see their hive-shaped dwellings on **Skellig Michael**, a windswept rocky island off the Kerry coast. Wherever they went, these early saints attracted followers and their monasteries expanded without much planning. The monasteries became universities renowned throughout Europe, which was submerged in the Dark Ages, and produced beautiful manuscripts like the famously beautiful *Book of Kells*. The abbots held great power as spiritual lords and landlords; many of the petty kings were relations and left all their precious goods in the monasteries, using them as a sort of bank. From the 6th century onwards, much of the missionary spirit of the Irish monks was directed outwards to the Continent. They founded Bobbio in Italy and other religious houses and the interchange of ideas between the Continent and Ireland was far greater than was once thought.

The Viking Invasion

The tranquillity of Ireland, 'land of saints and scholars', was brutally interrupted by the arrival of the **Vikings** or **Norsemen**. They were able to penetrate right into Ireland through their skilful use of the rivers and lakes. They struck for the first time in 795, but this was only the start of a 300-year struggle.

Much treasure from the palaces and monasteries was plundered, for the buildings had no defences; so the monks built round towers in which to store their precious things at the first sign of trouble. Never had the Gaels been threatened like this before. Eventually the Norsemen began to settle down and they founded the first city-ports—Dublin, Wexford and Waterford and started to trade with the Gaels.

Military alliances were made between them when it helped a particular king in the continuous struggle for the high kingship. After a short period of relative calm another wave of Norsemen invaded and the plundering began again; but **Brian Boru**, who had usurped the high kingship from the O'Connors, defeated the Vikings at Clontarf in 1014 and broke their power permanently. Unfortunately, for the Gaelic people, Brian Boru was murdered by some Vikings in his tent just after the victory at Clontarf. Now havoc and in-fighting became a familiar pattern, as the high kingship was fought for by the O'Briens, the O'Loughlins and the O'Connors. The Gaelic warriors wasted themselves and their people, for no one leader seemed strong enough to rule without opposition. The next invaders saw that their opportunity lay in the disunity of the Irish.

The Norman Invasion and Consolidation

In the mid 12th century the Pope gave his blessing to an expedition of **Anglo-Normans** sent by **Henry II** to Ireland. The Normans were actually invited over by the King of Leinster, **Dermot MacMurragh**, who had made a bitter enemy of **Tiernan O'Rourke** of Breffni by running off with his wife, Devorgilla. He also backed the wrong horse in the high kingship stakes, and the united efforts of the High King Rory O'Connor and O'Rourke brought about a huge reduction in MacMurragh's kingdom. So he approached Henry II, offering his oath of fealty in exchange for an invasion force of men with names like Fitzhenry, Carew, Fitzgerald, Barry—names you still see in Irish villages. The Normans were adventurers and good warriors: in 1066, William, Duke of Normandy had taken the crown of England by force with only 5000 men. Now, in 1169, several Norman nobles decided to try their luck in Ireland, and they found it easy to grab huge tracts of land for themselves. The Gaels had faced so few attacks from outside their country that they were unprepared to do battle. Their weapons were very inferior to those of the Normans; their main advantage was their knowledge of the bogs, mountains and forest, and their numbers. The Normans had a well-equipped cavalry, who rode protected by a screen of archers. Once they had launched a successful attack, they consolidated their position by building moats, castles, and walled towns. **Strongbow**, one of the most powerful of the Norman invaders, married MacMurragh's daughter and became his heir, but his successes and those of the other Norman barons worried Henry II. In 1171 Henry arrived in Ireland with about 4000 troops and two objectives: to secure the submission of the Irish leaders and to impose his authority on his own barons. He achieved both aims, but the Gaelic lords still went on fighting. In fact, the coming of the Normans began a military struggle which was to continue over four centuries.

The Bruce Invasion

In 1314 **Robert Bruce of Scotland** decisively defeated English forces at Bannockburn, and was in a position to try to fulfil his dream of a united Celtic kingdom, by putting his brother **Edward** on the throne in Ireland. At first his invasion was successful, but he left a trail of destruction behind him. The year 1316 was marked by famine and disease exacerbated by the war. His dream brought economic and social disaster to Ireland, and when Edward Bruce was defeated and killed at Dundalk few of his allies mourned his death. The Normans' control fluctuated within an area surrounding Dublin known as the Pale, and they became rather independent of their English overlord; in some cases, such as the de Burgos (Burkes), they became more Irish than the Irish. The Gaelic lords in the north and west continued to hold their territories. To do so they imported Scottish mercenary soldiers, called **gallowglasses**, who prolonged the life of the independent Gaelic kingdoms for more than two centuries after the defeat of Edward Bruce.

The Nine Years' War: Elizabethan Conquest and Settlement

Since the Norman invasion, Ireland had been ruined by continual fighting. By the late 16th century the country was in the doldrums and it is little wonder that **Queen Elizabeth** preached the need for a Crusade-style war to bring civilization to Ireland. Elizabeth had an interest in Ireland; many of the Irish nobles had been educated at her court, and she endowed and founded Trinity College, Dublin. However, the basic reason for her preoccupation with Ireland was security. She was determined to bring the Irish more firmly under English control, especially the Ulster lords who had so far maintained almost total independence. Elizabeth took over the Irish policy of her father which had never been fully implemented, her government decided that all the Gaelic lords must surrender their lands to the Crown, whereupon they would be regranted immediately. At this time Ulster, today the stronghold of Protestantism, was the most Gaelic and Catholic part of Ireland, and it was from here that the great **Hugh O'Neill** and **Red Hugh O'Donnell** launched a last-ditch struggle against Elizabeth. Initial successes bolstered the rebels' morale. Elizabeth, recognizing the gravity of the situation, sent over her talented favourite soldier, Essex.

Most of his troops died from disease and guerrilla attacks, and with no reinforcements he had little alternative than to make a truce with O'Neill. Disgrace and execution were his reward. In February 1600 Lord Mountjoy arrived in Ireland with 20,000 troops. Risings at Munster were crushed and with them the aspirations of Connacht and Leinster. The Gaelic chiefs seem to have been ruthless in their allegiances. They had hailed O'Neill as Prince of Ireland but now, anticipating defeat, they deserted him. O'Neill's hopes were raised by the long-promised arrival of Spanish troops at Kinsale in 1601, but they only numbered 4000. When they did do battle against Mountjoy, the Irish were left confused when the Spaniards failed to sally out as arranged.

The Flight of the Earls

O'Neill returned to Ulster on the 23 March 1603 and made his submission to Mountjoy, only to learn in Dublin later that Queen Elizabeth had died the very next day. He is said to have wept with rage. Amongst all the nobles, only he might have been able to unite the Irish and beat Elizabeth. O'Neill had his titles and lands returned to him, but the Dublin government, greedy for his property, began to bait him. It took his land at the slightest excuse and forbade him to practise Catholicism; so, abandoning hope and his followers, he sailed to Europe. This 'Flight of the Earls' took place on the 14 September 1607, from the wild and beautiful shores of the Swilly. It symbolizes the end of Gaelic leadership and a new period of complete domination by the English. The Irish lords took themselves off to the courts of France and Spain or into the foreign armies. If you glance through the lists of famous generals and politicians in Europe, a few Irish names will leap up at you from the pages: in Spain, Wall and O'Donnell; in Austria, the minister Taafe; in France, Admiral Macnamara and General Lally Tullindaly. The Flight of the Earls had become glorified in stories; but on the whole, the eponymous nobles were vicious and uncultured, contributing nothing to the mainstream of European thought. They had spent most of their energies warring among themselves and at the last moment deserted their country and left the Irish peasants with no leadership at all.

The Confederation, Cromwell and the Stuarts

By the 1640s, Ireland was ready for rebellion again—there were plenty of grievances. **James I**, a staunch Protestant, dispossessed many Gaelic and old English families in Ireland because they would not give up Catholicism, and he began the '**plantation**' of the most vehemently Catholic province, Ulster, with Protestants. Previous plantations had not worked because of inclement weather, but James knew that the Scots would be able to skip about the bogs as well as the Irish! When **Charles Stuart** came to the throne, many Catholic families hoped that they might be given some religious freedom and retain their estates, but nothing was legally confirmed. In 1633 **Black Tom**, the Earl of Strafford, arrived with the intention of making Ireland a source of profit rather than a loss to the king. In his zeal to do so he succeeeded in alienating every element in Irish society. His enemies amongst the Puritans in Ireland and England put pressure on the king to recall him and he was eventually executed. English politics became dominated by the dissension betweeen the Roundheads and the Cavaliers and the hopeless Irish took note. Their maxim was 'England's difficulty is Ireland's opportunity'. Charles tried to deal with the growing unrest in Ireland by giving everybody what they wanted, but he no longer had enough power to see that his laws were carried out. The Gaelic Irish decided to take a chance and rebel; many of them came back from the Continental armies hoping to win back their old lands. In October 1641 a small Gaelic force took over the whole of Ulster and there were widespread uprisings in Leinster. In Ulster, the Gaelic people had been burning for revenge and the new planted families suffered terribly. This cruel treatment has not been forgotten by Ulster Protestants.

The Dublin government was worse than useless at controlling the rebels, who continued to be successful. While the government waited for reinforcements from England, they managed to antagonize the old English, for they made the mistake of presuming that they would be disloyal to the Crown, and so viewed them with suspicion. The old English families decided to throw in their lot with the rebels since they were already considered traitors, but on one condition: a declaration of loyalty from the Gaelic leaders to the Catholic English crown which was now seriously threatened by the Puritans.

The Confederation of Kilkenny

By February 1642 most of Ireland was in rebel hands. The rebels established a provisional government at **Kilkenny**, and Charles began to negotiate with them hoping to gain their support against the Puritans. Things were too good to last. The destructive factors that had ruined many Irish uprisings before and since, came into play: personal jealousy and religion. The old English were loyal to the king and wanted a swift end to the war; the Gaelic Irish were only interested in retrieving their long-lost lands and were ready to fight to the bitter end. This disunity was exacerbated by the rivalry between the Gaelic commander, **Owen Roe O'Neill** and the commander of the old English army, **Thomas Preston**. In October 1645 the Papal Nuncio arrived and the unity of the Confederates was further split: he and O'Neill took an intransigent stand over the position of the Catholic Church, which Charles I could not agree to.

The rebels won a magnificent victory over the Puritan General Munro at Benburb, but O'Neill did not follow it up. The confederates, torn by disunity and rivalry, let opportunities slip past and they lost the initiative. Eventually they did decide to support the king and end their Kilkenny government, but by this time Charles I had been beheaded and his son had fled into exile. The Royalists were defeated at Rathmines in 1649 and the way was left clear for the Puritan leader, **Cromwell**, who landed in Dublin soon after. Cromwell came to Ireland determined to break the Royalists, break the Gaelic Irish, and to avenge the events of 1641 in Ulster. He shared the Puritan hatred for the Catholic Church: it is easy to forget how extreme both religious viewpoints were then. Cromwell thought that the priests had engineered the rising—of the Irish character and their grievances he knew little and cared less. He started his campaign with the **Siege of Drogheda**, and there are the most gruesome accounts of his methods. When his troops burst into the town they put Royalists, women, children and priests to the sword; in all 3552 dead were counted, whilst Cromwell only lost 64 men. Catholics curse Cromwell to this day. The same butchery distinguished the taking of Wexford. Not surprisingly, he managed to break the spirit of resistance by such methods and there were widespread defections from the Royalists' side. Owen Roe O'Neill might have been able to rally the Irish but he died suddenly. Cromwell's campaign only lasted seven months and he took all the towns except Galway and Waterford. These he left to his lieutenants.

By 1652 the whole country was subdued, and Cromwell encouraged all the fighting men to leave by granting them amnesty if they fled overseas. The alternative to exile was, for many families, something that turned out to be even worse: compulsory removal to Connacht and County Clare. Some had been neutral during all the years of fighting, but that was never taken into account. Cromwell was determined that anyone suspect should go to Hell or Connacht! So if you want to track down the really ancient Irish families, find out if they came from Connacht. The government had lots of land to play around with after that. First of all they paid off 'the adventurers', men who had lent them money back in 1642. Next, the Roundhead soldiers, who had not been paid their salaries for years, got Irish land instead. Thus the Cromwellian Settlement parcelled out even more land to speculators and rogues.

Stuart and Orange

After the **Restoration of the Monarchy** in 1660, the Catholics in Ireland hoped for toleration and rewards for their loyalty to the Stuart cause. They felt threatened by the fast-expanding Protestant community, mostly dissenters, who had been given religious freedom under Cromwell. Charles did not restore many Catholic estates because he had to keep in with the ex-Cromwellian supporters, but Catholics were given a limited amount of toleration. However, with the succession of Charles' brother **James**, who was a Catholic, things began to brighten up. In Ireland, the Catholic Earl of Tyrconnell became commander of the army in 1685 and, later, chief governor. By 1688 Roman Catholics were dominant in the army, the administration, the judiciary and the town corporations, and by the end of the year Protestant power in Ireland was seriously weakened.

James frightened all those Protestants in England who had benefited from Catholic estates. They began to panic when he introduced sweeping acts of toleration for all religions. His attempts to re-establish the Catholic Church alienated the country to such an extent that the Protestant aristocracy invited **William of Orange** over in November 1688 to relieve his father-in-law of his throne. James fled to France but soon left for Ireland, which was a natural base from which to launch his counter-attack. By the date of his arrival in March 1689, only Enniskillen and Londonderry were in Protestant hands.

The Siege of Londonderry and Battle of the Boyne

The subjugation of the city of Londonderry was James' first aim. In a famous incident celebrated in Orange songs, a group of apprentice boys shut the city gates to the Jacobite army, and so began the famous Siege of Londonderry. The townspeople proved unbreakable, even though food supplies were very low and they were reduced to eating rats and mice and chewing old bits of leather. Many did die of starvation during the 15 weeks of the siege, but just as they were about to give in, the foodship *Mountjoy* forced its way through a great boom built across the Foyle. This military and psychological victory was of enormous significance in the campaign. When William himself arrived at Carrickfergus in June 1690, James decided to confront him at the Boyne. William of Orange had an army of about 36,000 comprised of English, Scots, Dutch, Danes, Germans and Huguenots, against James' army of about 25,000, made up of Irish and French. William triumphed, as the result of his numerical and strategic superiority. James deserted the battlefield and Ireland with haste.

In the **Battle of the Boyne** James seems to have completely lost his nerve. The Jacobite forces had to retreat west of the Shannon to Limerick, and William promptly laid siege to it. So weak were its walls that it is said they could be breached with roasted apples. The defence of Limerick was as heroic as that of Londonderry. Patrick Sarsfield slipped out with a few followers and intercepted William's siege train and destroyed it. William then gave up and left for England leaving Ginkel in charge. The next year the French King Louis XIV sent over supplies and men to fuel the Jacobite cause, as he hoped to divert William in Ireland for a little longer. The Jacobite leader St Ruth, who landed with them, proved a disaster for the Irish; Sarsfield would have been a better choice. Ginkel took

Athlone and Aughrim in June and July of 1691, after two battles in which stories of courage on the Jacobite side have provided inspiration to patriot poets and musicians. The last hope of the Catholic Irish cause was now Limerick.

The Treaty of Limerick

Sarsfield skilfully gathered together what Jacobite troops were left and got them back there. (St Ruth had been killed by a canonball, and rather typically had appointed no second-in-command.) Ginkel tried to storm the town from both sides, but still Limerick held out and he began to treaty with Sarsfield. Honourable terms were made for the Jacobites, and Sarsfield signed the famous **Treaty of Limerick** in October 1691. The next day a French fleet arrived and anchored off the Shannon estuary, but Sarsfield stood by the treaty. The treaty seemed to guarantee quite a lot. Catholics were to have the same rights as they had had under Charles II and any Catholic estates which had been registered in 1662 were to be handed back. Catholics were to be allowed free access to the bar, bench, army and parliament. Sarsfield was to be given a safe passage to the Continent with his troops. But the Treaty was not honoured, except for the last clause which got all the fighting men out of the country.

This was one of the dirtiest tricks the English played, and to be fair to William of Orange he wanted the treaty to be enforced, but being new and unsure of his support he complied with the treachery. Eleven thousand Irish Jacobites sailed away to join the French army, forming the Irish Brigade. Over the years many came to join them from Ireland, and were remembered in their native land as the **Wild Geese**.

The Orange/Stuart war still lives vividly in the imagination of the people today. The Siege of Londonderry has become a sign of Protestant determination: 'no surrender 1690' is scrawled, usually in bright red paint, on the walls and street corners of Loyalist areas in Northern Ireland. The Battle of the Boyne is remembered in a similar way. Here is an old, old anecdote. An old man is asked by a youth (or a foreigner), 'Who is King Billy?' His reply is, 'Away man, and read your Bible.'

The Penal Laws

The defeat of the Catholic cause was followed by more confiscation of land, and the **Penal Laws**. What had happened was that a bargain had been struck with the Protestant planters. They would be allowed to keep a complete monopoly of political power and most of the land. In return they would act as a British garrison to keep the peace and prevent the Catholics from gaining any power. To do this they passed a series of degrading laws. Briefly they were as follows. No Catholic could purchase freehold land. Any son of a Catholic, turning Protestant, could turn his parents off their estate. Families who stayed Catholic had their property equally parcelled out amongst all the children, so that any large estates soon became uneconomic holdings. All the Catholics were made to pay a tithe towards the upkeep of the Anglican Church. All priests were banished. No Catholic schools were allowed and spies were set amongst the peasants to report on 'hedge schools', a form of quite sophisticated schooling that had sprung up; priests on the run taught at these schools and celebrated Mass. A Catholic could not hold a commission in the army, enter a profession nor even own a horse worth more than £5. These anti-religious laws had the opposite effect to that intended: Catholicism took on a new lease of life in Ireland. In addition, **economic laws** were introduced that put heavy taxes on anything that Ireland produced—cloth, wool, glass and cattle—so that she could not compete with England. The trading regulations were very disadvantageous to the non-conformist Ulster Protestants and many of them left.

The worst thing about these Penal Laws was the moral effect. It became heroic to break the law, and necessary to smuggle and steal; the country turned itself into a huge secret society using every means to outwit the authorities. To be a Catholic meant that you had to lie to protect your priest, and if you were a farmer there was no point in making a profit—any Protestant was allowed to come and claim it. It was not always as bad as that; the harshness of the laws did not reach to every part of Ireland. Sometimes a family, part of which became Protestant, would come to an agreement. The Protestant end held on to the Catholic property in trust and then handed it back when the laws were relaxed or repealed. The Protestant landlords were nervous at first and grabbed as much as they could while the going was good, until this became a habit. They felt under no obligation to their Irish tenants, whom they tended to despise and could not understand. Many of them never bothered to learn more than a few words of Gaelic. Not all of them were bad, but they were resented anyway for being alien in religion, race and customs.

Then, gradually things began to relax; the Catholics had been well and truly squashed. The Protestants began to build themselves grand and beautiful houses, the draughty, damp tower houses could be left to decay. (Irish squires were famous for their hard drinking; the expression 'plastered' comes from the story of a guest who was so well wined and dined at a neighbour's housewarming party that he fell asleep against a newly plastered wall. He woke up next morning to find that his scalp and hair had hardened into the wall!)

As the 18th century progressed, however, there were signs of aggression amongst the peasantry; agrarian secret societies were formed with names like the **White Boys**, **Hearts of Oak**, and the **Molly Maguires**. They were very brutal and meted out rough justice to tenants and landlords alike. If any peasant paid rent to an unfair landlord, he was likely to be intimidated or have his farm burnt down. In Ulster, peasant movements were dominated by sectarian land disputes. The Catholics were called the **Defenders** and the Protestant groups the **Peep-O'Day Boys**. In the 1770s the Penal Laws were relaxed a little and Catholics were allowed to bid for land, and they incensed the Protestants by bidding higher. After a particularly bad fight between the two sides which the Protestants won, the **Orange Order** was founded in 1795. A typical oath of one of the early clubs was, 'To the glorious, pious and immortal memory of the great and good King William, not forgetting Oliver Cromwell, who assisted in redeeming us from popery, slavery, arbitrary power, brassmoney and wooden shoes'.

The **American War of Independence** broke out in 1775 and Ireland was left undefended. There were fears of an invasion by France or Spain and a general feeling that there ought to be some sort of defence force. The **Volunteers** were organized with officers from the Protestant landowning class; but as the fears of invasion receded they turned their considerable muscle to the cause of political reform, and Britain began to fear that they might follow the example of the American colonies. When America sought independence, Irish Protestants and Catholics alike watched with approval, particularly since many of the rebel Americans were of Ulster/Scots blood. The landowners had their own parliament in Dublin, but all important matters were dealt with by London. A group of influential landowners began to think that Ireland would be much better off with an independent Irish parliament. In 1783, the British Government, influenced by the eloquence of the great speaker **Henry Grattan**, acknowledged the right of Ireland to be bound only by laws made by the King and the Irish parliament. Trade, industry and agriculture began to flourish, and the worst of the Penal Laws were repealed or relaxed.

Grattan's Parliament

Grattan's Parliament was really an oligarchy of landowners, but at least they understood the problems of the economy and tried to bring a more liberal spirit into dealings with Catholics and dissenters. Grattan wanted complete Catholic emancipation, but for that the Irish had to wait. Yet Trinity College was made accessible to those of all religious persuasions, although Catholics were forbidden by their bishops to go there. The great Catholic Seminary at Maynooth was founded, and endowed with money and land from the Protestant aristocrats, who were worried that the priests educated at Douai might bring back with them some of those frightening ideas of liberty and equality floating around France. Dissenters were given equal rights with the Established Church at this time.

Dublin was now a handsome Georgian city, a centre for the arts, science and society— duelling was the national pastime! All this pleasure was expensive so landowners began to sublet their estates to the landhungry tenants. All the dirty work was done by an agent who also pocketed most of the profits, but the system enabled landlords to live in idleness and keep large houses in Dublin. In the early 1790s, fear and anger swept through Europe in the form of the French Revolution and the governments of Europe, whether Catholic or Protestant, drew nearer together in mutual fear.

Many, who at first were delighted with the revolution in France, became disgusted with the brutality of its methods. The Irish government disbanded the Volunteers and got together a militia and part-time force of yeomanry. It was nervous of a French invasion and increasingly of a middle-class organization, the 'United Irishmen', who were sick of a government which only spoke for a tiny proportion of the population.

Wolfe Tone and United Irishmen

The aim of the United Irishmen was to throw open the Irish parliament to all Irishmen, irrespective of their rank or religion. Many United Irishmen were from Ulster nonconformist backgrounds. Initially the movement was to be non-violent, but when war broke out between England and France, all radical societies were forced to go underground. No liberal ideas could be tolerated during the war effort. **Wolfe Tone** was a Dublin lawyer and a prominent United Irishman; he crossed over to France to try and persuade the French Directory to help.

The Protestant Wind

Wolfe Tone succeeded brilliantly in arguing a case for French intervention and on the night of 16 December 1796, the last great French invasion force to set sail for the British Isles slipped past the British squadron blockading the port of Brest. Five days later 35 ships with 6000 men aboard arrived and anchored off Bantry Bay. Unfortunately, the frigate carrying the Commander-in-Chief, General Hoche, had become separated from the rest of the fleet during the journey and so it was decided not to land until he arrived. But their good fortune deserted them. After waiting through one clear, calm day the wind changed and blew from the east, and it is remembered in all the songs as a 'Protestant Wind'. The fleet endured the rain and storm for three days, then the ships cut cable and headed back for France. Only Wolfe Tone and his ship, *The Indomitable*, remained and, as Tone put it, 'England had not such an escape since the Armada'.

Meanwhile, in the Irish countryside, increasingly brutal attempts were made by the militia and the yeomanry to stamp out sedition. In Ulster, where the United Irishmen were strong, efforts were made to set the United Irishmen against the Orangemen, many of whom had joined the yeomanry. This continual pressure forced the society to plan rebellion. However, government spies had infiltrated its ranks, and two months before the proposed date many of the leaders were arrested. By this time many Irish peasants had joined the United Irishmen, inspired by the heady doctrine of Tom Paine's *Rights of Man*. The increased power of the Irish parliament had not meant more freedom for them; on the contrary the heretics and alien landlords now seemed to have more power to persecute them in the forms of tithes and taxes. Yet the Gaelic-speaking peasants had little in common with the middle-class agitators, and their anger was even more explosive.

The 1798 Rebellion

In May 1798 the rebellion broke out. The United Irish leaders had planned a rebellion believing that they could count on an army of over 250,000. However, the absence of leadership and careful, efficient planning resulted in local uprisings with no central support; even those which achieved some success were quickly crushed. In Wexford, the United Irishmen led by Father Murphy succeeded in capturing Enniscorthy and all the county except New Ross. It took a general, a month of warfare and a pitched battle lasting 12 hours to defeat the rebels. The battle of Vinegar Hill, with its grisly and indiscriminate reprisals against Protestants, ended in the rebels' defeat, and the usual brutal consequences. In Ulster there were two main risings, under **McCracken** and **Munro**. The risings both enjoyed brief success during which time the rebels treated any Loyalist prisoners well—a marked contrast to what had happened in other counties. But the sectarian battles between the Peep-O'Day Boys had already soured the trust of the Catholics, and many of them did not turn up to help the mixed bunch of United Irishmen. Poor Wolfe Tone and others who had started the society with such hopes for affectionate brotherhood saw their ideals drowned in a sea of blood. Nugent, the commander of the government forces in Ulster, decided to appeal to the rebels who had property to lose, especially those in the rich eastern counties, and he proclaimed a general amnesty if the Antrim rebels gave up their arms. The rebels of Down did not get off so humanely; when they had been routed and shot down they were left unburied in the streets for the pigs to eat. McCracken and Munro were executed.

The Races of Castlebar

Whilst the war between France and England became more embittered, Wolfe Tone succeeded in raising another invasion force. On 22 August 1798, **General Humbert** arrived in Killala Bay with 1000 men and more arms for the rebels, although most of them had dispersed. Humbert captured Ballina and routed 6000 loyalist troops in a charge called the 'Races of Castlebar'. But there were not enough rebels and Humbert had to accept honourable terms of surrender in September. Only a few weeks later, another unsuccessful French expedition arrived with Tone on board and entered Lough Swilly. It was overcome by some British frigates and Wolfe Tone was captured. He appeared before a court martial wearing a French uniform and carrying a cockade. The only favour he asked was the right to be shot, which was refused, whereupon he cut his own throat with a penknife and lingered in agony for seven days.

The rebellion of 1798 was one of the most tragic and violent events in Irish history, and it had the effect of making people try to bring about change in a non-violent way. In the space of three weeks, 30,000 people, peasants armed with pitchforks and pikes, women and children, were cut down and shot. The results of the rebellion were just as disastrous. The ideas of political and religious equality were discredited, because of the deaths and destruction of property. The British Government found that an independent parliament was an embarrassment to them, especially since the 'Protestant garrison' had not been able to put down the peasant rising without their help.

The Union

Pitt, the British prime minister, decided that union between Great Britain and Ireland was the only answer. First he had to bribe the Protestants to give up their power and many earldoms date from this time. Then the **Act of Union** was passed, with promises of Catholic emancipation for the majority. Pitt really did want to give them equality, for he saw that it was a necessary move if he wished to make Ireland relatively content. Unfortunately Pitt was pushed out of government, and **George III** lent his considerable influence to those opposed to Catholic emancipation. He claimed, with perfect truth, that the idea of it drove him mad. The Union did not solve any problems: the Catholics felt bitterly let down and the temporary Home Rule of Grattan's parliament was looked back to as an example. Irreconcilable nationalism was still alive and kicking. Union with England was disadvantageous to Ireland in the areas of industry and trade and many poorer Protestants were discontented—although from now on the Ulster non-conformists supported the Union, for many had been disillusioned by the vengeance shown towards Protestants by the Catholic peasantry. The terms of the 1801 Act were never thought of as final in Ireland, although the English failed to understand this.

The Liberator: Daniel O'Connell

Catholics still could not sit in parliament or hold important state offices or get to the senior judicial, military or civil service posts. Between the Union and 1828 many efforts to have something done about this came to nothing. Then the Catholics found a champion among themselves: a Catholic lawyer called **Daniel O'Connell**. Daniel O'Connell came from an old Catholic Irish family; he had been sent to school in France where his uncle was a general in the French army. His glimpses of the French revolutionary army had left him completely against violence whatever the political end. The rising of 1798 confirmed in him the belief that 'no political change is worth the shedding of a single drop of human blood'. O'Connell founded the **Catholic Association** which, amongst other things, represented the interests of the tenant farmers. Association membership was a penny a month and brought in a huge fighting fund. Most important of all, the Catholic priests supported him, and soon there were branches of the association everywhere.

A turning point for Irish history and the fortunes of Daniel O'Connell came with the Clare election in 1828, when the association showed its strength. O'Connell had an overwhelming victory against the government candidate when all the 40-shilling freeholders voted for him. The whole country was aflame: they wanted Daniel at Westminster. Wellington, the Prime Minister of the day, was forced to give in, and the **Emancipation Bill** was passed in April 1829. But this was not a gesture of conciliation, for at the same time he raised the voting qualification from 40 shillings to a massive £10. Protestant fears had been raised by the power of such a mass movement, for tenant farmers had dared to vote in opposition to their landlords, even though voting was public. To English Catholics Daniel was also a 'Liberator'.

For 12 years O'Connell supported the Whig government and built up a well-disciplined Irish party whose co-operation was essential to any government majority. He was then able to press for some very necessary reforms, and when the viceroy and his secretary were sympathetic much was achieved. But with the return of the Conservatives in 1840, O'Connell decided it was time to launch another popular agitation campaign, this time for the repeal of the Union. His mass-meetings became 'monster meetings', each attended by well over 100,000 people. The government refused to listen on this issue; British public opinion was firmly against it and in Ulster there was a distinct lack of enthusiasm. Daniel O'Connell arranged to have one of his biggest meetings yet, at Clontarf, where Brian Boru had defeated the Vikings. The Government banned it and O'Connell, unwilling to risk violence, called it off. He himself was arrested for conspiracy and sentenced by just the sort of packed jury he had been trying to abolish. Luckily for him, the House of Lords was less frightened and more just; they set aside his sentence. But by then O'Connell's influence had begun to fade, and some Irish began to look to violence to achieve their aims.

The Young Irelanders

Within the Repeal Association was a group of young men who called themselves the **Young Irelanders**. They had founded *The Nation* newspaper to help O'Connell, but they soon began to move in a different direction. They believed that culturally and historically Ireland was independent of England. They fed their enthusiasm on the painful memories of 1798 and composed heroic poetry which they set to old ballad tunes. They were useless at practical politics and did not have the support of the clergy. In 1848 they responded to the spontaneous and romantic uprisings in Europe with one of their own. It was a dismal failure and alienated many people who had been in favour of the Repeal of the Union. The movement was not to become respectable again until 1870.

The Great Hunger

The diet of an ordinary Irishman was six pounds of potatoes and a pint of milk a day, and he lived in miserable conditions. The Cromwellian and Williamite plantations, together with the effect of the Penal Laws, left the Catholics with only 5 per cent of the land. Except in the North, where a thriving linen industry had grown up, the people had to make their living from farming. Absentee landlords became more of a problem after the Union, their agents greedier and their rent demands even higher. It was the farmer at the bottom of the pyramid who paid heavily for what he got. From 1845–49 the **potato blight** struck, with tragic results.

The population of Ireland, as in the rest of Europe, began to rise quickly in the late 18th century, perhaps because the potato could feed large families on small plots of land. Anyway, the marriage age, which had previously been very high, dropped right down and more babies were born. The most deprived and populated area of Ireland was the west, where the potato was the only crop that would grow; it alone sustained the fragile equilibrium of large families on tiny holdings. The scene was set for agricultural and social catastrophe. As the potato rotted in the ground, people ate turnips, cabbage, wild vegetables and even grass, but these could not supply more than a few meals. Gradually, thousands of people began to die of starvation, typhus fever, relapsing fever and dysentery. You may ask yourselves what was done to help them? Very little by the government, quite a lot by individuals and private charities. Every day corn and cattle were leaving the country; nothing was done that might interfere with the principle of free trade and private enterprise. The government's attitude was rigid, though they did allow maize in, a crop in which nobody had any vested interest. Food distribution centres were set up and some relief work was paid for by the government. But this was not very sensible sort of work; mostly digging holes only to fill them in again. Something constructive like laying a network of railway lines might have interfered with private enterprise! Out of a population of eight and a half million, about one million died and another million emigrated.

Emigration

The Irish had been emigrating for years; first to escape persecution by fleeing to the Continent and then as seasonal labour for the English harvests. The Ulster Scots had set the first pattern of emigration to America. They had found that Ireland was not the promised land, after being lured over there by grants of land and low rents. Bad harvests, religious discrimination and high rents sent them off at the rate of 4000 a year. Not many Catholics followed, for there were still restrictions on Catholic emigration. After the Napoleonic wars and the agricultural slump, 20,000 of the brighter and wealthier Catholics went to America; by then America was more liberal in its attitude towards Catholics. Boat fares over were very cheap and the opportunities in the New World seemed less biased in favour of the rich upper classes. Many Irish went to Australia as convicts or free settlers. But the heaviest years of emigration were just after the famine, especially to the USA. The people travelled under appalling conditions, and boats were called 'coffin ships'. It took six to eight weeks to get to America in those overcrowded and disease-ridden conditions. By 1847 nearly a quarter of a million were emigrating annually.

Irish priests followed their flocks out to America and Australia and founded churches wherever they were needed, so a distinct Irish Catholic Church grew up. Such an influx of starving, diseased Irish Catholics was quite another thing to the steady flow of a few thousand Ulster Scots, and initially a lot of people were prejudiced against them. Most of the emigrants left Ireland loathing the British in Ireland. Their children grew up with the same hatred, and sometimes became more anti-British than the Irish left in Ireland. This bitterness was soon transformed into political activity, aided by the Young Irelanders who had fled to America. Many of the emigrants had come from the west where the Gaelic language and culture existed undisturbed. The rest of Ireland, especially the east, was quite anglicized and became more so with the development of education and transport.

America and Irish Politics

By 1858 the Irish Catholics in America had reorganized themselves as the **Fenian Brotherhood**. James Stevens founded a sister movement in Ireland called the **Irish Republican Brotherhood** (IRB). The Fenians called themselves after the legendary Fianna Warriors and were dedicated to the principal of Republicanism. In Ireland, aided by money from America, the Fenians started up the newspaper, *The Irish People*, which was aimed at the urban worker. When the American Civil War was over many Irish American soldiers came over to help the Fenians in Ireland, but their military operations were always dismal failures. In 1867 the government quickly crushed their uprising and felt confident enough to give the leaders long prison sentences. The clergy opposed any revolutionary secret societies and supported action only when it was through constitutional channels. But Fenianism remained a potent force. John Devoy in America and Michael Davitt of the Irish Land League, were imaginative enough to see that violence was not the only way to fight high rents. They made a loose alliance with Parnell, the leader of the Irish Party in the House of Commons.

John Devoy was head of the **Clan-na-Gael**, an organization which cloaked Fenianism. In America, through the Fenians, Parnell was able to collect money for the land agitators. John Devoy gave money and moral support to the revolutionaries in their fight for independence. The Clan created good propaganda for the Nationalists and, between the death of Parnell and the rise of **Sinn Fein** (the new Nationalist party), did everything it could to drive a wedge between the USA and England, and to keep the States neutral during the First World War. It even acted as an intermediary between Germany and the IRB who were negotiating for guns.

The Irish Americans played such an important part in Irish politics that it is worth jumping in time for a moment to recount subsequent events. In 1918 **Eamon de Valera**, born in America, was elected by Sinn Fein head of a provisional government. He came to America with high hopes during the War of Independence in Ireland. He wanted two things: political recognition from the government for the Dail Eireann—the Irish parliament set up in

Dublin in 1919—and money. He failed in his first aim: he was rebuffed by President Wilson, himself of Ulster Scots blood, and very proud of it too. But the President belonged to the strain of Presbyterian emigrants who had flung themselves wholeheartedly into the making of America, and helped draw up the Constitution. They had forgotten the hardships they suffered in Ireland and did not continue to bear grudges. However, de Valera got plenty of money, 6m dollars in the form of a loan, but he fell out with Devoy. He founded a rival organization called the **American Association for the Recognition of the Irish Republic** (AARIA). When Ireland split over the solution of partition and there was a civil war, the Republicans, who rejected the partition, were supported by the AARIA, whilst the Free Staters had Devoy and Clan-na-Gael behind them. The leading spirit of the AARIA was **Joseph McGarrity**, who later broke with De Valera when he began to act against the IRA. His group and their successors have continued to give financial support to the IRA during the present troubles in Northern Ireland.

Now to return to the efforts of the British government to forestall the repeal of the Union and the efforts of various organizations to bring it about.

Tenants' Rights and the Land War

The Union Government was blamed by many in Ireland for the tragic extent of the famine, but the government was blind to the lessons it should have taught them. The famine had only intensified the land war and the 1829 Act simply enabled the impoverished landlords to sell their estates, which the peasants had no money to buy. So the speculators moved in, seized opportunities for further evictions and increased the rents. They cleared the land for cattle rearing and were more brutal towards the peasants than the old landlords. Tenant resistance smouldered, stimulated by the horrors of the famine.

Michael Davitt organized the resistance into the **National Land League**, with the support of Parnell, the leader of the Irish Party in the House of Commons. In the ensuing **Land War** (1879–82), a new word was added to the English language—'boycott'. The peasants decided not to help an evicting landlord with his crops and he had to import some loyal Orangemen from Ulster to gather in the harvest. The offending landlord was a Captain Boycott. The tenants wanted the same rights that tenants had in Ulster and fair rent, fixity of tenure and freedom to sell at the market value. They also wanted a more even distribution of the land. At that time 3 per cent of the population owned 95 per cent of the land.

But one of the greatest barriers to reconciliation was the mental block the English had about Ireland. Behind all the agitation at this time, and all the obstruction the Irish Party caused in parliament, was a desire for the repeal of the Union. But the politicians saw the problem as religion, over-population, famine, anything but nationalism. It did not enter English heads that the Irish might not want to be part of Britain. The Union, in their eyes, was surrounded by a sort of aura: with it, Irishmen were on an equal footing with the rest of Great Britain, they were part of the Empire. The Union was also a security against foreign attack and must stay. Only one man said anything sensible on the subject and he was not listened to. **J. S. Mill** said that England was the worst qualified to govern the Irish, because English traditions were not applicable in Ireland. England was firmly *laissez-faire* in her economic policies, but Ireland needed economic interference from the government. This the English politicians had resolutely refused to do during and after the famine. Gladstone and other Liberals were aware of the discontent. They tried to take the sting out of Irish Nationalism by dealing with the individual problems one by one, believing that then the nationalist grievance would disappear.

Killing Home Rule with Kindness

One of the first things to be dealt with was religion, for it could not be kept out of politics. The Protestant Ascendency, by virtue of education, contacts, etcetera, still monopolized powerful positions, despite Catholic emancipation. This frustrated the middle classes and created an Irish Catholic national distinctiveness. There may have been no legal barriers any more, but there were unofficial ones.

The Anglican Church of Ireland still remained the Established Church until 1869, and until then the Irish peasant had to pay tithes to it. The Catholic hierarchy wanted a state-supported Catholic education, but the government tried to have interdenominational schools and universities. This never satisfied the Catholic Church and consequently, much later on, it supported the illegal nationalist organizations. Unfortunately the government were unwilling to establish the Catholic Church in Ireland as they would have had problems with the Protestants in Ulster, so although the Catholic Church had consolidated its position, it was not conciliated.

The distress of the peasant farmers had, by this time, become identified with nationalism, so the government set out to solve the economic problems, thinking that this would shatter the nationalists. But they acted too late. Only in 1881 were the demands of the tenants met. Large amounts of money were made available to tenants to buy up their holdings, and by 1916 64 per cent of the population owned land. (Many of these new owners had the same surnames as those dispossessed back in the 17th century.) But Britain was remembered not for these Land Acts, generous as they were, but for the Coercion and Crime Acts which Balfour brought in to try and control the unrest and anarchy which existed in some parts of the country. The **Land Purchase Acts** took away the individual oppressor and left only the government against whom to focus discontent. The peasants had been given more independence and the landlords were virtually destroyed, so the Union became even more precarious. The Nationalists could not be bought off.

Home Rule for Ireland?

Parnell forced the government to listen, often holding a balance of power in the House of Commons, and for a while he managed to rally the whole Nationalist movement behind his aggressive leadership. The bait of universal suffrage was enough for the Fenians to try and overthrow the Union from within the system. The **Secret Ballot Act** in 1872 made this even more attractive than abortive rebellions. But the Home Rule League did not succeed, even though Gladstone and the Liberals, who were at that time in Opposition, had promised to support it. First of all, Parnell was a weakness as well as a strength. His aggressive tactics alienated many Englishmen and his Protestant origins upset some of the Catholic hierarchy, who thought he should have concentrated a little more on pushing the Catholic university they wanted. Also, his affair with Kitty O'Shea and involvement in a divorce case shocked many Victorians and non-conformists in the Liberal Party. They demanded that he should be dropped from the leadership of the Irish Party, and when the Catholic hierarchy heard this, they also began to scold 'the named adulterer' and turned their congregations against him. Another reason for the failure of the Home Rule Bill was that the predominantly Protestant and industrial North of Ireland had no wish to join the South. The North thought that it would be overtaxed to subsidize the relatively backward agrarian South, and the Protestants were frightened of being swamped by the Catholics. Their fear gave them a siege mentality; Parnell's divorce case was like a gift from heaven and gave them a reprieve. English opinion was still against Home Rule and it was only because the Irish Party had made a deal with the Liberals that there was any hope of their succeeding. With the fall of Parnell, the Irish Party split and lost most of its importance.

Parnell's fall in 1891 and the failure of the 1893 Home Rule Bill initiated a resurgence of revolutionary nationalism. The younger generation were shocked by the way in which the Catholic Church within Ireland condemned Parnell over the O'Shea case. And, as the moral authority of the Church was cast aside, so was one of the barriers to violence. Parnell's failure to work things through Parliament seemed to indicate that only violence would work. Young people began to join the Irish Republican Brotherhood (IRB), founded by James Stevens, and even the Church began to show more sympathy because at least nationalism was preferable to the aesthetic socialism that was creeping into Dublin. Many of the priests had brothers and sisters in illegal organizations and it was inevitable that they would become emotionally involved.

Gaelic Cultural Renaissance

There was a new mood in Ireland at the end of the 19th century. The people were proud of being Irish and of their cultural achievements. Unfortunately only 14 per cent of the population spoke the Gaelic language (the famine and emigration that followed had seriously weakened its hold); English was taught in schools, knowledge of it led to better jobs and opportunities, and Irish music and poetry were neglected except by a few intellectuals. However, it was in the stories of Ireland's past greatness, her legends and customs, that many diverse groups found a common ground. In 1884 the **Gaelic Athletic Association** started to revive the national game—hurling. Everybody knows how important cricket is to the English village green. Now Irishmen were actively and publicly participating in something very Irish. In 1893 the **Gaelic League** was formed. Its president was **Douglas Hyde**, who campaigned successfully for the return of Gaelic lessons to schools and as a qualification for entry to the new universities. He never wanted the League to be a sectarian or political force, but it did provide a link between the conservative Catholic Church and the Fenians and Irish Nationalists. 'The Holy Island of St Patrick' developed an ideal: that of the Catholic, devout, temperate, clean-living Irishman. (England was seen as the source of corruption, whilst Patrick Pearse and de Valera made revolution seem respectable.) The Gaelic League and the Gaelic Athletic Association were used by the IRB as sounding boards or recruiting grounds for membership.

The Liberals returned to power in 1906 and things began to look brighter for Home Rule. In 1910 John Redmond led the Irish Party and held the balance of power between the

Liberals and the Conservatives. In 1914 Asquith's **Home Rule Bill** was passed, although it was suspended for the duration of the First World War. But six years later Ireland was in the middle of a war of independence and the initiative had passed from the British into the hands of the revolutionary nationalists. Why did this happen? The British Government had left Home Rule too late; the time lag between when it was passed and when it actually might be implemented gave the Irish public time to criticize it and see its limitations. The nationalists began to despair of ever finding a parliamentary solution, for the British could now not force the North into Home Rule and were shutting their eyes to the gun-running which had been going on since the formation of the Ulster Volunteers. The Irish people were rather lukewarm about organizations like the IRB and its associated new Sinn Fein Party, founded by Arthur Griffith, but an event on Easter Monday in 1916 changed all that.

Easter Rebellion 1916

Plans for a national rising with German support were made. The support did not arrive and in a confused situation a rising commenced in Dublin. It happened very quickly. Suddenly the tricolour of a new Irish Republic was flying from the General Post Office in Dublin. Two thousand Irish nationalist volunteers, led by **Patrick Pearse** of the IRB, stood against the reinforcements sent from England and then surrendered about a week later. People were horrified at first by the waste of life, for many civilians got caught up in the gun battles; but then the British played into the hands of Patrick Pearse. All 14 leaders were executed after secret trials. The timing of the uprising was no coincidence. Pearse and the others wanted it to be a blood sacrifice and the resurgence of the nationalist spirit which followed after such a sacrifice was comparable to the resurrection of Christ.

The executions happened before there could be any backbiting as to why the whole thing had been a muddle. Suddenly they were dead, and pity for them grew into open sympathy for what they had been trying to obtain. The Catholic Church was trapped in the emotional wave which advocated revolution. The party which gained from this swing was the Sinn Fein; it was pledged to non-violent nationalism and was the public front of the IRB. John Redmond, the leader of the Irish Party at Westminster, had urged everybody to forget their differences with England and fight the common enemy which was Germany, but the Irish Nationalists, who were negotiating with the Germans, saw things in a very different light. Many Irishmen did go and fight for Britain, but the feeling was that Redmond was prepared to compromise over Home Rule and shelve it until it suited the British.

When in 1918 conscription was extended to Ireland even more people decided that **Sinn Fein** was the only party which could speak for them. It won all the Irish seats bar six. Redmond's party was finished. The only problem was that 44 of the Sinn Fein members were in English jails; those that were not met in Mansion House and set up their own Dail Eireann. American-born Eamon de Valera made an audacious escape from Lincoln prison and was elected the first President of the Irish Republic in 1919. The Irish Volunteers became the **Irish Republican Army** and war was declared on Britain.

The North

Meanwhile in the North they had found a leader to defend the Union in the Dublin-born **Edward Carson**. He was a leading barrister in London (he cross-examined Oscar Wilde in that notorious law suit), and was openly supported by the Conservatives in England. A solemn **Covenant of Resistance to Home Rule** was signed by hundreds of thousands of Northern Unionists. They would fight with any means possible not to come under an Irish parliament in Dublin. After the Easter rising of 1916, Carson was assured by Lloyd George that the six northeastern counties could be permanently excluded from the Home Rule Bill of 1914. When the **War of Independence** broke out in the South, the British offered them partition with their own parliament whilst remaining within Britain. Today they still feel their ties are with a liberal Britain, not the Catholic South. (Remember that in the Republic there is no divorce and limited contraception, mixed marriages are discouraged, and the Welfare State is very limited. Protestants find it disturbing that the Roman Catholic Church's influence is so strong in every facet of social and political life, although the old-fashioned strict Catholicism prevalent until the 1970s is definitely on the wane).

The War of Independence

The British Government had been caught out by the Declaration of Independence by the Dail. The British were engaged in trying to negotiate a peace treaty at Versailles and the Americans had made it very clear that they sympathized with the Irish. Ammunition raids, bombing, burning and shooting began in Ireland, mainly against the Irish Constabulary. The British government waited until the Versailles Conference had come to an end and then started to fight back. The **Black and Tans** were sent over to reinforce the police, and Lloyd George tried to play it down as a police situation. The Black and Tans got their name from the mixture of police and army uniform they wore. Their methods were as brutal as those of the IRA and it became a war of retaliation.

Michael Collins was in charge of military affairs for the IRA and he set up an intelligence system which kept him well informed about British plans; he waged a vicious, well-thought-out campaign against the Black and Tans. By July 1921 a truce was declared because the British public wanted to try to reach a compromise. In October an Irish delegation, which included Griffith and Collins, went to London to negotiate with Lloyd George. They signed a treaty which approved the setting up of an Irish Free State with Dominion status, similar to Canada. The British were mainly concerned with the security aspect and they made two stipulations; that all Irish legislators should take an oath of allegiance to the Crown and that the British Navy could use certain Irish ports.

Civil War

The Republicans (or anti-treaty side) in the Dail were furious. They regarded it as a sell-out. They did not like the oath, or the acceptance of a divided Ireland. Michael Collins saw it as a chance for 'freedom to achieve freedom' and when it came to the debate on it in the Dail, the majority voted in favour of the treaty. De Valera was against the treaty and, as head of the Dail, he resigned; **Arthur Griffith** succeeded him. In June, when the country accepted the treaty, civil war began. The split in the Dail had produced a corresponding split in the IRA; part of it broke away and began violent raids into the North. The remainder of the IRA was reorganized by Michael Collins into the Free State Army. When he was assassinated, a man just as talented took over, **Kevin O'Higgins**. This period is remembered as the **War of Brothers**, and it was bitter and destructive. Men who had fought together against the Black and Tans now shot each other down.

Finally, the Republicans were ready to sue for peace. De Valera, who had not actively taken part in the fighting but had supported the Republicans, now ordered a ceasefire. The bitterness and horror of the civil war has coloured attitudes to this day. The differences between the two main parties, **Fine Gael** (pro-treaty) and **Fianna Fail** (anti-treaty), are historical rather than political, although perhaps in foreign policy Fianna Fail has taken a more anti-British line. Fine Gael held power for the first 10 years and successfully concentrated on building the 26-county state into something credible and strong. In 1926 de Valera broke with Sinn Fein because they saw the Dail and the government in power as usurpers, as bad as the British, and refused to take up their seats. De Valera founded his own party, Fianna Fail. De Valera was a pragmatist and succeeded in disappointing none of his supporters; the new state wanted a change and in 1932 he formed a government. He soon made it clear that Ireland was not going to keep the oath of allegiance or continue to pay land annuities (the repayment of money lent to help tenants pay for their farms).

De Valera

In 1937 de Valera drew up a new **Constitution** for Ireland. It declared Ireland a Republic and seemed a direct challenge to the Northern Ireland Government. Article 5 went like this: 'It is the right of the Parliament Government established by the Constitution to exercise jurisdiction over the whole of Ireland, its Islands and territorial seas'. Article 44.1.2. recognized: 'The special position of the Holy Catholic, Apostolic Roman Church as the guardian of the Faith professed by the great majority of its citizens'.

Both parties had trouble with extremists in the 1930s; Fine Gael had to expel General O'Duffy of the Fascist Blue Shirt movement, and Fianna Fail were embarrassed by their erstwhile allies in the IRA. De Valera dealt with the situation by setting up a military tribunal and declaring the IRA an illegal organization. The IRA did not die but went underground and continued to enjoy a curious relationship with the government and the public. When it got too noisy it was stamped on; but the IRA continues to be regarded nervously and with respect, for its ideals and its members' intransigence seem to be in line with Ireland's dead patriots.

Northern Ireland

The North Today

It is very difficult to be impartial about the 'Troubles' in Northern Ireland—they have been tragic and frightening. With the ceasefire holding at the time of writing, there is hope for the future, albeit very cautious. The basic reason for the 'Troubles' is that the Catholic minority in the North did badly with all the reshuffling that went on in the 1920s, and once the State was set up they were treated as second-class citizens.

The series of events that lead up to the present situation is discussed in more detail below. Before you read on, you may find it useful to look at the glossary of Northern Irish political parties and terms at the end of this chapter.

Discontent Amongst Ulster Catholics, 1921–69

The Ulster Protestants make up two-thirds of the population of Northern Ireland, and the Catholics the rest. Under the leadership of Edward Carson and James Craig, the Ulster Protestants had managed to wrestle their bit of Ulster from the rest of Ireland, and preserve the Union with Britain. They utterly repudiated the idea of a Catholic Gaelic Republic of Ireland, and held themselves aloof from events in the Free State, later the Republic. The Unionists regarded the Catholics as the natural enemies of the state, and their treatment of them stored up plenty of trouble for the future. No attempt was made to woo the Catholic Nationalists, perhaps because the Protestant leaders directed all their energies into preserving the Union. Unionists have a beleaguered mentality because they are constantly in a great state of anxiety about being turfed out of the Union with Britain and into the Republic of Ireland. They were anxious in the 1920s, and they are so now. Remember also that, for hundreds of years, a distrust and rivalry had grown up between the two religious groups over land. The feeling was tribal, and compounded by bloodshed over land fights. The **Government of Ireland Act** in 1920 gave Westminster supreme authority over Northern Ireland. The **Ireland Act** of 1949 enshrined the constitutional guarantee which gave the Stormont Parliament the right to decide whether Northern Ireland would remain in the UK or not.

All Catholics were and still are regarded as supporters of the **IRA**, an organization which was indeed a real menace to this shaky state. It was seen as imperative that Catholics should never be allowed into positions of power and influence. Sir Basil Brooke (1888–1973) was typical of the type of blinkered cabinet minister who ran the government for years. He, along with James Craig (1871–1940), first Prime Minister of Northern Ireland, encouraged Protestants to employ only Protestants, for he, like others, believed that the Catholics were 'out to destroy Ulster with all their power and might'. He became Prime Minister in 1943 and played an active role in linking the Orange Order, of which he was a leading member, with the government of the time. In describing the situation one wants to use the word 'apartheid', although the set-up was not as extreme as that which existed in South Africa. Protestant businesses tended to employ Protestants and Catholics employed Catholics. There were few mixed housing areas or marriages. The Catholic priests fiercely defended their right to run Catholic schools—as they still do.

Government went on at a mainly local level through county and town councils. The Loyalists ensured that they always had a majority on the council through the use of gerrymandering. The local voting qualification also favoured Protestants, who were often wealthier, for the franchise was only granted to house-owners or tenants, and the number of votes allocated to each person could be as high as six, depending of the value of their property. Because the Protestant rulers controlled housing schemes and jobs, the working-class Protestants were given the lion's share of any housing or jobs that existed. Northern Ireland had a much lower standard of living than the rest of the UK, and any advantages were eagerly grasped by these workers, who displayed little feeling of worker solidarity with their fellow Catholics. They never could escape from their religious prejudices and preoccupations to unite against the capitalists, although the ruling class had feared their alliance during the 1922 riots over unemployment.

The Catholics themselves were ambiguous about the State; most of them in the 1920s were Republicans, and they never gave up hope that the Dublin Government might do something about it. Many believed that the Six Counties could not survive, and in the beginning Nationalist Republican representatives refused to sit at Stormont. On the other hand, others had watched with horror the bloodshed and bitterness which resulted from the Civil War in the Irish Free State. After being educated, the bright ones emigrated rather than fight the system. The IRA attempted over the next 50 years to mount a campaign in the North, but they never got anywhere. They managed a few murders, but a big campaign in 1956–62 which killed 19 people failed miserably. The local Catholics did not back them, and the **B Specials** (the Protestant-dominated special police force) did their job well. The trouble was, 'the Specials' irritated and harassed law-abiding Catholics, which left them with a feeling of injustice.

For the time being the Protestant Unionists were able to dominate Catholic Nationalists in elections in a proportion of about four-to-one. This gave them a feeling of security, which was also bolstered by the gratitude of the British government for their loyalty and help during the Second World War, when the North of Ireland had been a vital bulwark for the rest of the UK.

The Civil Rights Movement—British Troops Move in

Yet things had to change, for as young and educated Catholics and Protestants grew up they began to agitate about the obvious injustices, and the **Civil Rights Association** was formed in 1967. Unfortunately, the marches which drew attention to their aims also attracted men of violence on both sides, and as the marches turned into riots, the Protestant Loyalists, including the **Royal Ulster Constabulary** (RUC) and B Specials, seemed to be in league with the Protestant mobs against the Catholics. At this point the discredited IRA failed to seize their opportunity to woo the Catholics, who were confused and frightened. The Catholics welcomed the British troops, who were brought in to keep the peace after the Loyalists and police beat up Civil Rights marchers at Burntollet, and later the inhabitants of the Bogside in Londonderry, in January 1969.

At that time **Terence O'Neill** had taken over from Lord Brookeborough as Prime Minister at Stormont. Although of the same Unionist Ascendancy stock, he realized that something must be done to placate the Nationalists. The few liberal gestures that he made towards the Catholics and the Republic opened up a Pandora's box of fury and opposition amongst the Protestant Unionists, who found a leader in the **Reverend Ian Paisley**. The reforms O'Neill planned over housing and local government came too late, and he was swept away by the Protestant backlash when he called a General Election in April 1969. The brutality with which the police had broken up the Civil Rights marches had stirred support for the IRA, and the Summer Marching Season was marked by even more violence.

The IRA Exploit Events

The IRA organized itself to exploit the situation. It split into two after an internal struggle, and the murders and bombings which dominated events after this time are mainly the work of the Provisional IRA, commonly called the IRA. The British army lost the confidence of the Catholic community it had come to protect through heavy-handed enforcement of security measures. Besides, the IRA posed as the natural guardians of the Catholics, so there were cheers amongst the Catholic Nationalists when the IRA killed the first British soldier in October 1970. The IRA aimed to break down law and order; any method was legitimate, and any member of the army or police was a legitimate target to their mind.

The Stormont government hastened to pass some much needed reforms between 1969 and 1972. The RUC was overhauled, and the B Specials abolished. A new part-time security force was set up within the British Army and called the **Ulster Defence Regiment** (UDR). In 1971 a new Housing Executive was set up to allocate houses fairly, irrespective of religious beliefs. The IRA managed to conduct a destructive bombing campaign in the cities; innocent civilians were killed or injured and buildings destroyed. British soldiers responded to rioting in the Bogside in January 1972 by killing 13 people. A cycle of violence begetting violence began to spiral, and society divided along even more sectarian lines than before. The legacy of hatred, psychological distress and bitterness that has built from this time is terrible to contemplate.

British Attempts to Solve the Problem

In 1972 the Stormont government and parliament were suspended by the British government, which had always retained full powers of sovereignty over it. Direct Rule from Westminster was imposed, and continues to be until a solution can be found. There is a **Secretary of State for Northern Ireland**, appointed by the British Prime Minister, and a body of English ministers and civil servants. Elected members from the different parties sit in Westminster and try to bring Northern Irish issues to the attention of the House.

Internment was brought in in August 1971, and large numbers of terrorist suspects were imprisoned without trial. This hardened Catholic opinion against British justice, and the practice was gradually phased out after a couple of years. Subsequently, the **Diplock system of Criminal Courts** was introduced, which means alleged terrorists are tried by judges who sit alone without juries. It was justified by the amount of intimidation that the jury could be subjected to. Various power-sharing initiatives between the largely Protestant Unionist parties and the Catholic and Republican SDLP did not get off the ground, so Direct Rule continues.The suspension of the Stormont Parliament removed the Constitutional guarantee of the 1949 Act but it was renewed in the 1973 Constitution Act which established the principle that any change would have to have majority consent.

The Sunningdale Agreement

In December 1973 the leaders of the Northern Irish parties, a new Executive, and Ministers from the United Kingdom and for the first time, the Republic of Ireland met together at Sunningdale, and agreed to set up a **Council of Ireland** which would work for consultation and co-operation between Northern Ireland and the Republic. The Agreement provided for a new type of Executive in Northern Ireland, in which power was shared as far as possible between representatives of the two communities in a joint government. It was the dawn of new hope for the province, but the Unionist masses and the Republican terrorists did not want this new co-operation to work. Faced with a general strike called by the Ulster Workers' Council which paralysed the province, the government did not use the army to break the strike, but allowed intimidation by 'Loyalist' paramilitary organizations to win the day. The Unionist members of the Executive resigned, and Direct Rule had to be resumed. Many people believe that if the Sunningdale Agreement had been implemented, much suffering could have been avoided, and the whole of Ireland might be a more stable place today.

The Victims of the 'Troubles'

Since then, the province has suffered sectarian killings, bombings, and the powerful propaganda of the hunger strike campaign by IRA prisoners in the early 1980s. The economy has been in the doldrums and the well-educated members of society, both Protestant and Catholic often leave; however there is now hope that things will improve, that the economy will pick up and foreign investors will look again at Northern Ireland. The Ulster people have suffered the gradual erosion of their society through violence, intimidation, and the subtler psychological effects that violence induces. On the positive side, the spirit and bravery of the Ulster people remains unbroken; manufacturing businesses continue to thrive and compete in international markets, and throughout the province you meet cheerful, humorous and down-to-earth people who are managing to cope. But the statistics in such a small population are grim. Between 1969 and 1994, around 3168 people have lost their lives, around 3300 people have been injured and maimed of which around 2200 have been civilians. The feelings of despair, fear and outrage in both communities led to extreme attitudes in the 1980s. The Reverend Ian Paisley and his colleagues have a huge following, whilst support for Sinn Fein increased considerably at the expense of the Constitutional Nationalists and the SDLP; more recently support for Sinn Fein has dropped.

The Anglo-Irish Agreement

In 1985, after initial efforts by **Garrett Fitzgerald**, the leader of the Fine Gael Party in the Republic, and **Margaret Thatcher**, the British Prime Minister, the New Ireland Forum met in Dublin. It was agreed that Northern Ireland would remain in the United Kingdom as long as the majority so desired, and that the Dublin Government should have an institutionalized consultative status in relation to Northern Irish Affairs.

The effect of the Agreement was largely positive, although gradual. Both governments made progress in the complicated area of extradition and cross-border security, especially after the general revulsion in the Republic against the IRA bomb attack in Enniskillen in 1987. Diplomatic tensions between Britain and the Republic eased. The British Government grasped the nettle of injustice over the conviction of the 'Guildford Four' and the 'Birmingham Six', prisoners convicted of bombings on mainland Britain. The re-opening of these cases and the subsequent acquittal of these prisoners dissipated much bad feeling in the Republic of Ireland where there is great scepticism about British justice in relation to the Irish. One of the most important achivements of the Agreement was that the Irish Government formally accepted 'the principle of consent' by the people of Northern Ireland. Any change in the Constitution Act of 1973 had to have majority consent. The Unionists were not mollifled by this, for it is enshrined in the constitution of the Republic that the Irish Republic claim the whole island, and this claim had not been given up. The Agreement made the world realise that the 'Brits out' solution would be no solution, because it would mean forcibly transferring a million-strong Protestant population into a united Ireland that did not really want them, and the probability of bloody civil war.

The strong emotional link between the English and the Northern Irish has changed since the beginning of the century. The Union was no longer regarded as sacrosanct; many English and Scots know little about the North, and resented the lives lost and money spent maintaining the Union. The Unionists understood this very clearly and felt even more threatened. The Nationalists had not rejected the IRA, who continued to work for the destruction of the six-county state through murder and bombing campaigns in Ulster. On mainland Britain and Europe, the IRA followed a campaign of bombing 'soft' British military targets, and assassinating British politicians, lawyers, and industrialists in order to turn British public opinion against the Union with Northern Ireland.

1990–1993

Inter-party talks began in Northern Ireland and before they broke down some progress was made in defining the three complicated relationships between the North and the UK, the North and the Republic, and the Republic and the UK. This meant there was a set of negotiating mechanisms for the peace process to be furthered. British policy continued to try and find the middle ground between opposing parties in the North, and it was hoped that the politics of the extremists would wither away.

The IRA carried out bombing attacks in the financial heart of London in 1992/93 and elsewhere. One such attack in a shopping centre in Warrington killed two children; there was worldwide revulsion, and a peace movement was launched in Dublin. The IRA could continue their campaign of violence indefinitely, but there were signs that key elements in the IRA wanted to try and change things through political action. In April 1993, **John Hume** of the SDLP started a dialogue with **Gerry Adams** of Sinn Fein. Both the British and the Irish Governments reacted furiously to this but popular nationalist support for the dialogue both North and South forced the governments to rethink their policy. Both Prime Ministers Major and Reynolds began a new policy of trying to draw the extremists into the political process and to aim at all party talks for a lasting constitutional settlement which would bring peace. The North had just suffered the horror in October 1993 of the IRA bomb in a Belfast chippie which killed 10 people; and then the terrible revenge by extremist loyalists who shot 14 people in a public house in Greysteel.

The Downing Street Declaration

On 15th December 1993, both the Irish and British Prime Ministers presented a **joint Declaration** which successfully managed to address the competing claims of the Nationalists and the Unionists. The British Government declared in the document that Britain 'had no selfish strategic or economic interest in Northern Ireland' and recognised the right of the people of Ireland North and South to self-determination. Both Governments affirmed that the status of Northern Ireland could only be changed with the consent of 'a great number of its people'. In the event of an overall political settlement the Irish Government declared it would drop its claim to the six counties contained in articles 2 and 3 of the Irish Constitution. The Irish Government would establish a forum for peace and reconciliation at some later date. Both governments offered a place at the negotiating table to the extremists on both sides if they renounced violence.

Ceasefire

After a disappointing reaction to the Declaration and prevarication for several months, the IRA eventually announced **'a complete cessation of military operations'** on 31st August 1994. In the following weeks the extremist unionist forces of the UFF, the UVF and the Red Hand of Ulster announced a **ceasefire**, conditional upon the IRA's continuing ceasefire. This outcome has brought great opportunities for eventual peace, and the fact that the day-to-day maiming and killing has ceased is a great relief to the people of Northern Ireland. Of course there are many irreconcilable aims on both sides of political opinion, and the politicians will have to make compromises. Amongst the many problems to solve is the great distrust on the Unionist side many fear a secret deal between Britain and the Republicans so the danger of a Unionist backlash is very real. Although the main Unionist party seems satisfied at the moment with British assurances, the Unionists have seen the British Government (Conservative) move from a unionist to a neutral position. They fear they may yet move, as Sinn Fein would like, to the role of 'persuading' the Unionists to join the Republic. All the people of Northern Ireland fear that the ceasefire may not be permanent—there have been ceasefires before, although this one has lasted the longest so far. Gerry Adams has said that a militant IRA could emerge in a few years' time if the causes of conflict are not resolved.

None of the terrorist groups has given up their arms (at the time of writing—February 1995). The IRA are demanding that the British Army and the RUC should disarm, and that all political prisoners be released. So there are major problems ahead over the question of IRA and UFF arms, and the future community policing in Northern Ireland. The IRA has been policing Catholic West Belfast for many years, to protect their own financial empire, and to control lawless youths. The RUC are not welcome in Nationalist areas, as the Nationalists see the RUC as a Unionist police force although the RUC has been trying hard to change its image. Historically there have always been very few Catholics in the RUC because of hostility to the force and fear of the IRA. One of the crucial issues to be worked out is who should police areas such as West Belfast. Another problem to be solved is the future of political prisoners, and how the rule of law can be reimposed on criminal activities and extortion rackets run by terrorist groups both republican and loyalist. However, the ceasefire is felt to be the irrevocable beginning of a new phase with the British Government slowly, and the Irish Government impatiently, moving towards the next step, a peace summit where the peace process can be decided.

The Republic Today

The Irish Republic has a titular Head of State, a **President** who is elected for seven years by the vote of the people. The President is empowered on the recommendation of the Dail to appoint the Prime Minister (Taoiseach), sign laws and invoke the judgement of the Supreme Court on the legality of Bills. He is also supreme commander of the armed forces. The Irish parliament consists of the President and two Houses: the Dail and the Senate. The Dail is made up of 166 members (TDs) elected by adult suffrage through proportional representation. The Senate is made up of 60 members: 11 are nominated by the Taoiseach; 49 are elected by the Dail and county councils from panels representive of the universities, labour, industry, education and social services. The average length of an Irish Government is three years.

In the 1970s and 1980s each Irish government has had to face unemployment, growing emigration and a huge national debt—in 1989 it was IR£24,827 million. The Republic is a major supporter of the **EU** and the **Maastricht Agreement** and has done extremely well economically from EU funding. Six billion pounds was allocated in regional structural funds. For many years Ireland was at the lower end of the EU GDP average which meant it often qualified for extra regional assistance, but recently its GDP has risen to above 80 per cent of the average so it might no longer be eligible. However, the addition of the new Scandinavian countries is likely to raise the average GDP.

The principle of neutrality so long adhered to in foreign affairs is no longer certain. Ireland has recently attended as an observer the **Western European Union** (WEU) defence body. Economically Ireland has become very attractive to high technology and computer investment, partly because of its young well educated population. Economic growth rates have been good, and emigration has slowed down.

The traditional lines of Irish parties are also changing from the pro- and anti-treaty (of 1921) stances. Mary Robinson as the Head of State has brought a new flexibility and dynamism into politics here. Her enthusiasm and energy in helping all parts of Ireland, including the North, has won her great popularity and a world profile.

Irish Political Parties

The origins of the two major parties, the Fianna Fail and Fine Gael, hark back to the violent differences between those anti the Free State Treaty, and those pro it. **Fianna Fail** has managed to establish itself as the dominant ruling party, although this dominance is definitely under threat as the general public is disillusioned with the incompetence and corruption revealed by a number of celebrated cases. At the time of writing the Taoiseach and Fianna Fail leader, Albert Reynolds had been forced to step down after a series of political blunders. He was replaced as party leader by Bertie Ahern.

Fine Gael is a more Socialist-inspired party with strong European inclinations. The **Labour Party** has found it difficult to gain popular support in the country as people have, up to now anyway, been very conservative and voted as their family do—either Fine Gael or Fianna Fail. This is changing now as Labour have increased their powerbase in the last 10 years in Dublin and Cork and formed coalition governments either with Fianna Fail or Fine Gael. Sinn Fein is the political arm of the Official IRA (which is a banned organization) but does not command much support in the Republic. The new government is a coalition of Fine Gael, led by the new Taoiseach, John Bruton, and the Labour Party.

A Glossary of Political Parties and Terms

The following labels and identities crop up in discussions on Northern Ireland again and again.

Unionist: refers to one who supports the Union with Great Britain, and has no wish to share an Irish nationality with the Republic of Ireland. There are two main Unionist parties in Northern Ireland. The Official Unionists were the original party and are, on the surface, more willing to discuss options to try and solve the crisis in the State. The Democratic Unionist Party (DUP), led by Ian Paisley, is more radical and Protestant. It is very anti any sort of co-operation with the Irish Republic, and anti-Pope.

Alliance: a label used for a party composed of moderate Unionists, both Protestant and Catholic, but it loses out to the more extreme parties.

Loyalist: a general term to describe anyone in favour of the Union with Great Britain.

Republican: a label which refers to anyone who supports a united Ireland. In Northern Ireland, the Socialist Democratic and Labour Party (SDLP), formed in 1970, is committed to achieving a United Ireland through peaceful and democratic means. It is linked, although only in its aims, to the Provisional Sinn Fein, the political wing of the IRA, which is less choosy about its methods.

Nationalist: interchangeable with the label 'Republican'.

IRA: is the label used to describe the Irish Republican Army, which did not disband after the Civil War in Ireland ended (1920–21). The IRA is outlawed in the Republic of Ireland and the United Kingdom. The objective of its members is to fight by the gun and bomb until the whole of Ireland is free of the British, and the six counties reunited with the rest of Ireland. In 1969, with the start of civil disturbances, the IRA was reinvigorated. Firstly it reorganized itself and split into two. The Marxist Socialist-inspired members call themselves the Official IRA (OIRA) and the traditionalists call themselves the Provisional IRA (PIRA) after the 'Provisional' government of Ireland set up in the GPO after the Easter Rising of 1916. The ideals of the 'Provos' are straightforward: a United Republic of Ireland, whatever the cost in terms of violence. The Provisionals are generally referred to as the IRA, since the Officials have dropped out of the action.

UVF and **UDA:** both the Ulster Volunteer Force and the Ulster Defence Association are illegal Protestant terrorist organizations that recruit from the working class. They are usually involved in revenge killings after IRA attacks.

RUC: Royal Ulster Constabulary. Reorganized in the 1970s, this police force manages much of the security of Northern Ireland in co-operation with the British army. The Catholic Nationalists in Northern Ireland regard it with suspicion, believing it to be biased by its largely Protestant Unionist membership. Any Catholics who join it are singled out for death by the IRA.

The B Specials: were a special, part-time reserve force within the RUC with special powers to search out IRA members. Catholics maintain that they beat up alleged members. They operated from the 1920s until it was disbanded in the early 1970s.

The Orange Order: a sectarian and largely working-class organization that originated as a secret Protestant working-class agrarian society known as the Peep-O'Day Boys. William of Orange (William III of England) became their hero, and the society changed its name to the Orange Order in 1795. Its members have a traditional fear of the Catholic majority in Ireland and are Unionist in politics. Orange Lodges are still active in Northern Ireland.

The Summer Marching Season: is a reference to the Orange and Hibernian marches during July and August. Each side commemorates opposing events in the history of Ireland. In the past, drums and equipment were lent between the two sides, but the present conflict has distilled into bitterness and hatred, and this has ceased. The Orange marchers, in particular, frequently take provocative routes through Catholic areas.

Gerrymandering: refers to the policy of concentrating large numbers of Catholics with Republican views in unusually big electoral districts, whilst Protestant Unionists were in smaller districts. This meant that the Protestant Unionists were always certain to win a larger number of representatives, district by district. Londonderry was a prime example: 87 per cent of the large Catholic population were placed in one ward which returned eight seats, whilst 87 per cent of the much smaller Protestant population were placed in two wards and they returned 12 seats. Gerrymandering gradually became the norm from the late 1920s until the electoral reforms at the beginning of the 1970s.

Civil Rights Movement: began in the 1960s, and was inspired by the American Civil Rights campaigner, Martin Luther King. The Civil Rights Association, founded in 1967, called for jobs, houses and one man one vote. It was supported by both Catholics and Protestants, and the leadership of the Association has been described as 'middle-aged, middle-class and middle-of-the-road'. The Civil Rights Movement was hijacked by a more Republican and Socialist element and the mob violence that attended the Civil Rights marches, and eventually lost out to the IRA.

Direct Rule: the British Government had always retained full powers of sovereignty on all matters over the Northern Ireland government at Stormont. Thus, when the riots and bloodshed began to get out of control, and the Stormont government seemed unable to implement reforms or control the police, Direct Rule was imposed in 1972. The Stormont Government and Parliament is still suspended, and Northern Ireland MPs sit in the British House of Commons.

Religion

The reminders and symbols of a religious faith and deep love of God are everywhere to be seen in Ireland. The images which fill my mind are of a child in white, showing off her dress after her first Holy Communion, rags caught in brambles around a holy well; cars parked up a country lane, everybody piling out for Mass, umbrellas held high and skirts fluttering. The people of Ireland invoke and refer to the Virgin Mary and to Jesus often in their everyday talk. Roadside shrines to the Virgin are decorated with shells and fresh flowers, and many people still stop what they are doing to say the Angelus at noon and at sunset. Grey Neo-Gothic churches dominate the small country town, whilst in the smaller villages the chapel or church is a simpler building, planted around with dark yews and beeches above which the ceaseless cawing of the rooks can be heard.

In Ireland everybody knows what you are—whether Catholic, Presbyterian, Church of Ireland, Baptist or Methodist; anything else is classed as 'heathen', and they feel sorry for you! The history of Ireland has had much to do with this feeling of religious identity, and, unfortunately, in the North this mix of politics and religion has produced individuals whose extreme Catholic or Presbyterian attitudes are reminiscent of 17th-century Europe. The bigotry that characterizes such attitudes has been a major factor in the political situation in the North today. Efforts are made by some of the clergy to organize ecumenical meetings but mostly their congregations ignore them.

Pre-Christian Ireland

The Irish have been religious for five thousand years, and there are plenty of chambered cairns (mounds of stones over prehistoric graves) to prove it. The Celts who arrived in about 500 BC seemed to have been a very religious people, and they had a religious hierarchy organized by Druids. These people worshipped a large number of gods, and central to their beliefs and rituals was the cult of the human head. They believed that the head was the centre of man's powers and thoughts. Their stone masons carved two-headed gods and the style in which they worked has a continuity which can be traced right up to the 19th century. There are heads in the Lough Erne district which are difficult to date. They could be pagan, Early-Christian or comparatively modern.

The origins of the earlier Tuatha Dé Danaan are lost in legend: they may have been pre-Celtic gods or a race of invaders, themselves vanquished by the Celts. They are believed to have had magical powers and heroic qualities. Today they are remembered as the 'wee folk' who live in the raths and stone forts. Here they make fairy music which is so beautiful that it bewitches any human who hears it. The wee folk play all kinds of tricks on country people, from souring their milk to stealing their children, and so a multitude of charms have been devised to guard against these fairy pranks. I can remember being told about the fairies who used to dance in magic rings in the fields; the trouble was that if you tried to go up to them they would turn into yellow ragwort dancing in the wind.

Early-Christian Ireland

Christianity is believed to have come to Ireland from Rome in the 4th century, although St Patrick is credited with the major conversion of the Irish in the 5th century. The Irish seem to have taken to Christianity like ducks to water, although much of our knowledge of early Christianity comes through the medieval accounts of scholarly (but possibly biased) clerics. One explanation for the ease with which Christianity took over is that the Christians did not try to change things too fast, and incorporated some elements of the Druidic religion into their practices.

An example of the assimilation of the Druidic religion by the Christians is the continuing religious significance of the holy wells. Ash and rowan trees, both sacred to the Druids, are frequently found near the wells, and Christian pilgrims still leave offerings of rags on the trees as a sign to the Devil that he has no more power over them. Patterns (pilgrimages) and games used to be held at the wells, although they often shocked the priest, who would put the well out of bounds and declare that its healing powers had been destroyed. There are many other everyday signs of the way that the spiritual life of the Irish people harks back to pagan times. In cottages and farmhouses you might see a strange swastika sign made out of rushes. This is a St Brigid's cross, hung above the door or window to keep the evil spirits away. Fairy or sacred trees are still left standing in the field even though it is uneconomic to plough round them—bad luck invariably follows the person who cuts one down.

Monasteries in Early-Christian Ireland

By the end of the 6th century the Church was firmly monastic, with great monasteries such as Clonmacnoise in County Offaly, and Clonfert in County Galway. These centres were responsible for big strides in agricultural development and were important for trade; they also became places where learning and artistry of all sorts was admired and emulated. The Ireland of 'Saints and Scholars' reached its peak in the 7th century.

The monks sought an ascetic and holy way of life, although this was pursued in a fierce and warlike manner. The ultimate self-sacrifice was self-imposed exile, and so they founded monasteries in France, Italy and Germany. The abbots, by the 8th century, had become all-powerful in Irish politics. Missionaries continued to leave Ireland and contribute to the revival of Christianity in Europe, and there was a blossoming of the arts with wonderful metalwork and painted manuscripts. By the 9th century, the monasteries were commissioning intricately carved stone high crosses, such as you can see at Ahenny in County Tipperary.

Religious Discrimination

Religious discrimination is long-established in Ireland. Over the centuries Catholics and Protestants have suffered by not conforming to the established church, although Catholics have undoubtedly received the greatest share of discrimination and persecution. The Huguenots arrived when Louis XIV revoked the Edict of Nantes in 1686. They were Calvinists and intermarried easily with the other Protestant groups. (The Huguenots were very skilled and established the important linen industry, as well as weaving and lace-making.) The Presbyterians were the biggest group of dissenters, most of whom were Scots who settled in Ulster during the 17th century. They had been persecuted in Scotland because of their religious beliefs and now they found that Ireland was no better: they were as poor as the native Irish, and many found life so hard that they emigrated to America. Quakers, Palatines (German Protestants), Moravians, Baptists and Methodists also settled in Ireland but their numbers have declined through emigration and inter-marriage.

Religion in Ireland Today

In the Republic of Ireland the Catholics make up 93% of the population, the Church of Ireland 2.8%, the Presbyterians 0.4%, the Jews 0.06%, the Methodists 0.2%, and the rest are small groups of other religious denominations or non-believers. In the Six Counties of Northern Ireland, the Catholics make up 34.9%, the Church of Ireland 24.2%, the Presbyterians 29%, the Methodists 5%, and others 6.9%. In the Republic the Catholic majority is obviously the controlling force in political and social life and the Protestant minority has bowed out gracefully. The Protestants used to represent almost 10% of the population but this figure has declined through mixed marriages.

In theory the modern state does not tolerate religious discrimination, and it is true that both Jews and Protestants have reached positions of importance and wealth in industry and banking. However, the Protestant classes had it so good during the hundreds of years of British Rule that it is not surprising that for a short time there was a legacy of antipathy towards anyone connected with the mainly Protestant Ascendency. Happily, the antipathy has nearly disappeared now, but instead there is an enormous amount of Catholic complacency, and the power of the Church is very powerful in the land. The bishops' exhortations on divorce, contraception, AIDS, etc. are listened to with great earnestness by the politicians. The sanctity of the family is held to be of the greatest importance. Recently there was a national referendum on the introduction of divorce, which had the priests thundering in the pulpits; and in the end the bulk of the people voted against it! Another referendum on this may well be held in the near future. Contraception is now readily available but women still go to England for abortions. Of course, in Northern Ireland, the laws of the land are quite secular, being laid down by the British government, but divorce is still quite unusual there, too, and the principal UK legislation on abortion, the 1967 Abortion Act, has not been extended to the province.

The parish priest is always a person of great importance in Irish society and he is usually very approachable. You might easily meet him in the village bar having a drink and a chat. Nearly every family has a close relative who is a priest or a nun, and Irish priests and nuns leave their native land in great numbers to serve overseas, taking their particular brand of conservative Catholicism with them.

Schooling is mostly in the hands of the Church (incidentally, Ireland has a very high standard of literacy and general education), and thankfully the days of the cane and the even crueller sarcasm of the priest-teachers described by so many Irish writers has disappeared. The people in the top positions in Ireland today mostly went to Christian Brother Schools (look in the Irish *Who's Who*). So did many county councillors and petty officials who organize Ireland's huge bureaucracy. The old-boy network is very strong for getting favours done, grants approved, and planning permission granted.

Irish people practise their religion faithfully in rural areas. The churches are full on Sundays, and visits to Knock, Croagh Patrick, and Lough Derg are taken many times in a person's lifetime. Holy wells are still visited, and Stations of the Cross go on even in ruined churches and friaries. But in the cities more and more young people and other disillusioned individuals have moved away from the church and some religious orders are forced to advertise for their priests! The numbing censoriousness of Catholicism and Protestantism in Ireland has become part of the island's image, just as the green hills, and constant rain. But it is a theme which has been overplayed, and the reality is that people are really very tolerant of other religious communities within their society; this applies to Northern Ireland too. Great community involvement and care comes directly from the churches, and the social events are enjoyable and fun. The Irish are amongst the most generous when it comes to raising money for world disasters, and this charity work is usually channelled through the Church.

Death and weddings are always occasions for a bit of 'crack', and there is also a party whenever the priest blesses a new house. Irish couples spend more on their engagement rings and their weddings than their English counterparts; it's a really big occasion. The Irish wake has lost many of its pagan rituals—mourning with keening and games involving disguise, mock weddings, jokes and singing. Nowadays, the dead person is laid out in another room and people come in to pay their last respects, and then spend the rest of the evening drinking, eating and reminiscing.

Irish Saints

Every locality in Ireland has its particular saint. The stories that surround him or her belong to myth and legend, not usually to historical fact. One theory is that all these obscure, miraculous figures are in fact Celtic gods and goddesses who survived under the mantle of sainthood. Included below is a short account of lives of some of the most famous saints, about whom few facts are known.

Brendan (*c.* 486–575), Abbot and Navigator

This holy man is remembered for his scholastic foundations, and for the extraordinary journey he made in search of Hy-Brasil, believed to be an island of paradise, which he had seen as a mirage whilst looking out on the Atlantic from the Kerry Mountains. His journey is recounted in the *Navigato Brendan*, a treasure of every European library during the Middle Ages. The oldest copies are in Latin and date from the 11th century. The account describes a sea voyage which took Brendan and 12 other monks to the Orkneys, to Wales, to Iceland, and to a land where tropical fruits and flowers grew. The descriptions of his voyage have convinced some scholars that he sailed down the east coast of America to Florida. Tim Severin, a modern-day explorer, and 12 others recreated this epic voyage between May 1976 and June 1977. In their leather and wood boat, they proved that the Irish monks could have been the first Europeans to land in America. (It is possible to see the boat at the Lough Gur Centre in County Clare.) Christopher Columbus probably read the *Navigato*, and in Galway there is a strong tradition that he came to the west coast in 1492 to search out traditions about St Brendan.

The saint's main foundation was at Clonfert, which became a great scholastic centre. One of his monks built the first beehive-shaped cells on Skellig Michael, the rocky island off County Kerry. Other foundations were at Annaghdown in County Galway, and Inisglora in County Mayo. Brendan is buried in Clonfert Cathedral, and he is honoured in St Brendan's Cathedral in Loughrea, County Galway, where the beautiful mosaic floor in the sanctuary depicts his ship and voyage.

St Brigid (died *c.* 525), Abbess of Kildare

Brigid, also known as Briget, Bride and Brigit, is the most beloved saint in Ireland and is often called Mary of the Gael. Devotion to her spread to Scotland, England and the Continent. The traditions and stories that surround her describe her countless generous and warm-hearted acts to the poor, her ability to counsel the rulers of the day, and her great holiness. Her father was a pagan from Leinster and she was fostered by a Druid. (This custom of fosterage in Ireland existed right up to the 19th century.) She decided not to marry and founded a religious order with seven other girls. They were the first formal community of nuns and wore simple white dresses.

St Brigid has her feast day on 1 February, which is also the date of the pagan festival Imbolc, which marks the beginning of spring. She is the patron of poets, scholars, black-smiths and healers, and is also inevitably linked with the pagan goddess Brigid, the goddess of fire and song. There is a tradition that St Brigid's Abbey in Kildare contained a sanctuary with a perpetual fire, tended only by virgins, whose high priestess was regarded as an incarnation and successor of the goddess. The two women are further linked by the fact that Kildare in Irish means 'church of oak', and St Brigid's church was built from a tree held sacred to the Druids. There is a theory that Brigid and her companions accepted the Christian faith, and then transformed the pagan sanctuary into a Christian shrine.

Kildare was a great monastic centre after Brigid's death, and produced the now lost masterpiece, the *Kildare Gospels*. Tradition says that the designs were so beautiful that an angel helped to create them. The St Brigid's nuns kept alight the perpetual fire until the suppression of the religious houses during the Reformation.

Brigid was buried in Kildare Church, but in 835 her remains were moved to Downpatrick in County Down, because of the raids by the Norsemen. She is supposed to share the grave there with St Patrick and St Colmcille, but there is no proof of this. In 1283 it is recorded that three Irish knights set out to the Holy Land with her head; they died en route in Lamiar in Portugal, and in the church there the precious relic of her head is enshrined in a chapel to St Brigid. The word 'bride' derives from St Brigid. It is supposed to originate from the Knights of Chivalry, whose patroness she was. They customarily called the girls they married their brides, after her, and hence the word came into general usage.

St Columban (died 615), Missionary Abbot

Columban, also known as Columbanus, is famous as the great missionary saint. He was born in Leinster and educated at Bangor in County Down under St Comgall, who was famed for his scholarship and piety. Columban set off for Europe with 12 other religious men to preach the gospel and convert the pagans in Gaul (France) and Germany. He founded a monastery at Annegray, which is between Austria and Burgundy, in AD 575, and his rule of austerity attracted many. Lexeuil, the largest monastery, and then Fontaines, were all established within a few miles of Annegray. When Columban was exiled by the local king, he and his followers founded Bobbio in the Apennines, between Piacenza and Genoa. Bobbio became a great centre of culture and orthodoxy from which monasticism spread. Its great glory was its library, the books from which are scattered all over Europe and are regarded as treasures. There are still many parishes in the region dedicated to St Columban.

St Colmcille (c. 521–97), Missionary Abbot

Along with St Patrick and St Brigid, Colmcille, also known as Columba and Columcille, is probably the most famous of the Irish saints. He spread the gospel to Iona and hence to Scotland. St Colmcille was a prince of Tyrconnell (County Donegal), and a great, great grandson of Niall of the Nine Hostages, who had been High King of Ireland. On his mother's side he was descended from the Leinster Kings. He was educated by St Finian of Movilla, in County Down, and also by Finnian of Clonard, and Mobhi of Glasnevin. He studied music and poetry at the Bardic School of Leinster, and the poems he wrote which have survived are delightful. A few are preserved in the Bodleian Library, Oxford. He chose to be a monk, and never to receive episcopal rank. He wrote of his devotion: 'The fire of God's love stays in my heart as a jewel set in gold in a silver vessel.'

In AD 545 he built his first church in Derry, the place he loved most. Then he founded Durrow and later Kells, which became very important in the 9th century when the Columban monks of Iona fled from the Vikings and made it their headquarters. In all, Colmcille founded 37 monastic churches in Ireland, and he produced the *Cathach*, a manuscript of the Psalms. At the age of 42 he set out with 12 companions to be an exile for Christ. They sailed to the island of Iona, off the west coast of Scotland, which was part of the Kingdom of Dalriada ruled over by the Irish King Aidan. He converted Brude, King of the Picts, founded two churches in Inverness, and helped to keep the peace between the Picts and the Irish colony. The tradition that he left Ireland because of a dispute over the copy he made of a psalter of St Finian is very dubious. The legend goes that the dispute caused a great battle, although the high king of the time, King Diarmuid, had tried to settle the dispute and had ruled against Colmcille, saying: 'to every cow its calf, to every book its copy'. The saint is supposed to have punished himself for the deaths he had caused by going into exile.

Colmcille was famous for his austerity, fasting and vigils. His bed was of stone and so was his pillow. From the various accounts of his life, Colmcille emerges as a charismatic personality who was a scholar, poet, and ruler. He died at Iona, and his relics were taken to Dunkeld (Scotland) in AD 849.

St Enda of Aran (died c. 535), Abbot

Famous as the patriarch of monasticism. He is described as a warrior who left the secular world in middle life. He had succeeded to the kingdom of Oriel, but decided to study for the priesthood. He was then granted the Aran Islands by his brother-in-law, Aengus, King of Cashel. He is said to have lived a life of astonishing severity, and never had a fire in winter, for he believed the 'hearts so glowing with the love of God' could not feel the cold. It is said that he taught 127 other saints, who are buried close to him on the islands.

St Kevin of Glendalough (died c. 618), Abbot

Many stories surround St Kevin, but we know he was one of the many Irish abbots who chose to remain a priest. He lived a solitary contemplative life in the Glendalough Valley where many people followed him, attracted by his rule of prayer and solitude. He played the harp, and the Rule for his monks was in verse. He is supposed to have prayed for so long that a blackbird had time to lay an egg, and hatch it on his outstretched hand. His monastery flourished until the 11th century. In the 12th century St Lawrence O'Toole came to Glendalough and modelled his life on St Kevin, bringing fresh fame to his memory. The foundation was finally destroyed in the 16th century.

St Kieran (c. 512–549), Abbot

St Kieran, also known as Ciaran, is remembered for his great foundation of Clonmacnoise, where the ancient chariot road through Ireland crosses the Shannon River. Unlike many Irish abbots he was not of aristocratic blood, for his father was a chariot-maker from County Antrim, and his mother from Kerry. St Kieran attracted craftsmen to his order, and Clonmacnoise grew to be a great monastic school, where, unusually for Ireland, the position of abbot did not become hereditary. Kieran died within a short time of founding the school. Many kings are buried alongside him, for it was believed that he would bring their souls safely to heaven.

St Malachy (1094–1148), Archbishop of Armagh

Malachy is famous as the great reformer of the Irish Church. He persuaded the Pope, Eugenius III, to establish the Archbishops of Ireland separately from those of England. He also ensured that it was no longer possible for important ecclesiastical positions to be held by certain families as a hereditary right. For example, he was appointed Bishop of Armagh, although the See of Armagh was held in lay succession by one family. It was an achievement to separate the family from this post without splitting the Irish Church.

The saint was educated in Armagh and Lismore, County Waterford, and desired only to be an itinerant preacher. His great talents took him instead to be Bishop of Down and Connor, and in 1125 he became Abbot-Bishop of Armagh. He travelled to France, where he made a lasting friendship with Bernard of Clairvaux, the reforming Cistercian. The Pope appointed him papal legate in Ireland, and whilst abroad he made some famous prophesies; one was that there will be the peace of Christ over all Ireland when the palm and the shamrock meet. This is supposed to mean when St Patrick's Day (17 March) occurs on Palm Sunday.

St Patrick (c. 390–461), Bishop and Patron Saint of Ireland

St Patrick was born somewhere between the Severn and the Clyde on the west coast of Britain. As a youth he was captured by Irish slave traders, and taken to the Antrim coast to work as a farm labourer. Much controversy surrounds the details of Patrick's life. Popular tradition credits him with converting the whole of Ireland, but nearly all that can be truly known of him comes from his *Confessio* or autobiography, and other writings. Through these writings he is revealed as a simple, sincere and humble man who was full of care for his people; an unlearned man, once a fugitive, who had learnt to trust God completely. Tradition states that after six years of slavery, voices told him he would soon return to his own land, and he escaped. Later, other voices call to him from Ireland, entreating him 'to come and walk once more amongst us'.

It is believed that he spent some time in Gaul (France) and became a priest; perhaps he had some mission conferred on him by the Pope to go and continue the work of Palladius, another missionary bishop who worked amongst the Christian Irish. It is believed that some confusion has arisen over the achievements of Palladius and Patrick. Patrick, when he returned to Ireland, seems to have been most active in the north, whilst Palladius worked in the south. He made Armagh his primary see, and it has remained the centre of Christianity in Ireland. He organized the church on the lines of territorial sees, and encouraged the laity to become monks or nuns. He was very concerned with abolishing paganism, idolatry and sun-worship, and he preached to the highest and the lowest in the land. Tradition credits him with expelling the snakes from Ireland, and explaining the Trinity by pointing to a shamrock.

One of the most famous episodes handed down by popular belief is that of his confrontation with King Laoghaire at Tara, known as the seat of the high kings of Ireland, and the capital of Meath. It was supposedly on Easter Saturday in 432, which that year coincided with a great Druid festival at Tara. No new fire was allowed to be lit until the lighting of the sacred pagan fire by the Druids. St Patrick was camped on the Hill of Slane which looks onto Tara, and his campfire was burning brightly; the Druids warned King Laoghaire that if it was not put out, it would never be extinguished. When Patrick was brought before Laoghaire, his holiness melted the king's hostility and he was invited to stay. Although Laoghaire did not become a Christian, his brother Conal, a prince of the North, became his protector and ally.

Certain places in Ireland are traditionally closely associated with St Patrick, such as Croagh Patrick in County Mayo, where there is an annual pilgrimage to the top of the 2510-ft (765 m) mountain on the last Sunday of July; and Downpatrick and Saul in County Down. The cult of St Patrick spread from Ireland to many Irish monasteries in Europe, and in more modern times to North America and Australia, where large communities of Irish emigrants live. The annual procession on 17 March, on St Patrick's Day in New York has become a massive event, where everybody sports a shamrock and drinks green beer. However, quite a few Irish believe St Colmcille should be the patron saint of Ireland, not this mild and humble British missionary!

Oliver Plunkett (1625–81), Archbishop of Armagh and Martyr

This gentle and holy man lived in frightening and turbulent times, when to be a practising Catholic in Ireland was to court trouble. He was born into a noble and wealthy family whose lands extended throughout the Pale. He was sent to study in Rome, and was a brilliant theology and law scholar. He became a priest in 1654 and in 1669 was appointed Archbishop of Armagh. Oliver was one of only two bishops in Ireland at that time, and the whole of the laity was in disorder and neglect. Apart from the hostility of the Protestants, the Catholics themselves were divided by internal squabbles. Oliver confirmed thousands of people, and held a provincial synod. He did much to maintain discipline amongst the clergy, to improve education by founding the Jesuit College in Drogheda, and to promulgate the decrees of the Council of Trent.

Oliver managed to remain on good terms with many of the Protestant gentry and clergy, but was eventually outlawed by the British government. The panic caused by the false allegations made by Titus Oates in England about a popish plot was used by Plunkett's enemies, and he was arrested in 1678. He was absurdly charged with plotting to bring in 20 thousand French troops, and levying a charge on his clergy to support an army. No jury could be found to convict him in Ireland, so he was brought to England, where he was convicted of treason for setting up 'a false religion which was the most dishonourable and derogatory to God of all religions and that a greater crime could not be committed against God than for a man to endeavour to propagate that religion'. He was hanged, drawn and quartered at Tyburn in July 1681. His head is in the Oliver Plunkett Church in Drogheda, County Louth, and his body lies at Downside Abbey, Somerset.

County Limerick

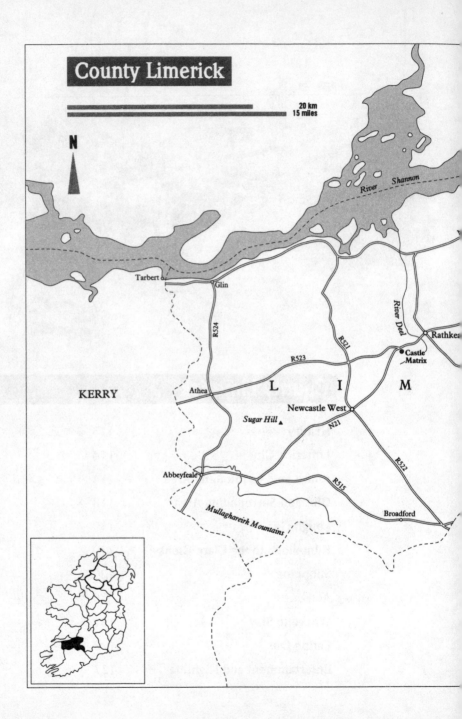

County Limerick

20 km
15 miles

N

River Shannon

Tarbert
Glin
R524
R521
River Deel
Rathkea
R523
Castle
Matrix
KERRY
Athea
L   I   M
Newcastle West
Sugar Hill
N21
Abbeyfeale
R515
R522
Mullaghareirk Mountains
Broadford

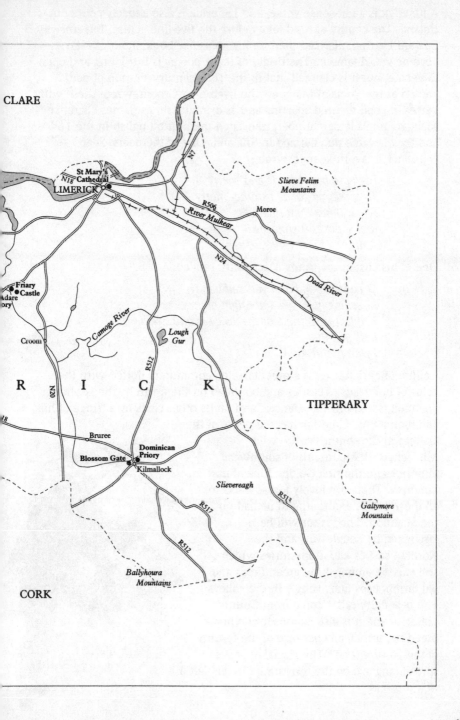

A limerick is a nonsense verse, and Limerick is also a lovely county in Ireland. The county existed long before the five-line stanza, but since Edward Lear popularized them in his nonsense book, limericks have become world-famous. The origin of these poems is intriguing and open to debate, but it is claimed that in the 18th century a group of poets known as the Poets of Maigue, who lived near Croom, wrote these witty verses in good-natured sparring and as drinking songs. James Clarence Mangan, himself a great poet, translated them into English in the 1840s and they became popularized in England. One of the poets, Sean O'Tuama, a tavern keeper, wrote:

> *I sell the best brandy and sherry*
> *To make my good customer merry*
> *But at times their finances*
> *Run short as it chances*
> *And then I feel very sad, very.*

One of his customers, Andy MacCraith, replied:

> *O Tuomy! you boast yourself handy,*
> *At selling good ale and bright brandy,*
> *The fact is your liquor makes everyone sicker,*
> *I tell you that,*
> *I your friend Andy.*

County Limerick itself is a quiet farming community dotted with the ruins of hundreds of castles and bounded on the north by the spacious Shannon, spreading like the sea, and on its other sides by a fringe of hills and mountains. Limerick has the peaks of the Galtees in the southeast, the wild Mullaghareirk Mountains of southwest Limerick and the rich Golden Vale of east Limerick. There are lovely forest walks in all these places and sailing to be had on the Shannon. The visitor will be fascinated by Lough Gur, and the Norman castles and monasteries which still survive amongst the green fields and old farmhouses lying snugly in the valleys. The best dairy cattle come from County Limerick and it is also famous for its horse-breeding, principally because of the fertility of the pasture land. (The glacial deposits spread long ago by the retreating glaciers left a rich topsoil.)

The population of County Limerick is around 160,000, of whom 60,000 live in towns. Besides work in the agricultural industry, there is some light industry, and the Shannon Free Airport Development Company provides a lot of jobs.

History

Not surprisingly in such fertile countryside, the monks founded important monasteries. That they were rich is proved by the bejewelled Ardagh Chalice found in a ring-fort in 1868, and now in the National Museum in Dublin. The Vikings, in search of new territory and loot, sought them out up the Shannon Estuary and destroyed many centres of learning. They founded a colony which was to become the city of Limerick. Next came the Anglo-Normans, also attracted by the rich lands. Amongst the principal families were the Fitzgeralds, the de Burgos, the de Lacys and the Fitzgibbons. But it was the Earls of Desmond, the head of the Fitzgeralds, who owned the most and ruled like independent princes, eventually quarrelling with their Tudor overlords in England. They and their supporters are known as the Geraldines. In the 16th century the Tudors tried to centralize their authority. So in 1571 the Geraldines, who by now were completely Gaelicized, started a revolt which ended in savage wars and ruin for their house.

Throughout the following centuries up to the present day, Limerick has played a significant role in the numerous uprisings against English rule. In 1650 there was the 12-month siege of Limerick against Cromwell which ended in capitulation. The Jacobite-Williamite war (1689–91) saw two more sieges in which the heroic General Patrick Sarsfield played his role (see 'Limerick City', below). William Smith O'Brien, a Limerick man, was one of the leaders of the abortive 1848 Rebellion, and three of the leaders of the 1916 Rising in Dublin were from the county. Edward Daly and Con Colbert were executed, but Eamon de Valera escaped that fate due to his American birth. Later he was one of the leaders of the War of Independence (1919–1921), and President of Ireland from 1959 to 1973.

Getting There and Around

By air: Shannon Airport.

By rail: There is a main rail terminal in the City of Limerick, ✆ (061) 418666.

By bus: Limerick City railway and bus depots are on Parnell Street. Bus Eireann runs a reasonable service from Limerick City, ✆ (061) 418855 for details.

By car: Cars available for hire from Shannon Airport. In Limerick City, contact Cara Rent-a-Car, Coonagh Cross, ✆ (061) 455811. Camper vans also available.

By hovercraft: Tours depart from Steam Boat Quay, Limerick, ✆ (061) 414147.

By bike: Raleigh Rent-a-Bike network operates throughout the county. Your local dealer in Limerick City is Emerald Cycles, 1 Patrick Street, ✆ (061) 416983.

Arthur's Quay, Limerick City, ✆ (061) 317522, all year.

Shannon Airport, ✆ (061) 41664, all year.

Adare, ✆ (061) 396255, May to October.

The dates of the festivals vary a little each year, and there may be one-off festivals in some towns, so do check details with the tourist offices.

17–25 March: The Band Music Festival, Limerick, ✆ (061) 410777. A mixture of concert bands, marching bands, parades and street entertainment.

May: Game and Country Fair, Adare, ✆ (061) 396770.

June: Paddy Music Expo, Limerick, ✆ (061) 400444. Showcase of traditional and contemporary Irish music.

July: The Ten Knights of Desmond Festival, Newcastle West ✆ (069) 62757/ (061) 317522.

End July/early August: Music Festival at Murroe, ✆ (061) 378219.

August: Limerick Agricultural Show, ✆ (061) 415519.

Limerick City

Limerick City has something rather drab about it which is hard to put your finger on. It is largely Georgian in character—a grid pattern of streets has been superimposed onto the older town which followed the curve of the River Shannon. The novelist Kate O'Brien came from the respectable middle class that moulded this city in the 19th century. She describes it as having 'the grave, grey look of Commerce'. Yet Limerick is doing its best to forget the hard times of the 1940s, '50s and '60s and has recently been given a substantial facelift. It has a reputation for smart clothes shops, and the Art School here has produced some talented clothes designers. For a city of its size it also has a buzzy nightlife. There is a lot of unemployment and emigration still, but new industries have been set up, and there is an Arts Centre, the Bell Table, which produces excellent shows and exhibitions.

It is a symbolic city, full of memories, and there is lots to see which reveals Limerick's more ancient past. It was founded in AD 922 by the Norsemen, and has always been an important fording place on the River Shannon. More concrete evidence of the past is the massive round tower of **King John's Castle** built in 1200, which is on the river guarding Thomond Bridge, and is one of the best examples of fortified Norman architecture in the country. In the wars of 1691 it was eventually surrendered to the Williamite Commander Ginkel after a fierce battering from his guns. The siege which preceded the surrender is stored away in the psyche of Irishmen. During the 1690s there were three struggles going on: the struggle of Britain and her Protestant allies to oppose the ascendancy in Europe of Catholic France, the struggle of Britain to subdue Ireland, and the struggle of the Protestant planter families and the Catholic Irish for the leadership of Ireland. The French supplied money and commanders to help Catholic James II wrestle his crown back from the Protestant William of Orange (*see* **History**, p.75). The majority of the Catholic Irish supported the Jacobite cause and many joined up. It is part of the Irish folk memory that the French commander, St Ruth, and King James were asses, and that the Irish Commander Patrick Sarsfield was intelligent, daring and brave. The Irish army had been beaten at the Boyne under St Ruth and had retreated to Limerick, where the walls were said to be paper thin. William began a siege whilst he waited for the arrival of big guns and artillery. Patrick Sarsfield led a daring raid on the siege train from Dublin and destroyed it. He rode through the night with 600 horses into the Clare Hills, forded the Shannon and continued on through the Slievefelim Mountains. Finally, he swooped down on William's huge consignment of guns and blew them skywards. His action saved Limerick from destruction for a time, whilst William abandoned the siege. When William III eventually did break through the Limerick walls, he sent in 10,000 men to wreak havoc, but the women and children of the city fought alongside their men, and they beat back the invaders. The second siege started the following year, and this time heavy losses were inflicted when the Williamite leader, Ginkel, gained control of Thomond Bridge. The promised help did not come, and there was nothing to do but negotiate an honourable treaty. This Sarsfield did, and he agreed to take himself and 10,000 Irish troops off to France, in what became known as 'The Flight of the Wild Geese'. But the terms of the treaty were not carried out and the Treaty Stone beside Thomond Bridge, where the treaty was supposed to have been signed, is now known as 'The Stone of the Violated Treaty'.

Old English Town and its Irish counterpart across the river are the most interesting parts of Limerick to wander in. The old Viking town of Limerick is on an island formed by the Shannon and what is called the Abbey River (a branch of the Shannon). It is known as English Town. The Vikings and later the Normans tried to keep the native Irish from living and trading in the city area so the Irish settled on the other side of the Abbey River—in Irish Town. A short circular walk takes you round the main places of interest. A great way of appreciating the beauty of the Shannon is to take a hovercraft trip up and down river (*see* 'Activities' p.113). From O'Connell street turn down Sarsfield street and cross the river by Sarsfield Bridge, then turn right up Clancy's Strand which gives you a good view of the city. Walk along until you come to Thomond Bridge which leads you into the Old Town, passing by King John's Castle. You may wander around the **Castle** (*open April–Oct, daily; Nov–Mar weekends only; adm; Ⓒ (061) 411201*) which has recently had a couple of floors converted into an interpretative centre with displays of various instruments of early warfare and details of the castle's role in Irish history. A riverside walk leads you from the castle to the beautiful 18th-century Custom House, which has been restored and is housing the Hunt Collection in 1995 (*see* below). Close by is the tourist office in Arthur's Quay. Walk down Nicholas Street to **St Mary's Cathedral**, which is the only ancient church building left in the city and which was built in 1172 by Donal Mor O'Brien, King of Munster. Inside are some superb 15th-century oak misericords (choir stalls) carved into the shapes of fantastic beasts.

A few minutes' walk over Matthew Bridge brings you to the **Granary** in Michael Street. This is a fine example of a recently restored 18th-century Georgian warehouse, now the home of the City Library and archive. The Bell Table Arts Theatre is situated in 69 O'Connell Street, to the southwest, and various Irish travelling theatre companies stop off here; well worth a telephone call to find out what's on. There is also a small gallery which shows the work of many local artists and is part of the international EVA Art Exhibition held at various venues around the city.

After the 1760s when the city walls were dismantled, English and Irish Town merged and Georgian streets and squares were built. St John's Square is full of lovely old buildings of *c.* 1750, some of which are being restored after years of neglect. The **Limerick Museum** (✆ (061) 47826) is in Nos.1 and 2 on the west side, and houses an impressive collection of items from the Neolithic, the Bronze and Iron Ages, including the famous 'Nail' or pedestal, formerly in the Exchange (now gone, except for a fragment of the façade in Nicholas Street), where the merchants of Limerick used to pay their debts. Hence the expression 'paying on the nail'.

To the southwest, close to the entrance to the People's Park off Pery Square, is **Limerick Art Gallery**, which has a collection of modern Irish paintings and holds some very interesting exhibitions. Beautiful lace is made by the Good Shepherd Sisters in Clare Street, on the Dublin Road, ✆ (061) 415183. You can visit them during working hours, and buy something exquisite which might in time become a family heirloom! Three miles (5km) from the city centre, off the N7 to Dublin, the **Hunt Collection** (*open Tues–Sat, 10–5; ✆ (061) 333644*) is temporarily at the University of Limerick, but is due to relocate to the Granary in Michael Street in 1995. John Hunt was a noted art historian and Celtic archaeologist who died in the 1970s. His collection was gathered over 40 years and contains a mixture of Bronze Age weapons, 18th-century silver, jewels, paintings and medieval artefacts, including the 9th-century bronze Cashel Bell, the largest in Ireland, found near Cashel town in 1849, and Early Christian brooches.

There is greyhound racing at the town course several nights each week. Look in the local newspaper for details.

Adare and Surrounding Area

To the west of Limerick, only 16 miles (26km) away, Shannon Airport is a free port area in which customs duties and formalities are suspended. There are hundreds of bargains for those flying out.

About 10 miles (16km) from Limerick, going southwest on the N20, **Adare** (*Ath Dara*: the ford of the oak tree), is set in richly timbered land through which the little River

Maigue flows. There is only a wide main street, set on both sides with pretty thatched cottages, many of which are either antique shops, craft shops or restaurants. One of them is the local tourist office. The village is noted for its fine ecclesiastical ruins, but first notice the newly restored village washing pool—opposite the Trinitarian Abbey, just off the main street. You can imagine the stories and scandal exchanged as the village women washed their clothes. The finest ruin is the **Franciscan friary** founded in 1464 by Thomas, Earl of Kildare. (The village belonged to the Kildare branch of the Fitzgeralds or Geraldines.) The friary was attacked and burned by parliamentary forces, but its ruins are very beautifully proportioned, and can be viewed at a distance from the long narrow bridge of 14 arches (*c.* 1400) on the outskirts of the village on the N20 going north. If you want to go right up to it, check with the golf club office at the entrance, as it is in the heart of the Adare Manor Golf Club.

The modern village has grown up around the rest of the ecclesiastical buildings. The **Augustinian priory**, now used as the Church of Ireland Church, was founded in 1315 by the Kildares. It was restored in 1807 by the first Earl of Dunraven. His family used to own the Gothic Revival-style manor house whose lush parklands surround the village. Adare Manor is now a luxury hotel. The church has some interesting carvings of animals and human heads, and gives a good idea of what an Irish medieval church must have looked like. **Desmond Castle**, on the banks of the Maigue, beside the bridge, was built in the 13th century on the site of an earlier ring-fort. It is a fine example of feudal architecture with its square keep, curtain walls, two great halls, kitchen, gallery and stables.

The area around Adare is known as the Palatine because of the number of Lutherans from Southern Germany who settled here in the 18th century. Their descendants, bearing such names as Ruttle, Shier, Teskey and Switzer, are still numerous in the area. **Rathkeale** (17miles/11km west of Adare) is the second-largest town in County Limerick, and is notable for its fine early-19th-century courthouse and doorways in the main street. It has a small museum devoted to the history of the palatines. **Castle Matrix** (*open 1 June–1 Sept, Sat–Tues, 11–5; adm; © (069) 64381*) about a mile (2km) to the southwest, is a fine Geraldine Castle built about 1410. The poet-Earl of Desmond, whose style epitomized the courtly love genre, lived here in the 1440s. The castle has been restored and houses a unique collection of documents relating to the Wild Geese, Irish soldiers who served so nobly in the Continental armies of the 17th and 18th centuries. It has the reputation for being the first place in Ireland, where the potato was grown. The story goes that the poet Edmund Spenser met Walter Raleigh here in 1580, and they became great friends. They were both as yet young and unknown, seeking to make their fortune in Ireland, where they had both been granted land. When Raleigh returned from his successful voyage to America, he presented some potatoes to their host, Lord Southwell, who evidently cultivated them with some success. The Methodist movement in North America was initiated at Castle Matrix: Palatine refugees on the estate were converted by John Wesley, and in 1760 Philip Embury and Barbara Ruttle Heck sailed to New York and founded a church there. It is now the headquarters of the Irish International Arts Centre and Heraldry Society. South of here was another Desmond stronghold at **Askeaton**. The ruins of the mostly 15th-century castle stand on a limestone island in the River Dee. It dominates the village and was the scene of fierce fighting in the 16th and 17th centuries. The Franciscan friary and the Church of Ireland are also of great interest.

Croom, right in the middle of County Limerick, is celebrated as the meeting place of the 18th-century Gaelic poets of the Maigue. Fortunately, their poetry is available in translation, and is unforgettable for its wit and feeling. It is here that the light verse of the 'limerick' was first popularized. An old castle of the Geraldines is hidden behind a wall on the southern approach to the village. Croom Mills Water Wheel and Heritage Centre ℂ (061) 397130 has a fine exhibition of local history and the part the mill played in the town's life. It has a good craft and coffee shop. **Knockfierna Hill**, 6½ miles (10km) southwest of Croom, is a fine place for a walk. It is held sacred to the Dé Danaan, King of the Other World, or Death, Donn Forinne. From the summit, on a clear day, you can see a great expanse of Ireland with mountains and the Shannon Estuary. The restoration of several famine houses and an exhibition on the famine years 1845–1849 is of great interest (ℂ *(069) 64526*).

Glin and Surrounding Area

Glin, a lovely village on the Shannon, is very near the car ferry at Tarbert which takes you across to County Clare. It is well worth a visit to **Glin Castle** (*open in May, 10–12 and 2–4, and at other times by arrangement with Madame Fitzgerald or Evelyne O'Sullivan, ℂ (068) 34112*) still the ancestral home of the Knights of Glin, part of the Fitzgerald tribe. (The present Knight of Glin is an art historian and stalwart campaigner on behalf of the historic buildings of this island which are so often left to decay.) The castle is Georgian Gothic and noted for its flying staircase, lovely plasterwork, and 18th-century furniture and paintings. The gardens are beautifully planned and tended, and are a fitting extension of this romantic house. (*Craft shop and restaurant at the Gate Lodge open Apr–Oct.*)

North of Glin is **Foynes**, a small port on a wide stretch of the Shannon Estuary. A very interesting hour can be spent at the Flying Boat Museum (*open Mar 31–Oct 31, 10–6; ℂ (069) 65416*). Between 1939 and 1945 Foynes was famous as a base for seaplanes crossing the Atlantic. The radio and weather room with original transmitters, receivers and Morse code is fascinating. Many high-ranking British and American military officers passed through Foynes during the Second World War.

Following the border with Tipperary southwards you come to **Athea**, a centre for traditional music, and a pretty place. All around are lovely hill walks and drives. **Abbeyfeale**, on the N21 south of Athea, is surrounded by rolling hills and is another centre of traditional music, song and dance. It is also the gateway to

Killarney and Tralee. To the east are the **Mullaghareirk Mountains** near the village of Broadford, which are mainly forested with the uniform evergreens so beloved of the Forestry Commission.

Lough Gur

Lough Gur, 11 miles (17km) south of Limerick City, is guarded by the remains of two castles built by the Earls of Desmond in an area rich in field antiquities. According to legend, the last of the Desmonds is doomed to hold court under the waters of Lough Gur and to emerge, fully armed, at daybreak on every morning of the seventh year in a routine that must be repeated until the silver shoes of his horse are worn away. As if to echo the story, the lake itself is horseshoe-shaped. Man has been here since 3000 BC and you can see stone circles, wedge-shaped graves and Neolithic house sites. The **Interpretative Centre** (*open 14 May–end Sept, daily, 10–6; adm; ℗ (061) 85186*) has an excellent audio-visual show explaining the history of the Lough Gur area from the Stone Age. The centre is very sympathetically built, inspired by Neolithic house styles.

Kilmallock to the Clare Glens

Kilmallock, about 11 miles (17km) south of Lough Gur on the R512, is in the rich land of the Golden Vale. It was built by the Geraldines (Fitzgeralds) and John's Castle still stands in the centre of town, while Blossom's Gateway is a remnant of the ancient walls. The town should have been as gracious as Adare, but nothing has been protected. There is a beautiful Dominican priory dating from the 13th century. A pillar in the aisle arcade shows the ball-flower ornament—very rare in Ireland, though common during the 14th century in England. **Bruree**, 4½ miles (7km) to the west of Kilmallock on the R518, is the place where Eamon de Valera grew up. The school he went to is now the **De Valera Museum**. An old corn mill with a huge mill wheel makes a striking image as you enter the village from the west.

Murroe (also spelt Moroe) and the Clare Glens are on the northeastern borders of Limerick, about 10 miles (16km) from Limerick City on R506. Murroe lies under the foothills of the Slievefelim mountains, and is dominated by the 19th–century **Mansion of Glenstal**, ℗ (061) 386103. Now a Benedictine monastery, it is famous as one of Ireland's public schools (run by the monks) and a centre for the promotion of ecumenicalism. The grounds are very beautiful in May and June when the rhododendrons are out. The monks will always make you welcome; they sell beautiful hand-turned wooden bowls etc. Glenstal used to be the family home of the Barringtons, who donated the **Glens of Clare** to the County Councils of Limerick and North Tipperary for the pleasure of the public. The Glens, a mile (2km) north of Murroe, are not so much glens as a scenic gorge with sparkling waterfalls. There is a nature trail which leads you through this beautiful wooded place. Murroe has traditional music recitals during the holiday season and is a pleasant area in which to stay. A further mile or so west, at **Clonkeen**, is a small rectangular church, about 12th-century, with a richly decorated Irish Romanesque doorway and north wall window.

A few miles to the northeast is the pretty Georgian town of **Castleconnell** with its neo-classical villas. It is famous as a base for salmon fishing on the Shannon and at one time was a spa. The scenic walk to the Falls of Doonass, the ruins of the O'Brien Castle in the village and the magnificent shell of Mount Shannon, an 18th century mansion, southwest of the village are all worth stopping for.

Shopping

 Chocolates: Leonidas Chocolates, O'Connell Mall, O'Connell Street, Limerick. Wonderful Belgian chocolates. Sonia's Chocolates, Denmark Street and 35 O'Connell Street, Limerick; delicious chocolates made in Limerick by the unemployed under the auspices of Sister Joan.

Crafts: Martin O'Driscoll, gold & silversmith, Potato Market, Merchant's Quay, ✆ (061) 415914. Irish crochet from Margaret Hogan, Main Street, Foynes. General crafts, woollens and tweeds from Irish Handicrafts, Arthur's Quay Shopping Centre; ceramics and stained glass from Workspace on Michael Street, Limerick, ✆ (061) 416800. All these are open during normal working hours.

Foods: Wholefoods/cheese: an excellent variety of local cheeses, organic veg and breads from Eats of Eden, Spaight's Shopping Centre, Limerick, ✆ (061) 419400; Glen-O-Sheen Cheddar, Kilmallock, ✆ (063) 86140.

Ham: County Limerick is world-famous for its ham. A good source is Hogan's Bacon Shop, 74a Little Catherine Street, Limerick, ✆ (061) 412542.

Venison: Irish Venison Co-op at the Limerick Food Centre, Rahun, ✆ (061) 412542.

Lace: From the Convent of the Good Shepherd Sisters, Clare Street (the Dublin Road), Limerick, ✆ (061) 415183. Open Mon–Fri, 9.45am–4.45pm.

Pottery: Orchard Pottery, Castleconnell, ✆ (061) 377181. Stoneware decorated with colourful Celtic designs.

Woollens: Michelina Stacpoole, luxurious fashion knitwear, Adare, ✆ (061) 396409. Also available at La Femme, Cecil Street, Limerick.

Activities

Golf: Shannon, between the airport and the estuary, ✆ (061) 471020. Adare, in the Manor Demesne; ✆ (061) 396204 and in the grounds of the Manor itself ✆ (061) 396566.

Horse-racing: 4-day meeting in December at Limerick.

Hunting: This is great hunting country. Contact the County Limerick Hunt through the Hon. Secretary, Limerick County Hunt, Adelaisk House, Bruff, ✆ (061) 82114; the Stonehall Harrier Hunt Club, the Hon. Secretary, Askeaton, ✆ (061) 393286.

Pony-trekking: At Rathcannon, Kilmallock, ✆ (063) 392026 and Crecora Equestrian Centre, ✆ (061) 355139.

Sailing: On the River Shannon, ✆ (061) 76364/(067) 376622.

Farm Visits: Glenroe Farm Trail includes Castleoliver Organic Farm, Ardpatrick. Gloster Old Spot pigs, Angora rabbits and Irish Draught horse. Glen O Sheen Close Cheese Farm, Ballinacourty; Lantern Lodge Deer farm, Ballyorgan; Molanna View Dairy Farm, Ballyorgan. You can go on a tour of all these very different farms, or visit them individually; ✆ (063) 91300 for details.

Where to Stay

luxury

Adare Manor Hotel, Adare, ✆ (061) 396566, is the original house of the Earls of Dunraven. A mixture of Victorian Gothic and Tudor Revival fantasy, it has beautiful grounds with horse-riding, clay pigeon shooting and an 18-hole golf course designed by Robert Trent Jones.

expensive

Dunraven Arms Hotel, Adare, ✆ (061) 396209, is an old-world hotel on the main street, with a colourful garden, pretty rooms and friendly staff. By contrast, **Jurys Hotel**, Ennis Road, Limerick, ✆ (061) 327777, is predictably modern and convenient.

moderate

The old-fashioned, comfortable **Railway Hotel**, Parnell Street, Limerick, ✆ (061) 413653, is family-run. **Castle Oaks House**, Castleconnell, ✆ (061) 377666, delightful Georgian house.

inexpensive

Mrs O'Shaughnessy offers comfortable accommodation in **Hollywood House**, Ballinvira, Croagh, Adare, ✆ (061) 396237, a pretty Georgian house 3 miles (4.8km) south of Adare. At **Millbank House**, Murroe, ✆ (061) 386115, Mrs Keays makes guests welcome in a farm setting. Trout- and salmon-fishing on the river which flows through the farm. From **Cooleen House**, Bruree, ✆ (063) 90584, Mrs McDonoogh's whitewashed Georgian farmhouse, you can hear the rustling of the little river that flows beside it. Very friendly service and fine old-fashioned bedrooms. Convenient for Shannon Airport, Mrs Johnson offers warm hospitality and good food at **Ballyteigne House**, Rockhill, Bruree, ✆ (063) 90575. Sample Mrs Sheedy-King's excellent home-cooking at **Flemingstown House**, Kilmallock, ✆ (063) 98093. From **Jackson's Turrett**, Clancy Strand, Limerick, ✆ (061) 326186, there are lovely views of the Shannon in Mrs Caball's cosy, en-suite rooms. **Reens House**, Ardagh, ✆ (069) 64276. 17th-century house on a dairy farm. A touch austere, **Limerick Hostel**, Barrington's House, George's Quay, Limerick, ✆ (061) 45222, has rooms for 2–4 people, singles IR£6.50. **An Oige** Hostel, 1 Pery Square, Limerick, ✆ (061) 31462, is another cheap option.

self catering

Rent an Irish Cottage, Kilfinane, ✆ (061) 411109, offer traditional-type cottages. **Adare Holiday Cottages**, Avenue Row, Adare, ✆ (061) 396566, are modern and practical.

expensive

Restaurant de la Fontaine, 12 Upper Griffin Street, Limerick, ✆ (061) 414461. Provincial France on the inside with robust but pricey country cooking and an extensive and exceptional French wine list. The **Mustard Seed**, Adare, ✆ (061) 396451. Delicious and imaginative food in a series of little dining rooms in pretty thatched cottage. Memorable smoked salmon with walnut oil.

moderate

Woodlands House, Knockanes, Adare, ✆ (061) 396118. Popular with locals; huge helpings of plain food. *Dinner and Sunday lunch only.* The **Silver Plate**, 74 O'Connell Street, Limerick, ✆ (061) 316311. Fish restaurant, cooking French-style. **Charcos**, Castleconnell, ✆ (061) 377533. Pub grub and restaurant with grill.

inexpensive/cheap

Bell Table Arts Centre Café, 69 O'Connell Street, Limerick, ✆ (061) 319866. Tasty lunches and great choice of cakes. *Daytime only.* Excellent snacks with good vegetarian options. Daytime only. **Vintage Pub**, Ellen Street, Limerick. Traditional pub with lunchtime snacks.

Foley's Pub, Lower Shannon Street, Limerick. Lunchtime meals such as ham and cabbage, Irish stew. **The Jasmine Palace**, Mall on O'Connell Street, Limerick, ✆ (061) 412484. Cantonese. *Open lunch and dinner.* **Matt the Thresher**, Birdhill, ✆ (061) 379227. On the road into Limerick. Excellent barfood, home-made bread; barstools made out of tractor seats. *Open all day.* **Oscar's**, Savoy Cinema Complex, Henry Street, Limerick. Always has a few moderately priced vegetarian options.

Ivan's, Caherdavin, Limerick, ✆ (061) 455766. A sandwich counter, take-away deli service and excellent breads. Good for picnic ingredients. *Open till 11pm.*

Entertainment and Nightlife

Lively arts: The Bell Table Arts Centre, 69 O'Connell Street, Limerick, ✆ (061) 319866. *Son et lumière* shows of Irish history at St Mary's Cathedral and King John's Castle, Limerick; adm, ✆ (061) 413157/310293.

Pubs and Clubs: Boxwell's, Patrick Street, Limerick; currently Limerick's 'hotspot' for the young and trendy. Brazen Head: O'Connell Street, Limerick. Popular pub and eatery which houses a club called 'Teds' for after-hours fun and frolics. The Works, Savoy Cinema Complex, Limerick, brand new 'hip' nightclub.

Traditional music: Nancy Blake's, Upper Denmark Street, Limerick, and at the Speakeasy on O'Connell Street, Limerick. Rambling House, Knockfierna Hill. Sean Collins Bar, Rathkeane Road, Adare.

County Kerry

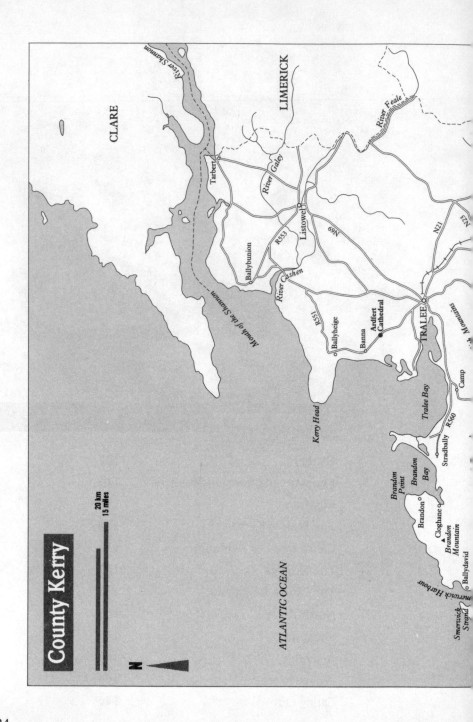

County Kerry

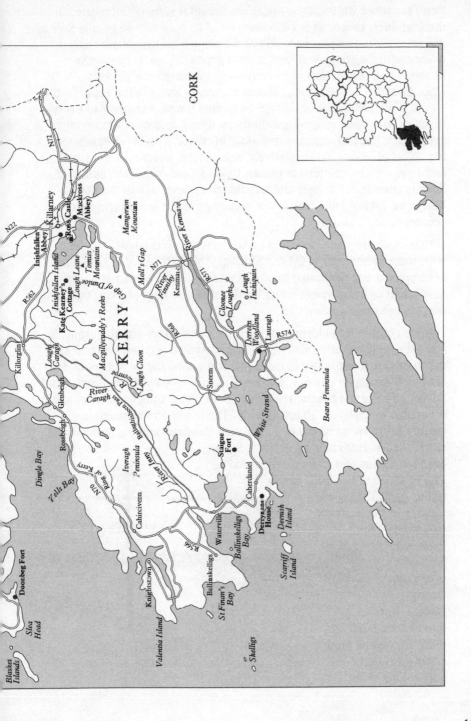

Kerry is packed with some of the most beautiful scenery in Ireland, and the friendliest people. It is a kingdom all of its own, whose people love to use words with flamboyance, skill and humour. An irregularly shaped county with long fingers of land reaching into the sea, it boasts the opulent lakes of Killarney at its centre—set amongst the wooded MacGillycuddy's Reeks, the grandest mountain range in the land. To the west are the peninsulas of Iveragh and Dingle, which are dear to every traveller who lands up amongst their splendour, and where mountains and sea are jumbled together in a glory of colour. The Beara Peninsula has an equal beauty but is relatively unexplored. Every year the small farmer re-creates a pattern of golden hayricks and cornfields, and wild flowers grow in the hedges and handkerchief fields where the black Kerry cow grazes, when she is not creating a traffic jam on the narrow country lanes.

Off the coast are some fascinating islands, which it is possible to visit with some perseverance. On the **Skelligs Rocks** the word of God has been praised and celebrated for six hundred years. **Valentia** is a soft, easy island by comparison; while the **Blaskets**, 3 miles (4.8km) out to sea, are beautiful but deserted.

The possibilities for enjoying yourself in County Kerry are numerous. If you are simply motoring around the narrow country lanes, you will see the most superb vistas of seascape, hill and valley. But do not try to do too much driving in one day, for the roads are very twisty and each bend holds more alluring beauty; the driver can end up doing too much, and it is possible to explore it all too quickly. The hotels and restaurants of County Kerry are generally of a very high standard, and the seafood and salmon are all that could be desired. Sailing, deep-sea fishing and water-skiing are all easy to arrange, as is golf, horse-riding, game fishing and walking in the heathery mountains. For those who most like to wander amongst gardens and into historic buildings, there are several properties open to the public. One of the

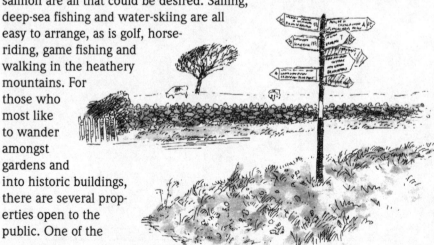

most famous is, of course, **Derrynane House,** the house of Daniel O'Connell, 'the Great Liberator', who won Catholic emancipation. Whatever you plan to do, expect some rainy weather and cloud, for Kerry is notoriously wet and warm. For those interested in the ancient past, Kerry is scattered with ogham stones, standing stones, forts and clochans (the stone huts of holy men). Interpretative centres have opened up to educate those interested in local history and to cater to the coach tours.

History

A brief historical outline must start, as always, back in the time of the Bronze Age, some 4500 years ago. Miners from Spain and Portugal were attracted by the precious metals to be found in the mountains, and it is still possible to find traces of their mines, and their assembly places which are marked with stone circles, rock carvings and wedge tombs. From the wealth of legend which remains of the later Bronze Age and Early Stone Age (500 BC) it is possible to build up an accurate picture of society as it was then. It was hierarchical, aristocratic, and warlike. There were no towns and cattle-raising and raiding dominated everything. Farmers lived in ring-forts and on crannogs for defensive reasons. Writing was confined to an archaic form of Irish which you can see on the ogham stones scattered around Kerry. Kerry beaches were the landing places for many of the legendary invasions, voyages and battles of Ireland's past. The miners who sailed into the bays from Spain are recorded in legend, as were the other waves of settlers.

Christianity came in the 5th century and great changes began. The old tribal centres went into a decline, and powerful new kingdoms emerged, often with an abbot-prince at their heads. A strong monastic structure grew up and some monasteries became great centres of learning. The monks learnt the art of writing and recorded the legends and sagas. Many of these centres were in inhospitable locations—the 'dysart' of some place names. In Kerry there is the wonderfully preserved 7th-century foundation on Skellig Michael.

In the upheavals and faction-fighting of the 11th and 12th centuries, three ruling families emerged in Kerry as definite clans: the MacCarthys south of Killarney; the O'Donoghues around Killarney; and the O'Sullivans around the Kenmare Rivers. These are names which crop up again and again in Kerry's history, right up to today. In the 13th century, with the arrival of the Anglo-Normans, the Fitzgeralds established strongholds throughout the region. They became the Palatine Earls of Desmond, and bought with them tenants and fighting men who introduced the common Kerry names of Browne, Landers, Ashe and Ferriter. The Earls of Desmond became so powerful that they were able to maintain an independence from the centralizing efforts of the English monarchs right up till the reign of Elizabeth I. They adopted many of the old Irish traditions; poetry and music flourished under their patronage. The last earl took part in a rebellion against Elizabeth, and lost his lands and his life, and the Gaelic way of life began to disappear. The country was reorganized in 1606 into the shape we know today, and the new landowners were largely English and Protestant. The political destruction of the 17th century is wonderfully recorded in the laments and satires of the poets of Munster. This short verse of David O'Bruadair (*c.* 1625–98) sums up what the poets felt:

> *Sad for those without sweet Anglo-Saxon*
> *Now that Ormonde has come to Erin*
> *For the rest of my life in the land of Conn*
> *I'll do better with English than a poem.*

Version by John Montague

Kerry produced perhaps the greatest Irish leader there has ever been in the shape of Daniel O'Connell, who in 1829 won Catholic emancipation, not only for the Irish, but for all Catholics under British rule. He came from an old Gaelic family who had managed to hold on to their lands and to get along with their Protestant neighbours. The famine of 1845–1849 and the emigration that followed reduced the population of Kerry as it did everywhere in Ireland. Nowadays Kerry is a land of small farmers and relies on the tourist industry.

Getting There and Around

By air: From the small airport at Farranfore there are flights from London with Manx airlines or Aer Lingus via Dublin, ✆ (066) 64644.

By boat: If you are planning to go west to County Clare and Galway, you can avoid Limerick City by taking the car ferry at Tarbert, across the Shannon River to Killimer. The ferry sails from Killimer every hour on the hour, and from Tarbert every hour on the half-hour; it takes 30 mins. The nearest international ferryport is Ringaskiddy, near Cork City, which has ferries to the Continent. Ferry service around the Ring of Kerry from Dingle: Tues, Wed, Thurs, Sat and Sun, IR£10.

By rail: Kerry is linked to Dublin by a good rail line from Killarney and Tralee; call ✆ (064) 31067 for information.

By bus: Bus Eireann provides a good bus service to many parts of the county, ✆ (066) 21211/23566.

By car: car hire from Brien Sheehy, Boherbue Road, Tralee, ✆ (066) 21080, or McElligots, Rathass, Tralee, ✆ (066) 23011.

By bike: Raleigh Rent-a-Bike network operates in Kerry, ✆ (01) 261333. The local dealer in Killarney is O'Callaghan's, College Street, ✆ (066) 31175. In Tralee, Jim Catall Himself Ltd, Staughton's Row, Tralee, ✆ (066) 21654.

To the islands: to visit the Skelligs, hire a boat from Caherdaniel or Derrynane Pier, or from Valentia Island—a matter of trying your luck with the local fishermen. One contact is Des Lavelle, who operates a scuba-diving school, ✆ (066) 56124. He also organises cruises around the islands starting from the Skellig Heritage Centre, ✆ (021) 273251 or (064) 31633. The Café Liteartha in Dingle,

$\mathcal{C}$ (066) 51388, often displays information in the window on boats and excursions out to the Skelligs and the Blaskets; there are now some 'official' boats that visit the islands—call Skellig Heritage Centre, $\mathcal{C}$ (066) 76306 for more information. Also, ask in Krugers Bar, Dunquin, $\mathcal{C}$ (066) 56127, about hiring a boat to the Great Blasket. A small boat ferries day-trippers from Dunquin Harbour at 11am, returning late afternoon, $\mathcal{C}$ (066) 56188 for more information. Bord Fáilte are loathe to recommend anyone because of the insurance requirements; the local boatman will not be covered and the trip is at your own risk.

Tourist Information

Killarney Town Hall, $\mathcal{C}$ (064) 31633, all year.

Kenmare, beside Heritage Centre, $\mathcal{C}$ (064) 41233, 9.30–7 in summer only.

Tralee, Godfrey Place, $\mathcal{C}$ (066) 21288, all year.

Dingle, $\mathcal{C}$ (066) 51188, April to end October.

Kenmare, $\mathcal{C}$ (064) 41233, seasonal office.

Festivals

Easter: Easter Folk Festival. Call Mr O'Callaghan, $\mathcal{C}$ (064) 33404.

May: Rally of the Lakes, car rally. Contact Mike Marshall, $\mathcal{C}$ (064) 32026. Ballybunion International Bachelor Festival, $\mathcal{C}$ (066) 21288.

May–September: Siamsa Tire, The National Folk Theatre of Ireland, Godfrey Place, Tralee, $\mathcal{C}$ (066) 23055, has a programme of evening entertainment based on Irish music, folklore and dance.

July: St Brendan's Festival, Dingle, ask for Rosie Ban, $\mathcal{C}$ (066) 51466. Irish Music Festival, Dingle. Contact Fergus O'Flahertie, O'Flahertie's Bar, Dingle, $\mathcal{C}$ (066) 51461.

August: Rose of Tralee Competition, $\mathcal{C}$ (066) 21322. **10–12 August**, Puck Fair, Killorglin, $\mathcal{C}$ (064) 31633/61193.

September: Listowel Harvest Festival and Races $\mathcal{C}$ (068) 21000/22675.

Kenmare and Surrounding Area

The route into Kerry via Cork is spectacular. However, instead of going straight to Killarney, you should explore around **Lauragh** and the **Cloonee Loughs**, for the waterfalls and lakes are lovely. An unmarked road off the R571 will take you up to a wonderful view over the Beara Peninsula and Inchiquin Lake. Across the lough is **Uragh Wood**, a survivor of the primeval oakwoods which once covered most of Ireland. These are sessile oaks, which are distinguished by their curious hunched branches. There is a beautifully planted garden at **Derreen Woodland** (*open April–end Sept, daily, 11–6; adm; $\mathcal{C}$ (064) 83103*) near Lauragh, on the Kenmare-Castletownbeare road (R571). The moist climate has given the plants a tropical vigour. As you walk through the winding paths and tunnels of deep shade cast by the bamboo and rhododendrons, there are glorious glimpses of sea and wild mountain country. The land, and thousands of acres around it, used to belong to Sir William Petty, who was responsible for the mapping of two-thirds of Ireland after the Cromwellian Conquest.

This is marvellous walking country, and you can base yourself in **Kenmare**, a pretty 19th-century town. Savour the view of the Kerry Hills, the Macgillycuddy's Reeks, the Caha Range on the Cork border and the broad estuary of the River Kenmare. Kenmare itself is full of excellent craft shops, coffee houses, bars, restaurants and a heritage centre, so leave yourself at least a couple of hours to wander around it. Cleo in Shelbourne Street is especially tempting. The colours of woven rugs, jerseys and tweeds perfectly echo the beautiful surrounding countryside.

There is a fine prehistoric stone circle along the banks of the River Finnihy. To get there, walk up a road to the right of the Market House. Follow this until you see a notice reading 'cul de sac', and walk up the little lane on the right to where it joins another lane to the left. On the left, behind a high ditch, is the stone circle. It is always accessible.

On the square above the tourist office is the **Kenmare Lace and Design Centre** where you can look at a display of the point lace made locally, buy it, and watch lace-making demonstrations. On the outskirts of town on the Killarney road (N71) is **St Mary's Holy Well,** which is still much visited as the waters are reputed to have strong healing powers. The road from Kenmare to Killarney (N71) is twisty but the landscape is spectacular. Once you have climbed to the top of the mountain and through Moll's Gap, you get wonderful views of Killarney's lakes and woods.

Killarney

Killarney is dedicated to making money out of tourists and no longer attractive in itself, yet the surrounding countryside remains beautiful and unspoiled. If you are willing to walk in the mountains and away from well-worn tracks, you will find that the luxuriant green of the woods, the soft air, the vivid blue of the lakes and the craggy mountains above will have the same charm for you as they have had for countless travellers since the 18th century. Remember to bring a raincoat, and expect at least one day when the mists will creep over everything.

Killarney does have one thing to offer sightseers: **St Mary's Cathedral**, built in silvery limestone in the 1840s to the design of Pugin. It is a very successful Early-English style building, austere and graceful. You will find it in Cathedral Place, a continuation of New Street. There are plenty of banks, shops, craft shops and restaurants to choose from, but avoid staying in the centre of the town as it gets so crowded. And expect to be approached by the jarveys, who gather with their ponies and traps on the street corner as you enter the town on the N71. They will guide you around the valley and take you for as long or as short a trip as you want. Be sure to negotiate the price for the ride before you start.

In July in Killarney Town are the **Killarney Races**, when the place is crowded with locals. They also come in their thousands for the **Killarney Rally** in May, part of the Benson and Hedges motor-racing circuit of Ireland. At about the same time, the Easter folk festival is held at various venues around the town.

Excursions from Killarney

A large part of the Killarney Valley is a National Park, at the centre of which is Muckross House and Abbey. The valley runs roughly north–south through a natural break in the great Macgillycuddy's Reeks range of mountains which run east–west. Lough Leane lies north of the range, and the Middle and Upper Lakes, mainly south of it.

It is possible to have great fun seeing the sights by pony and trap, also known as a jaunting car. Excursions from Killarney take up to a full day and during the trip you are regaled with stories by the jarveys. They have built up an international reputation for telling visitors exactly what they expect to hear—leprechauns, legends, you name it! A boat trip down the three lakes takes a whole day and is idyllic in good weather. There are half-day bus trips, and ponies may be hired to explore the Gap of Dunloe, on the outskirts of Killarney. This is only advisable for experienced riders. The Gap of Dunloe divides the Macgillycuddy's from the Purple Mountain and Tomies Mountain. The mouth of the Gap starts at Kate Kearney's Cottage (who was reputed to be a witch), a coffee shop off the Killorglin road 6 miles (10km) west of Killarney, and continues through to Moll's Gap on the Kenmare road (N71). Most people start from this end and hire a pony or sidecar. Cars are not welcome on this route until well after 7pm, as the horse traffic on the narrow unpaved road will not allow you to pass. The journey through the Gap is spectacular, with steep gorges and deep glacial lakes. A more detailed description is given below.

For those who prefer to be more independent and economical, hiking or biking will get you to the Gap of Dunloe, Muckross Abbey and Castle, Ross Castle and Innisfallen Isle. **Ross Castle** is 1.5 miles (2.4km) southwest of the town centre on a peninsula. It is a fine ruin dating from the 15th century, consisting of a tower house surrounded by a bawn (fortified enclosure). On the left of it there is a 17th-century house built by the Brownes, who became Earls of Kenmare. It is not possible to go inside the castle but from here you can hire a boat to **Innisfallen Island** (*IR£3–IR£4 per hour*), which is like a country in miniature with hills and valleys, and dark woods. Holly and other evergreens grow very thickly here. Near the landing stages are the extensive ruins of **Innisfallen Abbey**, founded about AD 600, a refuge for Christians during the Dark Ages in Europe. The Annals of Innisfallen, a chronicle of world and Irish history written between AD 950 and 1380, are now in the Bodleian Library, Oxford. The monastery lasted until the middle of the 17th century when the Cromwellian forces held Ross Castle.

About 3 miles (5km) from Killarney is the **Muckross Estate** on the Kenmare road. Muckross House and Abbey are part of an 11,000-acre estate given to the nation by Mr Bowers Bourne of California and his son-in-law, Senator Arthur Vincent. They had owned the property for 31 years. The estate has been made into a National Park and covers most of the lake district, with walks and drives to all the beauty spots, although cars are not allowed to some parts of the estate. **Muckross House** (*open all year, daily, 9–7 in summer, 5.30 in winter; adm, gardens free; for a small extra fee you can visit a traditional working farm within the estate; © (064) 31440*) was built in Tudor style by Henry Arthur Herbert in 1843, whose family were landlords in the area. The main rooms are furnished in splendid Victorian style. The rest of the house has been transformed into a museum of Kerry folklore with a craftshop in its basement. You can see a potter, a weaver and blacksmith at their trades. There is a very informative film of the geology and natural beauties of the park, which is put on every half-hour. The gardens around the house are delightful, and here you can see the native Killarney strawberry tree (arbutus)—an evergreen with creamy white flowers followed by fruits which resemble strawberries. Close by, overlooking the lower lake, is **Muckross Abbey**, a graceful Early-English ruin founded for the Observatine Franciscans in 1448. In fact, this area is a stage set for everything the tourist wishes to see, and the natural beauty of the setting is enhanced by superb gardens. There is a gigantic yew tree in the centre of the cloister.

The **Gap of Dunloe** can be approached further along the main Killarney–Kenmare Road (N71) and there is plenty to stop for en route. Notice the strawberry tree growing among ferns and oaks, and the pink saxifrage on the wayside. All of the following are well-signposted. You can stop and take the woodland path to the **Torc Waterfall**, found by following a rough road on the left just before a sign cautioning motorists about deer. The walk is very short, leading you through splendid fir trees to the 60ft (18m) falls. It is also possible to drive there and park. Return to the main road.

For another little detour to some falls, continue on past the Galway Bridge where you can follow the stream up into the hills to the **Derrycunnihy Cascades**. Maybe you will come upon a few sika (Japanese deer) or red native deer. The cascades are set in primeval oak woods, and this is a rich botanical site of ferns and mosses. Go back to the main road again (N71) and continue for 6 miles (9.7km) to **Ladies' View**, which gives you a marvellous view of the upper lake and a hideous tourist shop-cum-café. Now turn off right before

Moll's Gap and right
again along the dirt track. You are
now in the **Gap of Dunloe**, a beautiful wild
gorge bordered by the dark Macgillycuddy's Reeks, the
Purple Mountain and Tomies Mountain. You can explore the Gap with some arduous walking. This is some of the best ridge-walking country in Ireland. If you do go walking, even for a short stroll, you should carry good waterproof gear, as the weather comes straight in from the Atlantic. The Macgillycuddy's Reeks include Carrantuohill, at 3414ft (1040m), the highest mountain in Ireland.

If you are interested in seeing a fine example of ogham stones, take the main road for Killorglin (R567), past the Dunluce Castle Hotel. Turn right down a hill to a T-junction, and right again, over the bridge and up the hill. A signpost points left to a collection of ogham stones in a wired enclosure high on the bank. This is the best place in Kerry to see the weird ogham writing, the only form that existed before the arrival of Christianity. The lateral strokes incised into the stone and crossing a vertical line give the name of a man long, long dead.

Another fine view of the Killarney lakes and mountains can be seen from **Aghadoe Hill**. It is not at all touristy. In pagan times, the hill was believed to be the birthplace of all beauty, and lovers still meet here. The legend goes that whoever falls in love on Aghadoe Hill will be blessed for a lifetime. To get there from the centre of Killarney, take the Tralee road until you see a sign for Aghadoe Heights Hotel. The view opens up around the hotel. One of the youth hostels is also in this direction (*see* p.146).

The road which makes up the **Ring of Kerry** is 112 miles (180km) long, and takes about three hours to drive without any detours. Starting back at Kenmare, one can take the N70 and follow the coiling road south around the coast—stopping to enjoy the views, and perhaps setting off down the tiny R roads to get a better look at **St Finan's Bay**, **Bolus Head** and **Doulus Head**. The ring ends at Killorglin. (You can, of course, travel the Ring anti-clockwise, starting from Killarney on the Killorglin road. The views are equally good.)

Detour to the Interior

Alternatively, as the Ring does not venture deeply into the interior of the Iveragh Peninsula, you could do just that by travelling to the lake area of Caragh, Glencar and Lough Cloon, which will take at least half a day. This wild, mountainous landscape was the hunting ground of the legendary Fionn MacCumhail (Finn MacCool) and it is absolutely delightful. Myriad little roads lead up to these parts. Perhaps the simplest is the lonely road through the **Ballaghisheen Pass**, which is unnumbered and runs between Killorglin and Waterville. It actually branches off the N70 just north of Waterville by Inny Bridge. The Caragh River is famous for its early salmon, and the Macgillycuddy's Reeks cast their great height against the skyline all the way.

At the north end of Lough Cloon, up a small road to some farmhouses and then right along a track, is an ancient settlement with ruined clochans (beehive huts) and terraced fields. Up in the wild country, turn right at Bealalaw Bridge and continue on until you come to a right fork over the Owenroe River which takes you into the Ballaghbeama Gap and joins a larger road to Sneem. This takes you through a tortuous and breathtaking channel between two mountains, Knocklomena and Knockavulloge, named in Irish after the golden gorse which grows on their slopes. Traces of the Early-Bronze Age Beaker people have been found here in rock carvings. The Kerry Way, a signed route for walkers starts at Glenbeigh and follows a desolate and beautiful route through the Reeks.

Back to the Ring Again

Sneem is a quiet village (out of season) divided by the Sneem river. It has a good pub and was attractively laid out by an 18th-century landlord. On the central green is a recently erected monument to De Gaulle who once spent two weeks here; locals refer to it affectionately as 'Da Gallstone'.

About 10 miles (15km) west of Sneem, continuing on the N70, there is a signpost right to **Staigue Fort**—isolated at the head of a desolate valley, and about 2500 years old. The circular stone fort rises out of a field, and a large bank and ditch surround it. The fort has a tremendous atmosphere and ancient strength about it; the farmer who owns the field has been known to demand an entry fee. Beyond Castlecove village on the N70 is **White Strand**, which is superb for bathing.

West again on the N70, a mile (1.6km) from Catherdaniel is **Derrynane House** (*open May–Sept, 9–6; Oct–April, daily, 11–5; adm; © (066) 75113*), the home of Daniel O'Connell, 'the Great Liberator', who won Catholic emancipation in 1829. It contains many of his possessions and is beautifully kept as a museum. The mellow simplicity of the house is very appealing, and the video of his life well worth watching. He believed that 'no political change whatsoever is worth the shedding of a single drop of human blood.' His family typified the old Irish ways of hospitality. They got on easily with all their neighbours, whether the hard-drinking gentry or the fisherfolk. Daniel O'Connell himself was fostered out when a baby to some island people, a custom which has its roots in ancient Ireland. His aunt Eileen wrote a wonderful lamentation on the death of her husband, Art O'Leary, who was killed for refusing to sell his fine mare to a Protestant named Morris for the sum of £5. (Catholics under the penal laws of the time were not allowed to own a horse of greater value than this.) This extract is from the beginning, when she entreats his dead body to rise up:

> My love and my delight
> Stand up now beside me,
> And let me lead you home
> Until I make a feast,
> And I will roast the meat
> And send for company
> And call the harpers in,
> And I will make your bed
> Of soft and snowy sheets
> And blankets dark and rough
> To warm the beloved limbs
> An Autumn blast has chilled.

Translated by Frank O'Connor

The grounds have exceptionally fine coastal scenery, and form a park of 298 acres. **Derrynane Bay** has one of the most glorious strands in the country.

A few miles further round the coast, **Waterville** is the main resort of the Ring; palm trees and fuchsia imbue it with a Continental air. The people speak Gaelic, the Munster variety, and **Ballinskelligs Bay** is a favourite place for Gaelic-speaking students, who stay in the B&Bs here. The beach is very beautiful with splendid views. This area is a rich source of legend. The story goes that it was near Waterville that Cessair, the grand-daughter of Noah, landed with her father, two other men and 49 women. They were hoping to escape the Great Flood of the Bible story. The year, apparently, was 2958 BC! The women divided the three men amongst them but two of them died and the third, Fintan, was so reluctant to remain with the women that he fled and later turned himself into a salmon.

This peninsula was also the landing point of another invasion: the coming of the Celts. The 12th-century manuscript The *Book of Invasions*, or the *Lebor Gabala*, describes it as follows. The Milesians had got to Spain, and there they built a watch-tower from which they saw Ireland, and it looked so green and beautiful that they set sail for it. Their poet, Amergin, sang a poem of mystical incantations as he first touched the Irish shore. The poem itself is rather beautiful, and this is part of what he sings:

I am the womb: of every holt,
I am the blaze: on every hill
I am the queen: of every hive,
I am the shield: for every head
I am the grave: of every hope.

Version by Robert Graves

The *Book of Invasions* states that the Celts arrived on the 1 May 1700 BC. As you enter Waterville on the N70, on the skyline to your right is an alignment of four stones. This is supposed to be the burial place of Scene, wife of one of the eight leaders of the Milesians.

Cahirciveen to Killorglin

A theatrical tower guards the bridge and the inlet at **Cahirciveen**. It used to be the police barracks but is now a heritage and tourist information centre. The design is grandiose Victorian, and was used for many other police barracks all over the British Empire. This area is marked by turf-cutting and dominated by the holy mountain, **Knocknadobar**. From the summit at 2267ft (690m), you get a wonderful view of the Dingle Peninsula and the Blasket Islands. Closer to, Valentia Island and the little harbour village of **Knightstown** is a pretty place to stay. Valentia was chosen as the site for the first transatlantic cable in 1858; natives could get in direct contact with New York but not with Dublin! Above the village the famous blue-grey Valentia slates were quarried. The quarry is no longer in use, but has been converted into a religious grotto. The views across to the mainland are magnificent. The Skellig Heritage Centre is beside the road bridge that links the island to Portmagee (*see* below). The N70 continues around the peninsula, passing close to Knocknadobar Mountain and along Kells Bay, which is a good place to bathe. This wildly romantic landscape is peopled with heroes from Ireland's legendary past: Fionn MacCumhail and the warrior band, the Fianna, hunted these glens. Close by, in the locality of **Rossbeigh** and **Glenbeigh** the landscape is rich in memories of Oísín the son of Fionn, who came back here after his long sojourn in the land of youth. He had left with Niamh, a golden-haired beauty he had met on the Rossbeigh strand. It is fascinating to visit the Bog Village Museum at Glenbeigh (*open Mar–Nov, daily; adm*) which depicts life in the rural 1800s.

If you turn off the Ring of Kerry road (N70) here and drive up to the Ballaghisheen Pass, you can remember that this is where Oísín went looking for his companions in the Fianna, and from this great height surveyed the glens and mountains. He did not understand that three hundred years had passed whilst he was enchanted, and that they were long dead. This area is also strongly associated with the story of Diarmuid and Grainne (*see* p.200 and p.202), who stayed in a cave at Glenbeigh. The Ring of Kerry ends with the attractive town of Killorglin, which grew up around an Anglo-Norman castle on the River Laune. The castle is now ruined, but you can explore a similar one nearby at Ballymalis. It has been partly restored, and you can climb to the top of the 16th-century tower, which is great fun. It is always open, entry free. **Killorglin** is famous for its cattle and horse fair

held in August, when vestiges of an ancient rite are enacted: a wild goat from the mountains is captured and enthroned in a cage in the centre of town. He is a symbol of the unrestricted merrymaking to follow. The event is known as the **Puck Fair**, and there are various theories as to its origins (*see* p.65). Certainly, the '*craic*' (fun and entertainment) is good; book in advance if you want to stay overnight in the town.

The Skelligs

A trip to the **Skelligs** will take a whole day and is a highpoint of any visit to this part of the country. These rocky islands lie at the mouth of Ballinskelligs Bay and rise dramatically from the sea. The Small Skellig is covered in thousands of gannets, whilst the Great Skellig, or Skellig Michael, has on it an almost perfect example of an early monastic settlement which was in use between the 6th and 12th centuries. The Gaelic word *sceilig* means splinter of stone, and you can only wonder at the skill of the men who cut and shaped that stone.

A sea cruise around the islands can be taken from the Heritage Centre on Valentia Island, Cahirciveen or Dingle. If you wish to go yourself and stop off at the islands, boats can be hired at Caherdaniel or Derrynane pier. (For details, *see* 'Getting Around'.) At the time of writing, landings have been limited to Sun, Mon, and Tues during the high season. Check with the tourist office. Take a waterproof jacket, flat shoes, a picnic, and, if you are keen on birdlife, a pair of binoculars. The trip out there can be very rough, and it illuminates something of the need for solitude that those holy men hungered for. You land to the noisy fury of the seabirds, and approach the monastery up a stairway 540ft (164m) long, hacked out of stone over a thousand years ago.

On this barren rock half a mile long and three-quarters of a mile wide (800m by 1200m), there was little these holy men could do there except pray and meditate. The way of life must have been hard; sometimes the waves crashing around the rock reach enormous heights. You can see beehive huts, stone crosses, the holy well, oratories and cemeteries. These are laid out close together; the oratories and the medieval **St Michael's Church** are separated from the six cells or beehive huts by the holy well. The fresh water on this desolate island is provided from the rock fissures, which hold rainwater. The Vikings raided the monastery in AD 812 and 823, but in AD 956, Olaf Trygveson, the son of the King of Norway was baptized here. Whenhe became king he introduced Christianity to Scandinavia.

The monastery here grew independent of the authorities in Rome, as did the clerics in Ireland as a whole. The Celtic church refused to follow a 7th-century ruling about the time of Easter, and it was not until medieval times that the Skelligs fell into line. The **Skellig Heritage Centre** (*open May–Sept; © (066) 76306*) interprets the life of the monks on Skellig Michael through film, graphics and models. It also gives information about the birdlife, water-life and the lighthouse service. Books, crafts and snacks for sale.

Annascaul to Dingle Town

There are several ways into the peninsula. The most obvious is to continue on the N70 to Castlemaine and then to **Annascaul** on the R561, which passes the beautiful sandy beach at Inch. The spectacular way to get to Dingle, however, is via Camp on the R559, and the Glennagalt Valley—the Glen of the Madmen. Mad people were taken here to recover, helped perhaps by the magnificent scenery between the Beenoskee Massifs. (Incidentally, the Irish phrase for someone who has gone mad is 'he's away with his head'.) This is the way the old railway used to go, dropping down to Annascaul where you can get a drink at the South Pole Inn, called so because the former proprietor, Tom Crean, was with Scott in the Antarctic.

Dingle is a big fishing town. It has developed in the most attractive way. The gaily painted houses and busy streets lead you to the harbour where the fishing boats move gently in the swell of the tide. The catches off this part of the coast are terrific, but the boats are small and high-tech methods have not yet arrived. This adds greatly to the charm of the scene. The Roman Catholic church in the centre of the town is a dim, calm place full of a feeling of welcome. In a different way the cafés and bars invite one to linger, and give the town a delightful holiday atmosphere. James Flahire's Bar by the harbour is full of clutter and old-fashioned furnishings, and in Dick Mack's in Green Lane you can buy not only a pint but also a selection of footwear. Ireland used to have many such places, but they are rapidly disappearing. There are several good craft shops to browse in. The local celebrity and major attraction, however, is undoubtedly Fungi, a playful dolphin who wandered into the bay some years ago. His fame is such that the writer Vikram Seth has planned an opera in his honour.

If you decide to base yourself in Dingle for a few days, there are many beautiful places to explore nearby. You can walk in the **Slieve Mish Mountains**, where there is not only wild beauty but a fund of archaeological remains. To the northeast of Annascaul, on the right summit of Caherconree Mountain, is a rare example of an inland promontory fort. It dates from about 500 BC and is associated with Cú Chulainn, the great Ulster hero. (Notorious for his attraction to woman, in this story he rescues a damsel in distress, and carries her off to the North of Ireland.) From the great **Strand of Inch** you have views of the Blasket Islands. In the pubs, after ten in the evenings, you can listen to traditional music or singing, which just happens when the locals get together. Dingle comes from the Irish *daingean*, meaning fortress, but nothing remains of one now. The local people speak Irish amongst themselves, though you will find that they will switch to English when you are around, for courtesy's sake. West of Dingle is wonderful, austere country battered by the Atlantic wind and sea.

Ventry has a lonely white strand on which it is said the King of the other World, Donn, landed to subjugate Ireland. He had come to help the King of France avenge his honour as

Fionn had run off with his wife and daughter. The great Fionn MacCumhail and his Fenian knights won the day, of course (*see* **Old Gods and Heroes**, p.202).

On the road to Shea Head, just off the R559 at Fahan and about 3 miles (6km) past Ventry, there is a group of Early-Christian **clochans**—414 in all. Local farmers still build little clochans as storehouses for animals, and the continuity of style with the unmortared stone is such that you cannot tell the old from the new. Nineteen souterrains (underground passages and storage places) and 18 standing stones, two sculptured crosses and seven ring-forts are strewn all over the slopes of Mount Eagle; the most prominent is the powerfully built Doonbeg Fort, which can be seen from the road, surrounded by the sea on three sides. The fort is dated between 400 and 50 BC. It was well protected by several defensive, earthen walls and an inner stone wall. Inside, local people and livestock would have gathered when under threat by rival tribal groups. There is a souterrain leading from the inside of the fort to the entrance. The road from Fahan winds round the countryside to Shea Head, from where you can see the Blasket Islands.

The Blasket Islands

The Blaskets are made up of several tiny islands and the Great Blasket, all now uninhabited. Charles Haughey, the politician, owns one of them as a holiday retreat.

Some beautiful writing has sprung from the Great Blasket, produced just before the island way of life collapsed in the 1940s. The young emigrated because of the harsh living conditions, and the Great Blasket has been uninhabited since 1953. The accounts of island life left to us through the writing, record the warmth and the fun, as well as the misery and heartbreak, of their hard way of life. Their acceptance of death and life has great dignity, as does their sense of comradeship with the others on the island. There are three autobiographies written in the 1920s and 1930s: *The Islandman* by Tomas O'Crohan, *Twenty Years a-Growing* by Maurice O'Sullivan, and the autobiography of Peig Sayers. All are worth reading for the humour, pathos and command of the Gaelic language, which comes through even in translation. The **Dunquin Heritage Centre** (*open daily in high season; adm*) focuses on the story of the Blaskets.

You can visit the Blaskets from Dingle or Dunquin Harbour. Kruger's Pub in Dunquin is the place to enquire about boats and departure times. You might be lucky and persuade a local to take you out there in a **curragh**, the boat used for centuries by the Island men to catch the shining mackerel found in these waters. When you arrive, you will see that the Great Blasket is full of memories. If you have read the literature, you will recognize the White Strand where the islanders played hurling on Christmas morning. But the stone walls around the intensively farmed fields have now tumbled, and the village is a ruin. Tomas O'Crohan wrote at the end of his account: 'somewhere there should be a memorial of it all... for the like of us will never be again.' It is a pleasant walk up to the ruined hill-fort and there are wonderful views.

Back on the mainland again, heading north up round the peninsula, at **Ballyferriter** there is an active, friendly co-operative which grows parsley to export to France. They are also very keen on preserving their heritage—the Gaelic language, antiquities, and beautiful scenery. You can look around their heritage centre (*call © (066) 56100 for times of opening*). At **Ballydavid** the ancient industry of curragh-making goes on. The beaches around here are magnificent, in particular **Smerwick Strand**. In any of these you might find Kerry diamonds—sparkly pieces of quartz, a nicer souvenir than anything you could buy.

East of Ballyferriter lies the perfectly preserved **Oratory of Gallarus**—a relic of early Christianity. It is built of corbelled stone and is so watertight that not a drop of rain has entered it for a thousand years. The only missing section of the original building are the crosses which stood at each end of the roof ridge. Always accessible, and entry is free. At the crossroads above Gallarus, turn sharp left for **Kilmalkedar Church**, built in Irish Romanesque style in the 12th century. There must have been an earlier pagan settlement here as there are some ancient carved stones around the site. Nearby is the Saint's Road up the Brandon Mountain. This ancient track leads up to **St Brendan the Navigator's Shrine**. St Brendan climbed up to its summit to meditate and saw in a vision Hy-Brasil, the Island of the Blessed, and afterwards he voyaged far and wide looking for this ideal land. People still climb up here on the last Saturday in June to pray. An easier climb can be made from the village of **Cloghane** and the views from it are magical. It's not surprising that St Brendan saw Utopia from here!

The main (unnumbered) road from Dingle to Stradbally and on to Tralee (R560) takes you over the **Connor Pass**, the summit of which is 1500ft (497m) with great views over Dingle Bay. There are dark loughs in the valley and giant boulders are strewn everywhere. At the foot of the pass, a branch road leads off to Cloghane and Brandon,-both good bases for exploring and climbing the sea cliffs around Brandon Point and Brandon Head.

Tralee is the chief town and administrative capital of County Kerry. It is famous outside Ireland for the lovely Victorian song 'The Rose of Tralee'. The town was the chief seat of the Desmond family, but nothing remains of their strong castle. The old Dominican friary that the Desmonds founded was completely destroyed by the Elizabethan courtier soldier Sir William Denny, who was granted the town when the Desmond estates were seized. The town has suffered continually from wars and burnings, and today is largely mid-19th-century in character although there are some fine Georgian houses in the centre. The Courthouse has a splendid Ionic façade, and in Derry Street is an impressive 1798 Memorial. The Dominican Church of Holy Cross is by Pugin and contains ancient carved stones. In Abbey Street there is a modern church with a lovely chapel dedicated to the Blessed Virgin Mary, which contains some fine work in stained glass by that great artist Michael Healy, who worked at the turn of the century. The Ashe Memorial Hall, an imposing 19th-century building off Denny Street, is a very fine **County Musuem** (*open all year, Mon–Sat 10–6, Sun 2–6; adm; © (066) 27777*). The displays trace the history of Kerry from 5000 BC, and the exhibits include archaeological treasures found all over the county. Another attraction is the reconstructed town of medieval Tralee, you travel through the streets in a 'time-car'. The Tralee steam train leaves from Ballyard station; the 3km jaunt takes you to Blennerville working windmill, complete with restaurant and craft shops. It is possible to buy a 'passport ticket' which covers all Tralee's attractions. **Crag Cave,** Castle Island is an underground cave system at least 4km long (*signposted off the N21 Limerick to Tralee road; open all year; adm; © (066) 41244*).

North Kerry

North Kerry has none of the splendour of Dingle but a rather quiet charm, a taste of which you will get if you drive between Tralee and Tarbert on your way to County Clare.

Places to go in north Kerry include **Ardfert Cathedral** on the R551, a noble Early-English Romanesque building dating from the 13th century. Like many Irish ruins it is rather neglected, but therein lies much of its charm. Modern graves have been built inside the ancient walls, despite a stern warning from the Office of Public Works that this must stop. Open all the time, although restoration work seems to be ongoing. **Banna** and **Ballyheige** have lovely strands. The sand dunes are home to many interesting plants, and Lough Akeragh which runs alongside Banna is a haven for migrant birds from North America.

Nearly at Knappogue, Ballyduff is **Rattoo Round Tower and Interpretative Centre** © (066) 31501. **Listowel** has ambitions as a cultural centre and puts on a **Writers' Week** every year with a book fair, art and photography exhibitions, plus short-story-writing workshops (*dates change every year, so check with tourist office for details*). The attractive town is situated on the River Feale, with a ruined 15th-century castle in the square. It belonged to the Fitzmaurice family, Anglo-Normans who later showed consistent disloyalty to the Crown. Notice the naive sculptural groups based on patriotic subjects on some of the shopfronts. Many writers came from this area; of particular note is Bryan MacMahon, whose wonderful novel *Children of the Rainbow* will keep you entranced with its descriptions of the Kerry countryside.

On the coast, some 10 miles (16km) southwest of Listowel on the R553 is the delightful resort of **Ballybunion**. Besides good sea bathing, you can have a hot seaweed bath, which makes you feel very relaxed and seems to take away any aches and pains (*see* 'Activities'). **Carrigafoyle Castle** north of Ballylongford is a 16th-century O'Connor Castle. Always accessible, you can walk to the battlements by a winding stone staircase from which you get a stunning view.

If you are taking the car ferry across to County Clare from **Tarbert**, you may visit **Tarbert House** (*open May–mid August, 10–12 and 2–4; © (068) 36198*) with its fine Georgian furniture and lovely Irish Chippendale mirror. Also in Tarbert is the **Bridewell Courthouse and Gaol** © (068) 36500 which has an exhibition on crime and punishment in the 19th century. Also has a coffee shop and information point.

Killarney

Crafts: The Bricui, High Street and College Street; Blarney Woollen Mills and Serendipity in College Street, and Avoca hand-weavers at Moll's Gap. McBeas is a good little department store.

Ring of Kerry

Crafts: The Homestead Craft Shop and Sneem Craft Workshops. Gleann Bhride Handweavers, Waterville. Clay Pottery and Gallery in Cahirciveen. Sheeog Irish Handcrafts in Killorglin. Nostalgia for linen sheets, De Barra for Celtic jewellery.

Kenmare

Crafts: Kenmare Homespuns, the Craft Shop and Cleo for elegant tweed suits, linen and woven rugs. The Kenmare Lace and Design Centre, The Square, sells locally made lace, ℗ (064) 41679. Quill's Woollen Market, Kenmare, Brenmar Jon on Henry Street, ℗ (064) 41138 for designer knitwear.

Delicacies: Farmhouse cheese, yoghurt, pizzas and cheesecake from Lisette and Peter Kal, the White House, Tuosist, Kenmare, ℗ (064) 84500. (The Kals also hire out bikes and organize boat trips for fishing. Their house is signposted from the R571 going southwest from Kenmare.) The Pantry, 30 Henry Street, Kenmare, ℗ (064) 31326, for homemade bread, Capparoe goat's cheese, and various other picnic ingredients.

Dingle

Crafts: Commodum Craft Centre, Irish Crafts, Oliver McDonnell in Green Street, Dingle. Arts and Crafts in Strand Street, Dingle. Café Liteartha, Dykegate Street, Dingle, for Irish books and tapes. Pottery and tea shop in Ventry. Dunquin Pottery and Café in Dunquin. Handweaving and pottery by Louis Mulcahy in Ballyferriter at the Potadoireacht na Caoloigne Centre. Weaving by Lisbeth Mulcahy, Green Street, Dingle and silver jewellery by Brian de Staic, Green Street, Dingle.

Delicacies: wild smoked salmon from Ted Browne, Kilquane, Ballydavid, Dingle; ℗ (066) 55183. Delicious smoked bacon and black pudding from Norreen Curran, Green Street, Dingle; ℗ (066) 51398.

Tralee

Crafts and clothes: Carraig Donn Knitwear, Bridge Street, Tralee. Penny's Pottery, The Square, Tralee, ℗ (066) 59962 Lots of chunky lavender-blue pottery.

Delicacies: Seancara, Courthouse Lane, Tralee, for more excellent farmhouse cheeses, and homemade bread and lemon curd.

Deep-sea fishing: Mr N. O'Connor, Ventry, ✆ (066) 59947; Michael O'Sullivan, Waterville, ✆ (0661) 74255; George Burgum, Dingle, ✆ (066) 51337. Excellent deep-sea angling in the Kenmore River Estuary, Valentia Island and off Ballydavid Head.

Shore-angling: all round the Dingle Peninsula and Ring of Kerry. Ask in the Dingle tourist office for details.

Brown trout fishing: On Lough Leane and Lough Avaul and the Kenmare River.

Sea trout fishing: On the Inny River. Contact Club Med, ✆ (066) 74133; and the Butler Arms Hotel, Waterville, ✆ (066) 74144.

Salmon fishing: This is excellent on Lough Currane near Waterville. Contact the Waterville Fishery or Tourism development both on ✆ (066) 74366. Also, on River Laune and River Caragh. Contact Pat O'Grady on ✆ (066) 68228 or the Glencar Hotel, Glencar, ✆ (066) 60102.

Sailing and water-skiing: Parknasilla Great Southern Hotel, Parknasilla, ✆ (064) 45122. Dromquinna Manor, Kenmare, ✆ (064) 41657. The Aqua Dome, Ballyard, Tralee, ✆ (066) 28899. Waterworld complex.

Diving: in Ventry and Dingle Bays. You can go diving with an amazing and much loved friendly dolphin called Fungi who has been living in Dingle Bay for a few years. Boat trips to see him are organized by Mr Donegan, ✆ (066) 51720; or you can walk for 1km east of Dingle to the bay where he lives. Wet suits are available for hire from shops and boats, The Pier, Dingle or from Seventh Wave, ✆ (066) 51548, near the bridge, Dingle. Des Lavelle operates a scuba-diving school from Valentia, ✆ (066) 56124. Skelligs Aquatics, Caherdaniel, ✆ (0667) 5277.

Sea sports: Derrynane Sea Sports, Caherdaniel, ✆ (066) 75266, diving, sailing etc.

Surfing: Inch Strand, Srudeen Strand, near Dingle. (Bring your own surf board.)

Seaweed baths: Collins family, North Beach, Ballybunion, ✆ (068) 27469. Open June to beginning October. Cost IR£4.00.

Swimming: White Strand, near Castlecove, Derrynane beach, and Kells Bay near Rossbeigh. Beaches around Shea Head and Stradbally, Ballyheige and Banna Sands in North Kerry.

Lake tours: Killarney Waterbus; ✆ (064) 32638 or Lily of Killarney, ✆ (064) 31068.

Pony-trekking: in Tralee, ✆ (066) 21840. The management specializes in trekking through the Dingle Peninsula. For trekking in the Killarney National Park ✆ (064) 31686. Equestrian Centre, Ballintagart, Dingle, ✆ (066) 51454.

Horse-racing: in Killarney throughout May and July, contact Michael Doyle, ✆ (064) 31459 for details; in Tralee in August and in Listowel in September. Look in the local newspapers, or in the back of the free calendar of events available from any tourist office.

Horse-drawn caravans: D. Slattery, 1 Russell Street, Tralee, ✆ (066) 21722.

Golf: Waterville, ✆ (0661) 74133. Killarney, ✆ (064) 31034. Tralee, ✆ (066) 36379. Ballybunion, ✆ (068) 27146.

Walking: The Kerry Way, a signposted route between Killarney, the Black Valley, Lough Acoose and Glenbeigh; and the Dingle Way, between Tralee Camp, Annascaul and Dingle. Contact the tourist office in Killarney for detailed maps. General advice and help from Irish Wilderness Experience, 50 Woodlawn Park, Killarney, ✆ (064) 32922; and Arbutus Lodge Apartments, Aghadoe; ✆ (064) 31497. The 1:50,000 Ordnance Survey map no.78 'The Reeks' is good. For excellent information on walking, fishing, contact Tracks and Trails, ✆ (064) 54196 at 53 High Street, Killarney. Kerry Country Rambles, Killarney, ✆ (064) 54196.

Open farms: Muckross Traditional Farm, Killarney, ✆ (064) 31440; Churchtown Farm Park, Killarney, ✆ (064) 44440. Beechgrove Farm, Castleisland ✆ (066) 41217. Farm trail and raised bog.

Where to Stay

luxury

Park Hotel, Kenmare, ✆ (064) 41200. A château-style hotel with every modern comfort in rooms furnished with fine antiques. Everything about it is professional and first-rate.

Sheen Falls Lodge, Kenmare, ✆ (064) 41600. Beautiful location and sunny low-key décor. Food is lavishand imaginative. Helipad for visiting dignitaries.

expensive

Caragh Lodge, Caragh Lake, ✆ (066) 69115. Comfortable and well-furnished country house in a wonderful situation overlooking the lake, with a fine garden.

Parknasilla Great Southern Hotel, Parknasilla, ✆ (064) 45122. Comfortable hotel in a 19th-century mansion on the banks of the Kenmare River. Ask for a room in the older part.

Butler Arms Hotel, Waterville, ✆ (0667) 4144. A Grade A hotel and lovely place to stay if you like salmon or trout fishing.

moderate

Killeen House hotel, Aghadoe, Lakes of Killarney, ✆ (064) 31711. Friendly, cosy little hotel up in the hills of Aghadoe, 10 minutes from Killarney and away from the crowds.

Doyle's Townhouse, John Street, Dingle, ℘ (066) 51174. One of the most enjoyable places to stay in the county. The rooms are full of comfort and individuality, and the downstairs sitting-room has shelves and tables groaning with interesting books over which you can linger by a warm fire. The bar and restaurant next door are famous for their conviviality and good food.

Smugglers' Inn, Waterville, ℘ (0667) 4330. Family-run and on the beach.

Glendalough House, Caragh Lake, ℘ (066) 69156. Josephine Roder is an excellent hostess and has furnished her house with great love and care. Great views over the lake.

Listowel Arms, The Square, Listowel, ℘ (068) 21500. Old-fashioned country hotel.

Dromquinna Manor, Kenmare, ℘ (064) 41657. Very comfortable with lovely views over the water. Waterskiing nearby.

Lansdowne Arms, Main Street, Kenmare, ℘ (064) 41368. Friendly family-run hotel.

Lios Dana Natural Living Centre, Inch, Annascaul, ℘ (066) 58189. Holistic retreat holidays. Overlooking Dingle Bay.

Club Mediterranée, Waterville, ℘ (066) 74133. Shedding its sun image, lots of activities for the fit.

inexpensive

Hawthorne House, Shelbourne Street, Kenmare, ℘ (064) 41035. Extremely comfortable modern house, all bedrooms en suite. The food is delicious and lavish.

Carriglea House, Muckross Road, Killarney, ℘ (064) 31116. Very close to Muckross House and the National Park, so you can avoid the busy centre of town. Comfortable rooms, with own bathrooms.

The **Sugan Youth Hostel** in Killarney Town is good although fairly small, as is the restaurant beneath it, ℘ (064) 33104.

Lavelle Family, Valentia Island, ℘ (066) 76124. This peaceful place is a lovely base from which to explore. Fabulous views.

Mrs McKenna, **Mount Rivers**, Carhan Road, Cahirciveen, ℘ (0667) 2509. Comfortable rooms with bath in Victorian house.

The O'Shea family, **Benmore Farm**, Oughtive, Waterville, ℘ (0667) 4207. Old farmhouse on mountain road. They will arrange boat trips to the Skelligs.

Aisling House, Castlegregory, ℘ (066) 39134. Wonderful guesthouse: clean, comfortable and cheap, with a delicious breakfast.

Alpine House, Dingle, ℘ (066) 51250. All rooms with bath.

Mrs Curran, **Greenmount House**, Dingle, ✆ (066) 51414. Recommended by readers. Freshly squeezed orange juice and lots of choice for breakfast.

The **Old Stone Cottage**, Chiddaun, Dingle, ✆ (066) 59882. Comfortable little cottage.

Ferntock, Killorglin, ✆ (066) 61848. Well-run modern B&B, well-situated for golf and the 'Puck' festival.

Very cheap: The **'An Oige' Killarney International Hostel**, ✆ (064) 31240, is 2km outside Killarney at Aghadoe. A crumbly looking hulk of a building set in pretty grounds. A free bus meets trains from Dublin and Cork.

self-catering

Traditional 3-bedroom stone-built house in Ventry, ✆ (066) 59962. **Penny Sheehy** also has some recently built properties for rent.

2-bedroomed farmhouse in traditional style, **Patrick O'Leary**, ✆ (064) 45132. From £100 per week.

Ballintagart Hostel and Equestrian Centre, Dingle, ✆ (066) 51454. Converted 18th-century hunting lodge. Open fires & CH.

Bog View Hostel, Annascaul, Dingle Peninsula. Converted school with turf fires. Also does B&B and evening meals.

Modernised farmhouse, sleeps 6, close to Ballyferriter. Contact **Ms Naughton**, 20 Vineyard Hill Road, London SW19 7SH, ✆ (0181) 946 4782. From IR£180 a week.

3-bedroomed/3-star timber chalet with lush garden, Sneem. Call **Thomas Stans**, ✆ (064) 45100/(021) 273251 £400–£500 per week.

Eating Out

luxury

The **Park Hotel**, Kenmare, ✆ (064) 41200. Delicious French cuisine in grand surroundings.

expensive

Doyle's Seafood Bar and Restaurant, Dingle, ✆ (066) 51174. In a room reminiscent of an old Irish kitchen with stone floor and mellow wooden furniture, you can eat deliciously prepared seafood chosen by the very friendly and welcoming proprietors, John and Stella Doyle.

Nick's Restaurant and Pub, Lower Bridge Street, Killorglin, ✆ (066) 61219. Large portions of seafood and steaks. Packed with local people singing 'My Irish Molly' round the piano. Very friendly and great fun.

The **Strawberry Tree**, 24 Plunkett Street, Killarney, ✆ (064) 32688. One of the best restaurants in Killarney.

Sheen Falls Lodge, Kenmare, ✆ (064) 41600. Michelin-starred.

Beginish Restaurant, Green Street, Dingle, ✆ (066) 51588. Enthusiastic staff and delicious seafood with a conservatory at the back.

moderate

An Leath Phingin, 35 Main Street, Kenmare, ✆ (064) 41559. The Italian chef, Maria, makes her own fresh pasta and scrumptious sauces to go with it.

Foley's Seafood and Steak Restaurant, 23 High Street, Killarney, ✆ (064) 31217. Delicious seafood and lamb, also good vegetarian dishes.

Gaby's Restaurant, 17 High Street, Killarney, ✆ (064) 32519. Mediterranean-style café with delicious seafood. Very popular locally. It does not take bookings, so arrive early. *Lunch served Tues–Sat, and dinner at 6pm.*

The **Lime Tree**, Kenmare, ✆ (064) 41225. Newly re-opened as an American-style café.

The Half-door, John Street, Dingle, ✆ (066) 51600. Excellent and imaginative food. Very good value.

The Forge, Holy Ground, Dingle, ✆ (066) 51209. Steaks and seafood.

The **Smugglers' Inn**, Cliff Road, Waterville, ✆ (066) 74422. Good seafood in a restored farmhouse set on the beach. You can stay here very reasonably too.

Stone House, Sneem, ✆ (064) 45188. A guesthouse which produces reasonable Irish food. *Dinner only.*

Teach Cullain, Cahirciveen, ✆ (0667) 2400. Traditional Irish food, meat and fish.

Graney's Fish and Chip Shop, Dingle. Excellent and cheap take-aways.

Loaves and Fishes, Caherdaniel, ✆ (0667) 5273. Food hearty but stylish.

Packies, Henry Street, Kenmare, ✆ (064) 41508. Informal fish restaurant.

D'arcys Old Bank House, Main Street, Kenmare, ✆ (064) 41589.

inexpensive/cheap

Purple Heather, Henry Street, Kenmare, ✆ (064) 41016. Good for lunch-time snacks, homemade soups and seafood. Cosy fire in bar.

Sugan Bistro, Michael Collins Place, Killarney, ✆ (064) 33104. Near the railway station, a cheap wholefood bistro.

Anne's Kitchen, Annascaul. Healthy snack lunch.

An Café Liteartha, Dykegate Street, Dingle, ✆ (066) 51388. Bookshop and café serving sandwiches and soup.

The Islandman, Main Street, Dingle, ✆ (066) 51803 Very elegant bar/café/bookshop serving tasty food all day.

Whelans, on the Main Street, Dingle, ✆ (066) 51620. Good Irish stew.

Ashes Bar, Camp, ✆ (066) 30133. Seafood platter at lunchtime. More elaborate *à la carte* menu in the evening. Traditional music in the summer.

Ruth's Wholefood Kitchen, 76 Boherbue, Tralee, ✆ (066) 22665. On the road into Tralee, the restaurant has consistently good vegetarian food and fresh spring water from the owner's farm.

Pizza Time, The Square, Tralee, ✆ (066) 26317. Good pizza.

Lord Baker's, Main Street, Dingle, ✆ (066) 51277. Good bar food.

The **Blue Bull**, South Square, Sneem, ✆ (064) 45382.

The **Blind Piper**, restaurant and bar, Caherdaniel, ✆ (066) 75126. Good lively atmosphere in this pretty hamlet.

An Tailann, Brickwell Lane, off New Street, Killarney, ✆ (064) 33083. Vegetarian lunches and dinners in sweet little cottage.

Yer Man's Pub, 24 Plunkett Street, Killarney, ✆ (064) 32688. Authentic and cosy little pub, sandwiches at lunch and a good nightclub at the back.

The **Horseshoe** pub, Main Street, Kenmare. Popular, with a cosy fire; tables outside; serves food.

O'Donnatham's, Henry Street, Kenmare. Old-style new pub. Determined to establish a reputation for its traditional music.

County Cork

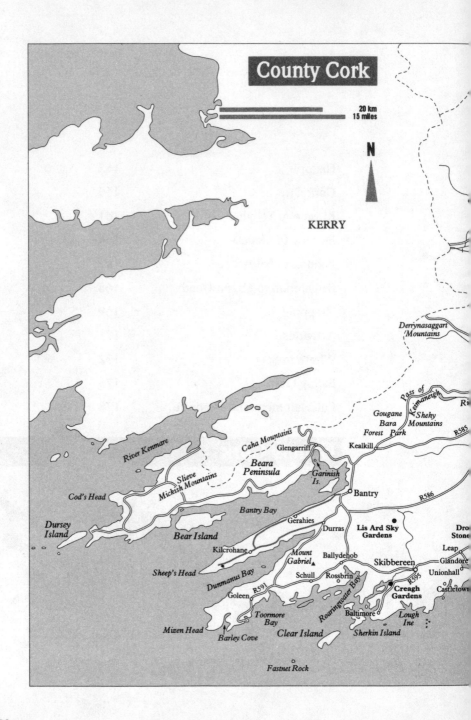

County Cork

20 km
15 miles

N

KERRY

Derrynasaggart
Mountains

Pass of Keimaneigh

Gougane
Bara
Forest Park

Shehy
Mountains

Ri

R585

Kealkill

Caha Mountains

Glengarriff

River Kenmare

Beara
Peninsula

Garinish
Is.

R586

Slieve
Mickish Mountains

Bantry

Cod's Head

Bantry Bay

Gerahies

Durras

Lis Ard Sky
Gardens

Dro
Stone

Dursey
Island

Bear Island

Kilcrohane

Mount
Gabriel

Ballydehob

Skibbereen

Leap

Glandore

Unionhall

Sheep's Head

Schull

Rossbrin

Creagh
Gardens

Castletow

Dunmanus Bay

R591

Goleen

Toormore
Bay

Roaringwater Bay

Baltimore

Lough
Ine

Mizen Head

Barley Cove

Clear Island

Sherkin Island

Fastnet Rock

150

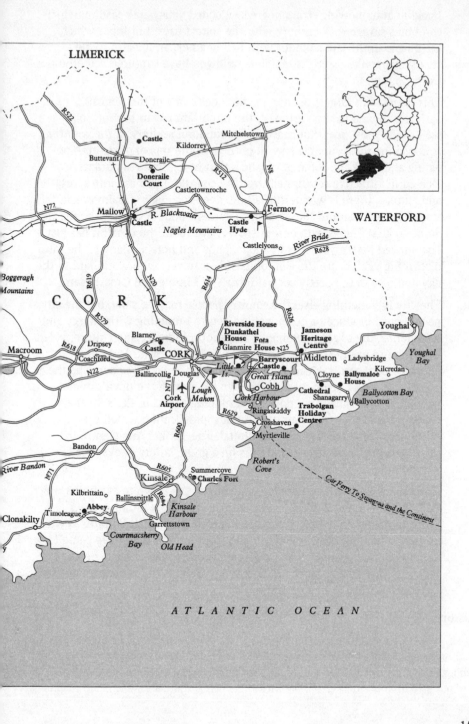

LIMERICK

Castle
Kildorrey
Mitchelstown
Buttevant · Doneraile
R512
N8
Doneraile
Court
Castletownroche
Fermoy
WATERFORD
N77
Mallow
R. Blackwater
Castle
Hyde
Castle
Nagles Mountains
Castlelyons
River Bride
R628
Boggeragh
Mountains
C O R K
R619
N20
R614
R626
Youghal
Riverside House
Dunkathel
House
Fota
House
Jameson
Heritage
Centre
Blarney
R579
Glanmire
House
Youghal
Bay
Macroom
R618
Dripsey
Castle
CORK
Barryscourt
Castle
N25
Midleton
Ladysbridge
Coachford
Little
Is.
Great Island
Cloyne
Kilcredan
N72
Ballincollig
Douglas
Cobh
Ballymaloe
House
Cork
Airport
Lough
Mahon
Cork Harbour
Cathedral
Shanagarry
Ballycotton Bay
Ballycotton
N71
R629
Ringaskiddy
Trabolgan
Holiday
Centre
R600
Crosshaven
Myrtleville
Bandon
Robert's
Cove
River Bandon
N71
R605
Kinsale
Summercove
Charles Fort
Car Ferry To Swansea and the Continent
Kilbrittain
Ballinspittle
Abbey
R600
Kinsale
Harbour
Clonakilty
Timoleague
Garrettstown
Courtmacsherry
Bay
Old Head

ATLANTIC OCEAN

Imagine quiet flowing rivers in green wooded valleys, a coastline which combines savage rock scenery with the softest bays, hillslopes which are purple in the late summer with bell heather, an ivy-clad castle standing amongst hayricks in a field, and you have captured something of Cork County.

This is Ireland's largest county and includes some of the richest agricultural land in the northeast, the important ocean port of Cobh, as well as the most beautiful coastal and mountain scenery in the country. It is also the most suitable spot to indulge in the relaxing pastimes of eating and drinking: some of Ireland's best hotels and restaurants are located in attractive settings all over the county. If you are into sports and culture, there is wonderful sailing, deep-sea angling, salmon and trout fishing, beautiful stately homes, gardens and, of course, the Blarney Stone to kiss! The growth of tourism has not spoilt the coast: it has just encouraged better quality craft shops, pubs and hotels. Many of the most discerning visitors are the Corkonians themselves, who work hard in the city and play in the pretty coastal resorts of Kinsale and Crosshaven.

The city is something else: the country people may be slow, but the city people have produced a cosmopolitan centre humming with energy and confidence, full of grand buildings and shops, industry and culture, aided by a wit and business sense that would be hard to beat. Dubliners alternate between jealousy and heavy sarcasm in trying to describe the place—the best I heard was 'God's own place with the devil's own people'. Corkonians think nothing of nipping across to Paris for the weekend, and there is an air of cultural sophistication which seriously challenges Dublin as the cultural capital. The Triskel Arts Centre in the city centre is excellent, and puts on a great variety of events all year round.

Corkonians are a mixed bunch, consisting of the down-to-earth working class and the monied middle class, which includes a rather genteel Protestant element whose forebears manned the British Empire; as well as quite a few 'blow-ins'—English and Continentals who have come for a variety of reasons and settled down to enjoy the way of life. The Cork accent is very strong, slow and sing-songy, so you will probably have to concentrate hard to understand it.

History

The history of Cork is similar to that of the rest of the Province; its well-watered and fertile lands attracted human settlement as far back as 6000 BC, when people lived by hunting, fishing, and gathering roots and berries. Kitchen middens found around the shores of Cork Harbour date from this time. From the Megalithic period there are stone circles, standing stones, and wedge tombs. Written history dates from the coming of Christianity. St Ciaran of Cape Clear is titled 'first born of the Saints of Ireland', and it is claimed that he arrived before St Patrick in the 5th century AD. Early church sites abound, and with the invasion of the Anglo-Normans in 1169 the Continental religious orders were set up in rich and beautiful abbeys. Some of their ruins remain. The Norsemen or Vikings mounted many raids on the Early-Christian settlements from the late 8th century onwards. They soon founded their own ports, settling down to trade with the native Irish, and so gradually became amalgamated into Gaelic society. The Anglo-Norman invasion brought advanced building techniques to Ireland: the Norman war-lords built themselves sophisticated castles, usually on a defensive site which had been used before. Their followers made themselves moated farmhouses. In the 15th century the ruling families built themselves tower houses; many ruins remain to add drama and interest to the countryside and coast-line. Comfortable domestic architecture did not develop until the 17th and 18th centuries, for the county was very unsettled whilst Celt and Anglo-Norman fought, made alliances with and against each other, and largely ignored the laws issued from London.

The administrators sent to implement English rule were successful after the Elizabethan wars of the late 16th century, when the land was planted with families loyal to the crown. Huge tracts of land were granted to men like Richard Boyle, who became Earl of Cork; and Sir Edmund Spenser, who wrote the long poem *The Faerie Queene* at Kilcolman Castle whilst he was Lord Deputy of Ireland. Beautiful Georgian houses survive from the 18th century, when the new landowners began to feel secure in their properties and build, plant and garden. It is possible to stay in some of these fine houses, which are not huge, but perfect in proportion and decoration.

By contrast, the oppressive laws introduced to control the Catholic population in the 1690s, the Rising of 1798 and the ghastly famine of the 1840s, all combined to create a peasantry that was poverty stricken. The Irish War of Independence was fought with ferocity in County Cork, with many burnings and cruelties on both sides, and the Civil War split family loyalties in two. Michael Collins (1890–1922), the dynamic revolutionary leader and one of the men responsible for negotiating the Anglo-Irish treaty of December 1921, was the son of a small farmer in Clonakilty. During the Civil War he was shot in the head by the anti-Treaty forces in an ambush between Macroom and Bandon (*see* pp.88–9).

Today, the memories of the Civil War are still alive, but the people are forward-looking and sophisticated. Industries such as whiskey, brewing, clothing, food processing, computers and pharmaceuticals have boomed around Cork Harbour, and the Cork City inhabitants enjoy the amenities of their beautiful county.

Getting There and Around

By air: Cork and Shannon International Airports.

By bus: Expressway buses from Dublin and other big towns, and a good local bus service in County Cork, ✆ (021) 506066/ 508188 Cork City Depot. Day tours and airport buses from Parnell Place, ✆ (021) 503399. Local buses from Patrick Street.

By rail: Cork is linked to Dublin and other areas by an excellent rail network. Trains from Kent Station, including a suburban service to Cobh. For all passenger enquiries, bus or train, ✆ (021) 504888.

By boat: To Ringaskiddy Ferryport near Cork City, between the Continent and Swansea, ✆ (021) 378036. Car and passenger ferry at Ringaskiddy Airport, 3¾ miles (6km) from the city centre, on the road to Kinsale. ✆ (021) 371185.

By car: Car hire from Kevin O'Leary, Bandon, ✆ (023) 41264. Parking: disc system operates; tickets available from shops and post offices.

Taxis: Co-op, City Centre, Cork, ✆ (021) 272222; and ABC, ✆ (021) 961961.

By bike: Bikes are available for hire from the Cycle Repair Shop, 6 Kyle Street, Cork, ✆ (021) 276255, Cycle Sane, 396 Blarney Street, ✆ (021) 301183, and from the Youth Hostel (central booking office), ✆ (01) 725399. Raleigh Rent-a-Bike network operates here. Your local dealers are Kramer's Bicycles, Glengariff Road, Newtown, Bantry, ✆ (027) 50278. Roycroft Bikes, Ilen Street, Skibbereen, ✆ (028) 21235/21810. Shortcastle Cycles, Shortcastle Street, Mallow, ✆ (022) 21843. J. O'Donovan, 4/5 South Main Street, Bandon ✆ (023) 41227.

getting to the islands

Sherkin Island: Ferry from Baltimore sails seven times daily during the summer months and takes about 10 minutes, ✆ (028) 20125 for more details.

Cape Clear Island: During June, July and August, the island is serviced by two ferries: one from Schull and one from Baltimore. The Baltimore ferry runs at least twice daily, May to September, ✆ (028) 39119. The Schull ferry operates from June to September, ✆ (028) 28138.

Bear Island: Off Castletownbere in Bantry Bay. Two ferries offer a frequent service in the summer months. Contact Colm Harrington, ✆ (027) 75000; or Patrick Murphy, ✆ (027) 75004.

Shearwater Cruises, Seaview Farm, Kilbrittain, ✆ (023) 49610, offers cruises to offshore islands leaving from Kinsale.

Tourist Information

Cork, Tourist House, Grand Parade, ✆ (021) 273251, all year.

Cork Airport, ✆ (021) 964347, June to September.

Skibbereen, Town Hall, ✆ (028) 21766, all year.

Youghal, Market House, Market Place, ✆ (024) 92390, June to September.

Bantry, ✆ (027) 50229, June to September.

Kinsale, ✆ (021) 772234, March to November.

Clonakilty, ✆ (023) 33226, July and August.

Glengarriff, ✆ (027) 63084, July and August.

Cork City

End April/early May: Cork International Choral and Folk Dance Festival; contact ✆ (021) 308308, John Fitzpatrick.

May: Garden Festival, ✆ (021) 353119 for details.

June: Cork Dry Gin Round-Ireland Sailing Race, a biennial event held in even-numbered years, starting in Dublin. Contact the tourist office.

July: International Folk Dance Festival, Cobh. Contact Noel O'Driscoll, ✆ (021) 504233.

Mid-July: Cork Sailing Festival, held in even-numbered years. Based at Crosshaven, Royal Cork Yacht Club. Contact Donal Healy, ✆ (021) 831023.

August: Cobh Regatta, ✆ (021) 811237.

September/October: International film festival, ✆ (021) 271711, Anne O'Sullivan.

Late October: Cork Jazz Festival, ✆ (021) 270463.

Co. Cork

March: Ballydehob Races, ✆ (028) 37191.

May: Aquatic and Vintage Car Weekends in Kinsale, ✆ (021) 774026. Bantry Mussel Festival; ✆ (027) 50360.

June: Kinsale Arts Week, ✆ (021) 774026. Charlesville Cheese and Song Contest; ✆ (063) 81407.

July: Walter Raleigh Potato Festival, Youghal; ✆ (024) 92390. Festival of West Cork in Clonakilty, ✆ (028) 21766. Maid of the Isle Festival, Skibbereen, ✆ (028) 21200. Cahirmee Festival, Buttevant, ✆ (022) 23556. Kinsale Regatta, Castletownshend, ✆ (028) 36146. Mallow Folk Festival Contact N. Doolan ✆ (022) 22218.

August: Mallow Horse Races, ✆ (022) 21338; Schull and Baltimore Regattas ✆ (028) 20125. Timoleague Harvest Festival, ✆ (023) 46120.

August: All Ireland Busking Festival, Youghal.

September/October: Gourmet Festival, Kinsale, ✆ (021) 774026 (Peter Barry).

Cork City

The name Cork comes from the Gaelic *Corcaigh*, which means 'a marshy place'. Ireland's second city, with a population of 135,000, is built on marshy land on the banks of the River Lee, and has crept up the hills. The river flows in two main channels, crossed by bridges, so that central Cork is actually on an island. It is a bit confusing if you are driving there for the first time, with its one-way roads and the crossing and recrossing of the river.

Until the Anglo-Norman invasion in 1172, Cork City was largely a Danish stronghold, though it first became known in the 7th century as an excellent school under St Finbarr.

The Cork citizens were an independent lot and although after 1180 English laws were nominally in force, it was really the wealthy merchants who were in charge and decided things. In 1492 they took up the cause of Perkin Warbeck and went with him to Kent where he was proclaimed Pretender to the English crown—Richard IV, King of England and Lord of Ireland. They lost their charter for that piece of impudence, but Cork continued to be a rebel city. William III laid siege to it in 1690 because it stood by James II, and it had to surrender without honour. In the 17th and 18th centuries it grew rapidly with the expansion of the butter trade, and many of the splendid Georgian buildings you can still see were built during this time. In the 19th century it became a centre for the Fenian movement, which worked for an independent republic. During the War of Independence 1919–21, the city was badly burned by the Black and Tans and one of Cork's mayors died on hunger strike in an English prison. But Cork is also famous for a more moderate character, Father Theobald Matthew (1790–1856), who persuaded thousands of people to go off the drink, though the effect of his temperance drive was ruined by the potato famine and the general misery it brought.

Cork still has a reputation for clannish behaviour amongst its businessmen, and for independence in the arts and politics, but you would be hard put to it to find a friendlier city to wander around, and you can easily explore it on foot.

City Centre

Cork's business and shopping centre is crowded onto an island, with elegant bridges linking the north and south sides of the city. The first thing you will notice about the city is its skyline which is still 19th-century (*see* pp58–9). Cork has spires and gracious wide streets. St Patrick's Street curves close to the river; one side of the street is lined with old buildings, the other by uninspiring modern office and shop fronts built after the burning in 1920. Here you will find a statue of Father Matthew. The covered **English Market**, off Patrick Street, is fun to wander round; notice the fountain with birds and bulrushes cast in

CORK

1 Bus Office	12 St Ann's Church, Shandon	22 English Market
2 Christchurch	13 St Finbarr's Cathedral	23 The Granary Theatre
3 Church of St Francis	14 The Lough	24 St Mary's Pro Cathedral
4 Crawford School of Art	15 Tourists Office	25 South Chapel
5 Fitzgerald Park	16 University College	26 To Cork Airport
6 G.A.A. Athletic Grounds	17 University Sports Ground, Mardyke	27 To Car Ferry at Ringaskiddy and Crosshaven
7 Mardyke Walk	18 Coal Quay	28 Cork Gaol
8 Marina	19 SS Peter & Paul Church, off Patrick St.	
9 Opera House	20 Court House	
10 Railway Station	21 Father Mathew Memorial Church	
11 Red Abbey		

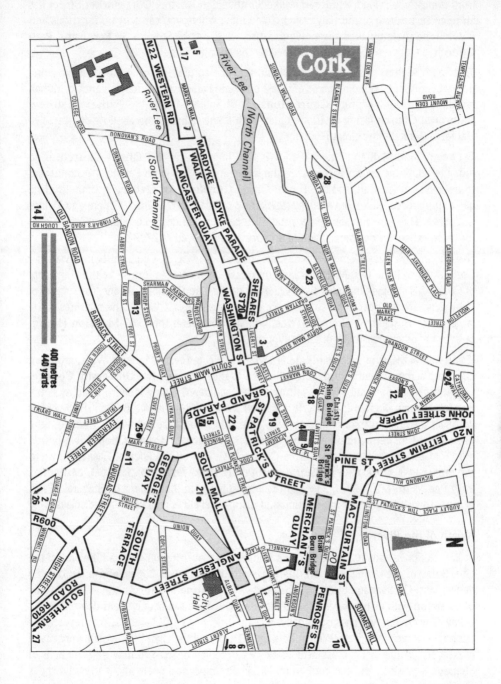

Cork

157

iron. It mostly sells food, and is rather like Smithfield in London. **Cornmarket Street** has an open-air flea market, usually called Coal Quay, where you can bargain for trifles and observe the sharp-tongued store owners. Also off St Patrick Street is **SS Peter and Paul Church**, a Gothic-style building designed by the younger Pugin.

The South Mall to the south of the island, and the adjoining Grand Parade have some pretty buildings. In Washington Street, east of Grand Parade, is the magnificent Corinthian façade of the 19th-century **Court House**. Off South Mall is the **Father Matthew Memorial Church** facing Charlotte Quay with a fine-stained glass window dedicated to Daniel O'Connell, 'the Great Liberator'.

Between South Mall and Grand Parade is the fine 18th-century **Christ Church**, used today to house the county archives. At the south end of the Grand Parade is a monument to Ireland's patriot dead, and the Tourist Office. **Crawford Art Gallery** in Emmett Place has a stunning collection of works by Irish artists such as Sean Keating, Orpen, and Walter Osbourne. There are also some very good 19th-century paintings. The Gallery Café is ideal for those exhausted by appreciation of art (*open daily; © (021) 273377*).

Nearby, in Park Street, are excellent craft shops to browse in. Opposite North Mall, on Cork Island still, the **Old Maltings** buildings have been adapted for use by the University of Cork. This complex includes a small theatre called **The Granary**. Swans, the symbol of Cork City, are fed near here, so there are often large flocks. Close to the maltings is the large Mercy Hospital, off Grenville Place, which incorporates the 1767 **Mansion House**, built as the official residence of the Mayor of Cork.

If you follow the river westwards along Dyke Parade and leafy Mardyke Walk, and then cut south across Western Road, you will come to the Oxbridge-style **University College**, which is grouped around a 19th-century Gothic square. The only modern building is the **Boole Library**, opened in 1985. It is named in honour of George Boole (1815–1864) who was the first professor of mathematics here, and who is credited with working out the principles of modern computer logic. The Roman Catholic **Honan Chapel** is a period piece of Celtic revivalism, copied from Cormac's Chapel on the Rock of Cashel. Close to the university is **Cork City Museum** (*open daily, Mon–Fri, 11–5, Sun 3–5, closed Sat; adm free, © (021) 270679*), a pleasant Georgian house in the gardens of Fitzgerald Park. It is worth visiting for local information and history and silver, glass and lace displays.

North of the River

St Patrick Street leads to the St Patrick's Bridge. Once over it, you enter a hilly part of the city. Some of the streets here are literally stairs up the steep slopes, and open only to pedestrians. Off Shandon Street, the bell-tower of **St Anne's Church**, the lovely **Tower of Shandon** with its two faces in white limestone and red sandstone, looks down into the valley. The church, which is open daily, was built between 1722 and 1726 to replace the church destroyed during the Williamite siege. The peal of the eight bells which were made in Gloucestershire in 1750 are dear to every Corkonian heart. You may ring the bells of Shandon for a small fee, and conjure up Father Prout's lyrical poem about the wild spells that they wove for him a hundred years ago:

'Tis the bells of Shandon
That sounds so grand on
The pleasant waters of the River Lee.

Skiddy's Almshouse, founded in 1584, stands in the churchyard. In about 1620, the Vintners Company of London settled a perpetual annuity of £24 for the benefit of 12 widows of Cork. Down by the river is North Mall, which has some fine 18th-century doorways. The 18th-century **Butter Market** used to be in this area, as was the slaughterhouse for vast numbers of cattle, which were then salted and used as provisions for the British Navy and many European ships before they made the long voyage to America. The **Old Butter Exchange** is now a centre for craft studios. The **Dominican Church of St Mary** by the River Lee was completed in 1839 and has a magnificent classical façade. It is in a very prominent position, which immediately dates it as post-Catholic Emancipation: Catholic churches built before that time were built away from the main centre of towns and cities. Further north is St Mary's Pro-Cathedral, begun in 1808, which has a fine tower. The Neo-Gothic **Cork City Gaol** on Sunday's Well Road (*open daily 9.30am–8pm © (021) 542478*) has been restored as a museum which depicts the life of a 19th-century prisoner and the social history of the period.

South of the River

South of the river, between Bishop and Dean Streets, is **St Finbarr's Cathedral**, which was built in the 19th century by wealthy Church of Ireland merchants on the site of the ancient church founded by Saint Finbarr. If you don't have time for much sight-seeing this building and the **Art Gallery** are musts. The cathedral's great spires dominate the city, and it has a beautiful west front, with three recessed doors, elaborate carving and a beautiful rose window. The building itself is in the Gothic style of 13th-century France and was built between 1867 and 1879 by a convinced medievalist and English architect, William Burges. His eye for detail was meticulous as well as humorous, and the whole effect is vigorous—a defiant gesture to Catholic Ireland. Also on the South Side, off Douglas Street, is the grey limestone tower of **Red Abbey**, a remnant of a 14th-century Augustinian friary. Close by, on Mary Street, is **South Chapel**, built in 1766 on an inconspicuous site. At this time, the penal laws may have relaxed, but a show of Catholicism was discouraged and disliked by the ruling classes.

The Suburbs

The **Church of Christ the King** on Evergreen Road, to the south at Turner's Cross, was designed by an American architect, Barry Bryne, in the 1930s. The carved figure of Christ crucified with his arms spread above the twin entrance doors is very striking.

Riverside House at Glanmire, 3¾ miles (6km) from the city on the Cork–Dublin road (*open May–Aug, Thurs–Sat, 2–6; at other times by appointment; adm; © (021) 821205/ 821722*), was built in 1602, and has exquisite plasterwork by the Francini brothers. The brothers were Swiss-Italian stuccodores, who came to Ireland in 1734 and adorned the ceiling of the dining-room with allegorical figures representing Time rescuing Truth from the assaults of Discord and Envy. Dr Browne, the Archbishop of Cork, was responsible for remodelling the original house in the 1730s and it remained in his family until the early part of this century. It has been restored by its present owners, Mr and Mrs Dooley, with the help of the Georgian Society.

Dunkathel House, also in Glanmire (*open May–mid-Oct, Wed–Sun, 2–6; © (021) 821014; adm*) is a fine Georgian house, worth visiting not only to see the antiques, but also to buy some. Afternoon tea here is very pleasant too. The house was built by a wealthy Cork merchant in 1790, and has a wonderful bifurcated (forked) staircase of Bath stone. There is a rare 1880s barrel organ which is still played for visitors. Gifts as well as antiques are for sale.

Twenty minutes' walk from the city centre via Barrack Street and Bandon Road is the **Lough**, a freshwater lake with feral geese. **Douglas Estuary**, via Tivoli (15 minutes from the centre by car), has hundreds of black-tailed godwit, shelduck and golden plover.

Cork City Environs

Approximately 5 miles (8km) southwest of Cork city on the N22 is **Ballincollig**, where you can visit the 19th-century **Royal Gunpowder Mills** on the River Lee (*open April–Sept; © (021) 874430*). This factory produced huge quantities for the British army. The restored visitor centre details the history of the mills; it also has an exhibition gallery, craft shop and café.

Blarney is 5 miles (8km) northwest of the city on the R617. This small village has a fame out of all proportion to its size because it is the home of the Blarney Stone. Legend tells that whoever kisses it will get the the 'gift of the gab'. This magic stone is high up in all that is left of **Blarney Castle**—its ruined keep (*open all year, Mon–Sat, 9–5 in spring; 9–6.30 in summer; and 9–sundown in winter; © (021) 85252; adm*). It is a magnet which attracts almost every visitor to Ireland, so expect to find the place crowded and full of knick-knacks. In the days of Queen Elizabeth I the castle was held by Dermot MacCarthy, who had the gift of plamas, the Irish word for soft, flattering or insincere speech. Elizabeth had asked him to surrender his castle, but he continued to play her along with fair words and no action. In the end the frustrated Queen is supposed to have said, 'It's all Blarney—he says he will do it but never means it at all.' The MacCarthys forfeited their castle in the Williamite wars of 1690, and it was later acquired by the St John Jefferyes family. The stone is probably a 19th-century invention, and today you can even buy yourself a certificate which guarantees you have kissed it. Try showing that to your prospective employer! The castle is well worth seeing for its own sake, as it has one of the largest and finest tower houses in Ireland, built in 1446 by the MacCarthy clan. The landscaped gardens surrounding it are also superb. You can also visit **Blarney Castle House and Gardens** (*open Mon–Sat, June–mid-Sept, 12–6; adm; © (021) 385252*), a Scottish baronial mansion with a charming garden.

Cobh (pronounced *Cove*) is 15 miles (24km) southeast of Cork city on the R624 off the N25. It is the great harbour of Cork and handles huge ships. There is an International

Dance Festival here in July; it is a rather nice place to stay, near to the city but without its bustle. The town is almost entirely 19th-century and is dominated by the Gothic **St Colman's Cathedral**, the work of Pugin and Ashlin (*open daily 10–6; adm; © (021) 811562*). Between 1848 and 1950 two and a half million people emigrated to America from here with many a sad scene enacted by the quay. The history of the port with its strategic position in the North Atlantic, the sinking of the liner *Lusitania* by a German submarine in 1915, and the story of the emigrants is recorded at the **Cobh Heritage Centre** (*open daily 10–6; © (021) 813591*) in the converted Victorian railway station. The Royal Yacht Club, near the railway station, was founded in 1720, and is the oldest such club in the world. It has a very good regatta in the summer and visiting yachtsmen and women are welcome and can use all the facilities of the club including the modern marina. The views from the hill above Cobh facing south onto the land-locked harbour, islands and woods are superb. If you want a stroll, make for the old **churchyard of Clonmel**, a peaceful place where many of the dead from the Lusitania are buried.

Fota House and Estate (*open April–Sept, weekdays 10–5; Sun 11–5; rest of the year, Sundays and public holidays only; © (021) 812678; adm*) over the Belvelly Bridge is on a magical little island in the River Lee Estuary (*see* p.58). The arboretum surrounding the house is luxurious and mature, with a collection of semi-tropical and rare shrubs. The house, which is mainly Regency in style, was built as a hunting lodge, and has a splendid neoclassical hallway. Sadly, at the time of writing the house is closed to the public due to deterioration of its structure. The University of Cork has sold a large portion of the island to a British development company who have already made a golf course and plan to build an hotel and holiday houses here. The house, arboretum and seventy acres of parkland were withdrawn from the development after a public outcry. The fine collection of Irish landscape paintings have been transferred to Limerick University Museum. The future of Fota Island is uncertain, so see it whilst you have a chance. There is also a bee garden and a wildlife park.

Kinsale to Youghal

Kinsale (*Cionn Saile*: tide head) is 18 miles (29km) southwest of Cork City on the R600. Its fame was established years ago as a quaint seaside town with delicious restaurants and carefully preserved 18th-century buildings; its popularity only seems to increase. It used to be an important naval port. In 1601 the Irish joined forces with Spain against the English, and the Spanish fleet anchored here before the disastrous battle of Kinsale, which led to the 'Flight of the Earls' and put an end to the rebellion against Elizabeth I and her reconquest of Ireland.

This is the perfect place for a relaxed holiday. **Multose Church** is the oldest building in town, parts of it dating from the 13th century. Inside are the old town stocks. The churchyard has several interesting 16th-century gravestones which in spring are covered in whitebells and bluebells, and in summer red valerian grows out of crevasses in every wall. There is an interesting museum in the old courthouse, with material associated with the life of the town and port through the centuries, © (021) 77220.

To the south, on the R604, near **Ballinspittle**, is a ring-fort at about AD 600. There are some superb sandy beaches at the resort of **Garrettstown**, a little further south on the R604, and splendid cliff scenery at the **Old Head of Kinsale** at the end of the road. Round the Old Head of Kinsale, just 7 miles outside the attractive village of Summercove, the remains of a 15th-century **De Courcy castle** overlook the blue and white-flecked sea. **Charles Fort** in Summercove (*open mid-June–early Oct, daily, 10–5; mid-April–mid-June, Tues–Sat, 9–4.30, Sun, 11–5.30; rest of the year, Mon–Fri, 10–4; adm; © (021) 772263*) was built in the 1600s (in the time of Charles II), as a military strong point. It is shaped like a star and you can wander round its rather damp nooks and crannies. The 18th/19th-century houses inside were used as barracks.

Crosshaven, 13 miles (21km) east of Cork city, on the Cork Harbour Estuary, is the play-ground of the busy Cork businessmen and their families. There are lovely beaches at **Myrtleville** and **Robert's Cove**, and a crescent-shaped bay filled with yachts and boats of every description. Approximately 11 miles from Cork City going east on the N25 is the attractive town of **Midleton**, which has benefited from the restoration of the 18th-century whiskey distillery. It is a fine building, self-contained within 11 acres, and you can take a tour around all the major parts—mills, maltings, corn stores, stillhouses and kilns. The waterwheel is still in perfect order, and you can see the largest pot still in the world with a capacity to hold more than 30,000 gallons. It stopped as a working distillery in 1975, and there is a mass of information charting the history of Irish whiskey. The **Jameson Heritage Centre** is off Distillery Road (*open March–Oct; © (021) 682821 for more details*). Southwest of Midleton is the fine **Barryscourt Castle** (*open to the public daily*), a quadrangular keep with square towers surrounded by a lawn; it overlooks the inner reaches of Cork harbour. The fast main road (N25) to Midleton and Youghal means that many people do not explore the peninsula opposite Crosshaven. Turn off at Midleton and follow the R629 to **Cloyne**, if you wish to visit its vast and ancient cathedral. This dates from the 13th century, and the round tower beside it is one of the only two surviving round towers of the county. You are allowed to climb this one to the top and the view is superb. Amongst the monuments in the cathedral is an alabaster tomb to George Berkeley, the philosopher who was bishop here from 1734 to 1753.

The R629 from Cloyne leads down to **Ballycotton**, a little fishing village set in a peaceful unspoilt bay. There is a pretty view out to Ballycotton Islands, which protect the village from the worst of the sea winds, and a fine bird sanctuary on the extensive marsh by the estuary. Close by is the welcoming and attractive **Ballymaloe House**, which is now a lovely hotel, famous for its restaurant, cooking school and craft shop. At Ladysbridge near Garryroe is a fine fortified house built of the local limestone, called **Ightermurragh Castle**. Over one of the fireplaces in Latin is an inscription which tells that it was built by Edmund Supple and his wife, 'Whome love binds in one', in 1641. Two miles (3.2km) to the southeast in Kilcredan's 17th-century Church of Ireland church are some fascinating limestone headstones with a variety of imaginative motifs. Sadly, the church has suffered the fate of many of that faith and is without a roof, and the carved tomb of Sir Robert Tynte has been ravaged by the weather. Just to the south is **Shanagarry**, famous for its pottery, and the old home of William Penn, the founder of Pennsylvania. You can buy the simple earthenware and glazed pottery there or at the **Ballymaloe House** craft shop.

Youghal (pronounced 'Yawl', from *eochaill*: a yew wood), is one of the most attractive seaside towns in Ireland, approximately 30 miles (48km) east of Cork City on the N25. If you can, try to arrange your trip so that you approach it from the lovely **Blackwater Valley**, which has some outstanding driving and walking country—if you like wooded banks, green fields, old buildings and twisting, unfrequented roads. Youghal was founded by the Anglo-Normans in the 13th century and was destroyed in the Desmond Rebellion of 1579. The Fitzgeralds, earls of Desmond, were a powerful Anglo-Norman family who joined forces with the Gaelic lords from Ulster to try and repel the armies of Elizabeth I. The town was handed over to Sir Walter Raleigh in the Elizabethan plantation period, when he became mayor of the town and lived in a gabled house called **Myrtle Grove** at the end of William Street (guided tours possible). Raleigh is said to have planted the first potato in the garden, an act which was to have far reaching consequences for the whole of Ireland's population. The town holds a potato festival each year to celebrate the arrival of the new spuds.

In the same street is the 15th-century Church of Ireland collegiate **Church of St Mary**. The inside of this large cruciform church is crowded with interesting monuments, including one to the Earl of Cork, Richard Boyle, looking very smug, surrounded by his mother, his two wives, and nine of his 16 sons. A memorial stands to the extraordinary lady, the Countess of Desmond, who died in 1604 at the age of 147 after falling out of a tree when gathering cherries. The church was founded by Thomas, the 8th Earl of Desmond, and restored in 1884, after being derelict for years. The most notable features are its Early-English west doorway, the massive pulpit, with its canopy of carved bog oak, and the large six-light east window (*c.* 1468) of stained glass with arms of the Desmonds, Sir Walter Raleigh, the Earl of Cork and the Duke of Devonshire.

The old part of town lies at the foot of a steep hill, whilst the new part has grown along the margin of the bay. The main street is spanned by a clock, weather vane and lantern known as the **Clock Gate** and erected in 1771. It houses the tourist office, art gallery and museum. Further down the street is the ruined **Tynte's Castle**, which was built in the 15th century. Portions of the old walls which once bounded the town still stand, but even in 1579 they were in a bad state, and were easily breached by the rebellious Earl of Desmond.

Fermoy to Mallow

Fermoy (*Mainistir Fhearmuighe*: the abbey of the plantations), 30 miles (48km) north of Cork City on the N8, used to be a garrison town for the British army and is built along both sides of the darkly flowing River Blackwater. People hereabouts are familiar with every fascinating detail of catching salmon. The town has an air of shabby gentility, for it has seen more prosperous days. Lord Fermoy, an ancestor of the Princess of Wales, is said to have gambled away his Fermoy estates in an evening. The Protestant church built in 1802 contains some grotesque masks. A few miles to the northwest, beside the old Glanworth road, is a megalithic tomb. It is a gallery grave and the huge capstone rests on an upright slab; inside are two chambers divided by a flat slab. It may have been a Queen's grave and is known as 'Labbacallee' which translates as the Hag's Bed.

Just outside Fermoy, overlooking the river to the west, is the beautiful, late-Georgian mansion, **Castle Hyde**. This was the home of Douglas Hyde, the first President of the Irish Republic and the founder of the Gaelic League. Sadly, it is not open to the public. **Castlelyons**, a few miles outside the town (turn left off the N8 going towards Cork), is a quiet and pretty hamlet where intimations of past history compel you to stop. Here is the ruin of the great house of the Barrys, a Norman family, and the remains of a 14th-century Carmelite friary.

To the north, **Mitchelstown** is famous for butter and cheese, an industry which employs a lot of people, although the cheese is rather boring—cheddar and a soft bland spread. It is also famous for its **caves**, a further 10 miles (16km) to the north on the Cahir road (N8) (*open daily throughout the year, 10–6; adm; ✆ (052) 67246*). The countryside around becomes richer as you travel west and enter the Golden Vein, a fertile plain which extends north of the Galtee Mountains. At Kildorrey, turn right off the N73 onto the R512 to go to Doneraile. Near here was the home of the novelist Elizabeth Bowen (1899–1973), whose works so beautifully describe the shades and subtleties of the Anglo-Irish. Her house, '**Bowens Court**', a beautiful 18th-century mansion, was demolished recently—a victim of the government's lack of interest in historic buildings.

Doneraile and Buttevant are in Edmund Spenser country, 40 miles (64km) north of Cork City, between the Blackwater and the Ballyhoura Mountains. Here he is said to have written *The Faerie Queene*, inspired by the sylvan beauty of the countryside, and so flattering Elizabeth I that she granted him lands. Tragically, Spenser's home, **Kilcolman Castle**, was burned and he and his wife had to flee, leaving their baby daughter to perish in the flames. **Kilcolman** is now a sombre ruin, in a field beside a reedy pool northeast of

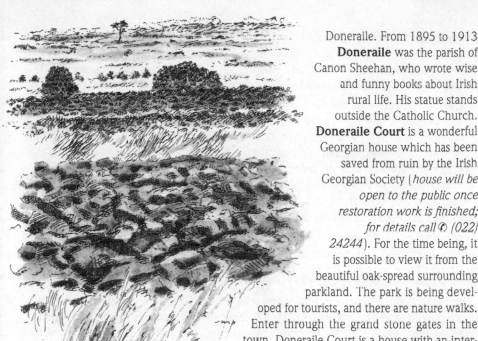

Doneraile. From 1895 to 1913 **Doneraile** was the parish of Canon Sheehan, who wrote wise and funny books about Irish rural life. His statue stands outside the Catholic Church. **Doneraile Court** is a wonderful Georgian house which has been saved from ruin by the Irish Georgian Society (*house will be open to the public once restoration work is finished; for details call ☏ (022) 24244*). For the time being, it is possible to view it from the beautiful oak-spread surrounding parkland. The park is being developed for tourists, and there are nature walks. Enter through the grand stone gates in the town. Doneraile Court is a house with an interesting story behind it: here Elizabeth Barry, wife of the first Viscount Doneraile, hid in a clock case to observe a masonic lodge meeting held in the house. Perhaps she laughed, but whatever happened she gave herself away, and all the masons could do was to elect her as a mason—the only woman mason in history. Nearby is the unique alkaline **Kilcolman Bog**. The home of many birds, you can arrange to visit it if you are involved in bird study. Contact the tourist office for details.

At **Buttevant** during July is the **Cahirmee Horse Fair**, which has been held for hundreds of years and is always good crack, with lots of other events happening at the same time. It is also worth looking at the ruined **Franciscan friary** which has ornate carved tomb recesses and a collection of carved stone built into the wall.

Mallow, 10 miles (16km) south, used to be a famous spa where the gentry of Ireland came to take the waters and have a good time. In the 18th century the spa inspired the anonymous verse which begins:

> *Beauing, belling, dancing, drinking,*
> *Breaking windows, damning, singing,*
> *Ever raking, never thinking,*
> *Live the rakes of Mallow...*

The old spa house is now a private house and the once-famous water gushes to waste. The town has pretty 18th-century houses, a timbered decorated **Clock House** and **Mallow Castle**, which is a still-impressive, roofless ruin of a fortified 16th-century tower house.

The **Mallow Races**, which happen intermittently throughout the spring, summer and autumn, is the only time the place really comes alive, though it is frequented by anglers and the **Folk Festival** in July is very cheerful. Just outside the town is **Longueville House** which produces delicious wine, and where you can eat and stay in great style.

At **Castletownroche** on the N72, 10 miles (16km) east of Mallow, notice the pretty Church of Ireland church on a rise above the river. To the north of it is **Annes Grove** (*open Easter–end Sept, Mon–Sat, 10–5; Sun 1–6; adm; © (022) 26145*) with its tranquil woodlands and walled garden. The sloping grounds surrounding the beautiful 18th-century house are planted in the style made popular by William Robertson in the late 19th century. Nothing is contrived and the massed plants lead up winding paths to the river and gardens. Rhododendrons, magnolias, eucryphias, abutilons and primulas obviously love it here, so vigorously have they grown.

Now head west to **Killarney**, from Cork or Mallow, via Macroom. From Mallow, the country lanes which take you through the **Boggeragh Mountains** are a maze, and rather fun if you have time to get lost for a while. They have a wild mystery, heightened by the green glow from the overgrown hedges which form an arbour overhead. Twenty miles (32km) further on, you arrive at **Macroom**, where J. P. Quilan's Pub is a welcome retreat for a drink or snack. The woodwork of the bar is superb and there is always a warm fire to welcome you. Macroom (*Maigh Chromtha*: sloping plain) is on the direct route to Killarney (N22), and is a favourite place for tourists and music enthusiasts. This is a gorgeous part of the southwest: scenes are lush with green pasture and bright-flowered with fuchsia and heather. The R618, west from Cork City, follows the lovely River Lee through **Dripsey** and **Coachford**. Dripsey woollen mills produce an excellent wool.

If you are heading for Killarney, plan your journey to include the **Pass of Keamaneigh** 5 miles (8km) west of Ballingeary on the R584 to Bantry. Here is a very beautiful forest park—**Gougane Barra**, 'the rock-cleft of Finbarr', a dramatic glacial valley with a shining lake in its hollow, into which run silvery streams. This is the source of the River Lee. In the lake is a small island, approached by a causeway, where St Finbarr set up his oratory in the 6th century. At the entrance to the causeway is **St Finbarr's Well** and an ancient cemetery. The island has a few 18th-century remains, some Stations of the Cross, and a tiny modern Irish Romanesque chapel which is often used for weddings. A popular pattern (pilgrimage) is made here every year on the Sunday nearest to the feast day of St Finbarr (25 September). After the Pass of Keamaneigh, strewn with massive boulders, you come into the colourful valley of the Owvane with a view of Bantry Bay. At **Kealkill**, 5 miles (8km) before Bantry, there is an ancient stone circle, reached by an exciting hilly road just off the R584.

Before describing Bantry, here is a brief description of the very attractive south Cork coast, starting off from the market town of **Bandon**, 20 miles (32km) southwest of Cork City on the N71. Bandon was founded by Richard Boyle, the Earl of Cork, in 1608. Over the gate of the then-walled town it is said that there were once the words, 'Turk, Jew or atheist may enter here, but not a papist.' A Catholic wit responded, 'He who wrote this wrote it well, the same is written on the gates of hell.' The River Bandon and its tributaries make for good fishing and walking, and, if you want to explore, **Kilbrittain**, **Timoleague** and **Courtmacsherry Bay** are unspoilt. Courtmacsherry is a sea-angling centre. **Timoleague** is dominated by the ruins of a **Franciscan abbey** founded in 1312. It has a fairly complete cloister and an outer yard, and is always accessible to the public. On the banks of the Argideen River are the varied and lush **Timoleague Castle Gardens** (*open daily from mid-May–mid-Sept, 11–5.30; adm; © (023) 46116 or (021) 831512*), with many rare and tender plants. To open shortly at **Clonakilty** is a model village depicting life in Ireland 40 years ago; it is typical of the theme approach to tourism that is becoming so common. Contact the Town Hall, Clonakilty for details. But it is still possible to experience the real thing and in this part of the country you find the typical Irish bar-cum-grocery shop, with old-fashioned lettering displaying the proud name of the owner.

A little further west, **Rosscarbery** is a charming old-fashioned village. It had a famous school of learning founded by St Fachtna in the 6th century, and a medieval Benedictine monastery. The very attractive 17th-century Church of Ireland church is on the old cathedral site. Inland to the west, in the valley of the little River Roury stands the ruin of Coppinger's Court, a ruined Elizabethan or Jacobean mansion, burnt out in 1641, which gives shelter to cows in winter. It stands to the left, off an unclassified road between Leap and Rosscarbery. From Roury Bridge, a country road (R507) winds to **Dromberg Stone Circle**, from where you can see across pastures and cornfields to the sea. It is dated between the 2nd century BC and 2nd century AD. A cremated body was discovered in the centre of the circle when it was excavated. The beaches of **Owenahincha** and, to the east, the **Longstrand** have wonderful sand. **Union Hall** and **Glandore** are two pretty resort villages on a narrow inlet 5 miles (8km) west of Rosscarbery, whose harbours are filled with highly painted boats.

Round the next headland, **Castletownshend** is a neat Georgian village on a steep hill, in the middle of which grows a huge tree. The village used to be the home of Edith Somerville (1858–1949), co-author of the humorous *Reminiscences of an Irish RM*. She is buried in the pretty Church of Ireland graveyard here, with cousin and co-author Violet Martin (1862–1915), who wrote under the pen name 'Martin Ross'.

Skibbereen, linked to Castletownshend by the R596, is a market town famous for its own weekly newspaper the *Southern Star*, previously called the *Skibbereen Eagle*. It is good for a read and sheds a lot of light on local preoccupations. In the ruins of the **Cistercian abbey** a mile west of Skibbereen on the Schull road, many hundreds of famine victims are buried. They were tipped into huge pits which were quickly covered over as disease killed more rapidly than hunger. Between Skibbereen and Drimoleague off the

R593, is an exciting and thoughtful enterprise still in the process of creation. The **Liss Ard Sky Gardens** (*open by appointment only* © *(028) 22368*) is a combination of artistic spaces and wildlife gardens extending for forty acres. Three and a half miles (5.6km) south of Skibbereen on the Baltimore Road are **Creagh Gardens** (*open all year, daily, 10–6; adm;* © *(028) 22121*), a romantic and informal garden planted amongst woods which lead to the river estuary. Best seen between April and June. All round Skibbereen and particularly to the west is some lovely country where knuckles and fingers of land reach into the sea, breaking off into islands like **Sherkin** and **Clear**. It is possible to get a boat from Baltimore (R595) to the islands. Negotiate with the local fishermen or take the regular ferry boat. St Kieran was born on Cape Clear, and the remains of a cross and holy well mark the site of his church. There is an important bird observatory here, as the island is on a major bird migration route; and also a youth hostel. The familiar Fastnet Rock mentioned in shipping forecasts is just off Cape Clear. This region used to be an O'Driscoll stronghold (the local Gaelic sept or tribe) until it was sacked by Algerian pirates in 1631, and the Irish people captured and sold as slaves along the Barbary coast. Near to Baltimore is the beautiful **Lough Ine**, just the place for a walk or picnic. It is connected to the ocean by a narrow channel and is very deep—down to twenty-five fathoms in places. The water is wonderfully clear, and the fauna and flora of great interest to divers.

Ballydehob to Mizen Head

Ballydehob is a colourful little village 10 miles (16km) away from Skibbereen on the N71, with a fine 12-arch railway bridge which lies at the head of Roaring Water Bay. About 2 miles (3.2km) south at **Rossbrin**, the ruin of an O'Mahony castle stands by the sea, the home of the 14th-century scholar Finin. A spectacular road runs from Schull, a few miles further west, up to **Mount Gabriel** (945ft/288m). If you decide to climb it, be careful of the prehistoric coppermines dug into the slopes. The view is out of this world. The R591 curls round the head of lovely **Toormore Bay**, past **Goleen** with its sandy beach (the Gulf Stream means that swimming is quite possible here), to Crookhaven with its boat-filled harbour. **Barleycove** is a sandy beach along which you can stretch your legs before you get to the splendid, sheer heights of **Mizen Head**. The soft, red sandstone cliffs banded with white fall down to the sea whilst flurries of birds glide on the air currents beneath you. The cliffs are high and nearly vertical, so be careful! A lighthouse on the islet below is linked to the mainland by a suspension bridge. Many ships have been wrecked here in the past. From the Mizen Head, the R591 goes to Durras at the head of Dunmanus Bay. The drive to Kilcrohane and Sheeps Head and then on to Gerahies is magnificent and very untouristy. The views spread across Bantry Bay and the Beara Peninsula.

Bantry has one of the finest views in the world. What you must not miss is **Bantry House** (*open daily all year except Christmas Day, 9–6; open until 8 on most summer evenings; adm; tearoom and craftshop; also B&B accommodation—see 'Where to Stay', below;* © *(027) 50047*) which has a glorious view and is directly above the town so you do not see the ugly petrol stations below it. You can go round the house on your own (accompanied only by the faint strains of classical music), with a detailed guide written by the owner which you then hand back when you have finished. Rare French tapestries, family portraits and china still have a feeling of being used and loved. The house and garden have definitely seen better days, yet this is one of the most interesting houses in Ireland, and certainly one of the least officious that is open to the public. The house was built in 1740, and added to in 1765. The owner, Mr Egerton Shelswell-White, is at present embarking on restoration work. He is an enthusiastic patron of music, and there are many fine concerts held in the library. The dining room is a stunning shade of bottle blue against which the gold-framed portraits, the china and silver look magnificent. Two of the portraits are of King George II and Queen Charlotte. They were painted at the sovereign's order and given to the first Earl of Bantry, from whom Mr Shelswell-White is descended, as a token of thanks for his efforts in helping repel the French invasion force of 1798. In the side courtyard of the house is an exhibition devoted to the 1798 Bantry Bay Armada. There is a 1:6 scale model of a frigate in cross-section and extracts from Wolfe Tone's Journal. Just outside the town on Glengarriff Road are the **Donemark Falls**, a pretty waterfall on an island. The owner of this land has made it into a rather eccentric garden, a mixture of natural and artificial charm with gnomes. The N71 takes you swiftly towards Glengarriff.

Glengarriff's humpy hills and wooded inlets look over limpid water and isles. (Mulroy Bay in Donegal is similar.) **Inacullin**, alias Garinish Island (*open May–Oct, daily 10–5; adm; © (027) 63040*), used to be covered only in rocks, heather and gorse until it was made into 37 acres of garden by a Scotsman, John Allen Bryce, in 1910. Now it is a dream island full of sub-tropical plants, with a formal Italian garden, rock gardens and a marble pool full of goldfish. It is an exceptional place, full of structure and outstanding plants, well worth the IR£4 plus return boat fares to the island. Bernard Shaw often stayed here. There are many boatmen willing to take you out to the island; in fact, they fight for your trade. You might walk in **Glengarriff Valley**, 'the bitter glen', and up to the hills hidden in the Caha Range, or drive up the Healy Pass Road, with its lovely mountain scenery gazing down on the indented sealine and the green woods. It is quite a testing zig-zag drive following the R574 road to Lauragh in County Kerry.

Shopping

Cork City and Environs

Antiques: Dunkathel, Glanmire, © (021) 821014. McCurtain Street, Cork (north side), has a variety of antiques and bric-a-brac. Also the flea market, Cornmarket Street.

Clothes: stylish linen and tweed for men and women from the House of Donegal, Paul Street.

Musical instruments: *uillean* pipes from A. Kennedy, St Johns, Clifton Road, Montenotte Park, Cork, © (021) 503762. Bodhrams (drums) from Crowleys Music Centre, 29 MacCurtain Street, © (021) 503426. Harps from L. Egar, Ardmuire, Herbert Park, Gardiner's Hill, Cork, © (021) 504832. Fiddles from Martin Faherty in the Shandon craft centre.

Crafts: a wide selection, of top-quality, from the Stephen Pearse Shop, Paul Street, and IDA Craft Centre, The Butter Exchange, Shandon.

Woollen goods: Blarney Woollen Mills. Blarney Castle Knitwear, Blarney.

Glass: Cork Crystal Glass Company, Blarney.

Hand-woven tweed: Rosemary Kelleher, 15 The Skiddys, Shandon, Cork, ✆ (021) 501283.

Contemporary art: Cork Art Society, Lavitt's Quay, ✆ (021) 277749.

Jewellery: Stephen O'Shaughnessy, 22 Patrick Street, Cork, ✆ (021) 270011.

Chain stores: (including A-Wear and Marks & Spencer) St Patrick Street and Merchant's Quay Pedestrian Centre.

Books: The Mercier Press, French Church Street, produces a wealth of books of Irish interest, and novels by Irish authors.

Food and flowers: The English Market, between Patrick Street, Grand Parade and Oliver Plunkett Street. Natural Foods, 26 Paul Street, for delicious bread and buns.

If you need a quiet drink after shopping, make for the traditional, old-fashioned bar called the Vineyard in Market Place, off St Patrick Street.

Co. Cork

Crafts: Ballymaloe Craft Shop, Shanagarry, Midleton, ✆ (021) 652531. Bantry House Craftshop, Bantry.

Handmade baskets: Morbert Platz, Ballymurphy, Innishannon, ✆ (021) 885548.

Handmade kitchen knives: Ballylickey, Bantry, ✆ (027) 50032. Ballymaloe Kitchen shop, Shanagarry ✆ (021) 652032.

Pottery: Macroom. Rossmore Country Pottery, Rossmore, Clonakilty, ✆ (023) 38875. Ian Wright, Corsits Pottery, Kilnaclasha, Skibbereen, ✆ (028) 21889. R. and J. Forrester, Bandon Studios, North Main Street, Bandon, ✆ (023) 41360. P. & F. Wolstenholme, Courtmacsherry Ceramics, Courtmacsherry, ✆ (023) 46239. Kinsale Pottery, Jagoes Mill, Kinsale, ✆ (021) 72771. Leda May Studios, Main Street, Ballydehob; ✆ (028) 37221. Stephen Pearce Pottery, Shanagarry, ✆ (021) 646807; West Cork Arts Centre, North Street, Skibbereen, ✆ (028) 22090.

Furniture: O'Donnell Design, Baltimore Road, Skibbereen.

Gift shop: Bantry House.

Leprechauns: Elizabeth Mans, Gort na Reagh, Kilcrohan, Bantry, ✆ (027) 67017.

Flutes: Colin Hamilton, Coolea, Macroom.

Smoked goods: Harbour Smoke House, Ballydevlin, Gooleen, Schull. Ummera Smoked Products, Ummera House, Timoleague, Bandon, ✆ (023) 46187. Phone first to buy their delicious smoked-salmon sausage.

Cheese: Gubbeen Cheeses, Gubbeen House, Schull, ℰ (028) 28231. Wonderful soft cheese, visitors welcome at the farm. Milleens Cheese, Eyeries, Beara Peninsula, ℰ (027) 74079. Delicious soft cheese. Telephone first. Cleire Goat's Cheese, and goat's milk ice-cream, summer only, Cape Clear, Skibbereen, ℰ (028) 39126. Garlic and plain semi-soft cheese. Ardrahan Cheese, Ardrahan House, Kanturk, ℰ (029) 78099. Gouda-type cheese. Coolea Cheese, Coolea, ℰ (026) 45204, strong flavoured semi-soft cheese; Ardsallagh goat's cheese and milk, Ardsallagh, Youghal, ℰ (021) 92545. Also comes bottled with olive oil.

Delicacies: Mannings Emporium, Ballylickey, ℰ (027) 50456. Local cheeses and whiskey cake. Fields, 26 Main Street, Skibbereen, ℰ (028) 21400. Good locally made herb sausages, cheese, country butter. Essential Foods, Bantry, ℰ (027) 61171. Local organic vegetables; Hudson's Wholefoods, Main Street, Ballydehob, ℰ (028) 37211, for assorted seaweeds, local cheese and delicious ice cream; Twomey's Butchers, 16 Pearse Street, Clonakilty, ℰ (023) 33365. Famous Clonakilty Black Pudding.

Market: Carrigaline Country Market held at the GAA Hall, Crosshaven Road, Carrigaline. Market every Friday, 10–11. Good vegetables, home baking and gorgeous flowers.

Fish: Castletownbere Fishermen's Co-op, The Pier, Castletownbere, ℰ (027) 70045. Fresh fish every day except Sunday. Fresh fish also available from The Pier, Ballycotton Bay, E. Cork, usually about 2 every day. If you miss it there's a good fish shop on the main street, ℰ (021) 613122.

Shrubs and Plants: Carewswood Garden Centre, Castlemartyr. Excellent variety of plants.

Activities

Salmon fishing: Carysville Fishery, Carysville House, Fermoy, ℰ (025) 31094/31712, book in advance. Derek Good, Inishannon, ℰ (021) 775133. Fishing tackle and local knowledge from I. O'Sullivan, 4 Patrick Street, Fermoy, ℰ (025) 31110; Vickery & Co, Main Street, Bantry; The Tackle Shop, 6 Lavitts Quay, Cork City; Trident Angling Centre, Kinsale, ℰ (021) 772301.

Deep-sea fishing: Boat hire from Peter Manning, Ballycotton Angling Centre, ℰ (021) 646773. International Sailing Centre, East Beach, Cobh, ℰ (021) 841348. Charles Robertson, Roycestown, Carrigaline, Crosshaven, ℰ (021) 372896. Marc Gannon, Woodpoint, Courtmacsherry, Bandon, ℰ (023) 46427. Carberry Charters Ltd, Ballinatoma, Union Hall, ℰ (028) 33463. Ted Brown, Green Gorse, Baltimore, ℰ (028) 20438. Nick Dent, Cappaglass, Ballydehob; ℰ (028) 20164.

Sea-swimming: At Ballycotton, Longstrand, Owendahincha, Goleen Beach, Barleycove, around Skibbereen and Schull.

Sailing schools: International Sailing Centre, 5 East Beach, Cobh, ℂ (021) 811237. Baltimore Sailing School, The Pier, Baltimore; ℂ (028) 20141.

Yacht charter: Rossbrin Yacht Charters, Rossbrin Cove, Schull, ℂ (028) 37165. Sail Ireland Charters, Trident Hotel, Kinsale, ℂ (021) 772927.

Hunting: Duhallow Hunt, ℂ (022) 21539. Muskerry Hunt, Mr Murphy, ℂ (021) 872966; South Union Hunt, ℂ (021) 293966.

Pony-trekking: The Rosscarbery Riding Centre, Rosscarbery, ℂ (023) 48232; The Henry Ford Homestead, Clonakilty, ℂ (023) 39117; Dunboy Riding Stables, Dunboy Castle, Castletownbere, ℂ (027) 70044.

Golf: Mallow Golf Club, Ballyellis, Mallow, ℂ (022) 21145. Fermoy Golf Club, Fermoy, ℂ (025) 31472. Muskerry Golf Club, Carrigrohane, ℂ (021) 385297. Cork Golf Club, Little Island, Cork City, ℂ (021) 353451. Douglas Golf Club, in the southern suburbs of Cork City, ℂ (021) 895297. Monkstown Golf Club, Parkgarriffe, Monkstown, ℂ (021) 841225/841686/841376. Youghal Golf Club, Knockaverry; ℂ (024) 92787. Fota Island, ℂ (021) 883700.

Trabolgan Holiday Centre: indoor pool, children's safari jungle etc.

Where to Stay

Cork City and Environs

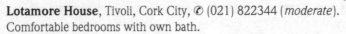

Jury's Hotel, Western Road, Cork City, ℂ (021) 276622 (*expensive*). Garden on the river, modern with sports facilities.

Lotamore House, Tivoli, Cork City, ℂ (021) 822344 (*moderate*). Comfortable bedrooms with own bath.

Arbutus Lodge, Montenotte, Cork City, ℂ (021) 501237 (*moderate*). Famous for its restaurant. Luxurious rooms.

The Metropole, McCurtain Street, Cork City, ℂ (021) 508122 (*moderate*). Old-fashioned with delicious breakfasts.

The Gables, Stoneview, Blarney, ℂ (021) 385330 (*inexpensive*). Old rectory, nicely furnished.

Isaac's, 48 MacCurtain Street, Cork City, ℂ (021) 500011. Hostel with self-service restaurant in converted warehouse.

The Fitzgeralds, Ashton Grove, Knockraha, ℂ (021) 821537 (*inexpensive*). Fine Georgian house, 7 miles (11km) north of Cork.

Co. Cork

Mrs Merrie Green, **Ballyvolane House**, near Fermoy, ℂ (025) 36349 (*expensive*). Lovely old Georgian house, beautiful grounds. Friendly family and lots of locally produced vegetables in the cooking.

Assolas Country House, Kanturk, ℂ (029) 50795 (*expensive*). Set amongst mature trees which reach down to the river, this 17th-century house is a superb place to get away from it all. Tennis, fishing and croquet within the grounds. Delicious food.

Ballymaloe House, Shanagarry, Midleton, ℗ (021) 652531 (*expensive*). Very pretty Georgian house, near the fishing village of Ballycotton. Elegant rooms, very friendly service, fabulous food, generous helpings. The whole Allen family are involved in the enterprise. You may be inspired to book into the cookery school here. Sea, river-fishing and riding can be arranged.

Longueville House, Mallow, ℗ (022) 47156 (*expensive*). There is a maze at the back of the house, and the only vineyard in Ireland; and long sloping views to the river and the ruined Callaghan Castle in the front. The food is superlative, and the service attentive.

Larchwood House, Pearson's Bridge, near Ballylickey, ℗ (027) 66181 (*moderate*). Family atmosphere and delicious cooking.

Scilly House, Kinsale, ℗ (021) 772413 (*moderate*). American owned. Attractive bedrooms with pretty views over garden and bay.

The **Marine**, Glandore, ℗ (028) 33366 (*moderate*). Simple hotel with lovely view of cove.

The **Commodore Hotel**, Cobh, ℗ (021) 811277 (*moderate*). Old-fashioned seaside hotel.

Bantry House, Bantry, ℗ (027) 50047 (*moderate*). Stately house, 1740, with bright rooms furnished in the simplest, yet most cheerful way. Fantastic views.

Seaview Hotel, Ballylickey, Bantry, ℗ (027) 50462 (*moderate*). Cosy, bright, Victorian house with spacious bedrooms. Two comfortable cottages for rent in the grounds.

The **Old Presbytery**, Cork Street, Kinsale, ℗ (021) 772027 (*moderate*). Characterful B&B with brass beds and restaurant.

The **Blue Haven**, Kinsale, ℗ (021) 772209 (*moderate*). The best hotel in Kinsale: small, cosy and comfortable with excellent food.

Mrs Vickery, **Bow Hall**, Castletownshend, ℗ (028) 36114 (*moderate*). Lovely Queen Anne house.

Mrs Sharp Bolster, Glenlohane, Kanturk, ℗ (029) 50014 (*moderate*). Comfortable Georgian house.

Mrs Sherrard, **Glenview House**, Ballinaclasha, Midleton, ℗ (021) 631680 (*moderate*). Pretty 18th-century house, lovely grounds with tennis and croquet. Good food.

Aherne's Pub and Seafood Bar, North Main Street, Youghal, ℗ (024) 92424 (*moderate*). Nice neat spacious bedrooms and wonderful seafood.

O'Donovan's Hotel, 44 Pearse Street, Clonakilty, ✆ (023) 33250 (*inexpensive*). Wonderful old-fashioned and characterful family-run hotel, with a fine public bar, in the town centre.

Seacourt, Butlerstown, ✆ (023) 40151 (*inexpensive*). Historic and beautiful house built in 1760. View of Seven Heads Peninsula. *Open June–end of August.*

Glebe House, Ballinadee, Bandon, near Kinsale. ✆ (021) 778294 (*inexpensive*). Splendid dinners and breakfasts in an attractive house.

Mrs O'Mahony, **Grove House**, Ahakista, Durras, ✆ (027) 67060 (*inexpensive*). Pretty old farmhouse on Sheep's Head Peninsula. For breakfast, honey from the garden and free-range eggs.

Mrs Hegarty, Ahakista, Bantry, ✆ (027) 67045 (*inexpensive*). Traditional farmhouse with lovely views.

Mrs O'Shea, **Magannagan Farm**, Derryconnery, Glengarriff, ✆ (027) 63361 (*inexpensive*). Good high teas.

Muckley Family, **Shangri La**, Glengarriff Road, Bantry, ✆ (027) 50244 (*inexpensive*). Friendly, cosy house.

Lettercollum House Hostel, Timoleague, ✆ (023) 46251 (*inexpensive*). Excellent restaurant.

Gabriel Cottage, Smorane, ✆ (028) 22521 (*inexpensive*). Vegan/vegetarian B&B.

Travara Lodge, Courtmacsherry, ✆ (023) 46493 (*inexpensive*). Comfortable with views of the bay and good home cooking.

self-catering

Mrs Harte, Cahermore, Rosscarbery, ✆ (023) 48227 Renovated farmhouse, oil fired aga cooker, sleeps 6. From IR£150 per week.

Hollybrook House, Skibbereen, ✆ (028) 21245. Several 19th-century properties on wooded estate. 8 luxury coastal cottages (sleep 6) with use of hotel facilities.

Terry Adams, Courtmacsherry, ✆ (023) 46198. From £200 per week.

Shiplake Hostel, Dunmanway, ✆ (023) 45750. Traditional farmhouse in the mountains, with self-catering kitchen where you can cook up the organic vegetables sold by the owners. They also sell wholemeal bread and delicious pizzas.

Blairs Cove House, Durras, near Bantry, ✆ (027) 61041. Apartments, IR£90–400 per week.

18th-century apartments, Castletownshend, contact Mrs Salter-Townshend, **The Castle**, Castletownshead, ✆ (028) 36100. Mrs Salter-Townshend also does B&B.

Mrs Kowalski, **Ashgrove Lodge**, Cobh, ✆ (021) 812483. 18th-century house, sleeps 5. From IR£200 per week.

Cashman Family, Garrison, Kanturk, ✆ (029) 50197. Thatched cottage, sleeps 6. From IR£130 per week.

Cork City and Environs

Arbutus Lodge, Montenotte, Cork, ✆ (021) 502893 (*expensive*). Well-established and excellent restaurant with a nationwide reputation. Moderately priced lunch; dinner is more lavish.

Cliffords, 18 Dyke Parade, Cork City, ✆ (021) 275333 (*expensive*). Smart restaurant in converted Georgian building that used to house the city library. One of few Irish restaurants to have a michelin star. Imaginative menu and impeccable service. Also own a small cheaper bistro next door.

Glandore, Jury's Hotel, Western Road, Cork, ✆ (021) 276622 (*moderate*). Good service and consistent quality.

Glassialley's, 5 Emmet Place, Cork, ✆ (021) 272305 (*moderate*). Salads, roasts, seafood.

The Huguenot, French Church Street, Cork, ✆ (021) 273357 (*moderate*). French cuisine.

Jacques Restaurant, 9 Phoenix Street, Cork. ✆ (021) 277387 (*moderate*). Interesting cooking and good vegetarian dishes.

The **Oyster Tavern**, Market Lane, ✆ (021) 272716 (*moderate*). Has the atmosphere of a gentlemen's dining room with white-aproned waitresses. The seafood is excellent.

Isaac's Brasserie, 48 MacCurtain Street, ✆ (021) 503805 (*moderate*). Fashionable 18th century converted warehouse. Zesty imaginative menu.

O'Reilly's, English Market (corner of Grand Parade), Cork, ✆ (021) 966397 (*inexpensive*). Tripe and drisheen (sheep's innards).

Baxters, Lavitt's Quay, Cork ✆ (021) 272139 (*inexpensive*). Cold meats and salads. *Lunch only Mon–Fri.*

Quay Co-op, 24 Sullivan's Quay, Cork. ✆ (021) 317660 (*inexpensive*). Good wholefood vegetarian restaurant, open lunch and dinner. Also a wholefood shop and bookshop.

The Long Valley, Winthrop Street, Cork, ✆ (021) 272144 (*inexpensive*). Pub selling delicious sandwiches.

Crawford's Art Gallery Café, Emmett Place, Cork, ✆ (021) 274415 (*inexpensive*). Run by one of the Allen Family of Ballymaloe fame, you can eat light and original food here for lunch or early supper. Good fresh orange juice and gooey cakes for a snack.

The Triskel Arts Café, Triskel Arts Centre, 15 Tobin Street, Cork, ✆ (021) 272022 (*inexpensive*). Filling lunchtime dishes. Very good soups.

Bewley's, Cork Street (*inexpensive*).

The Gingerbread House, Frenchchurch Street, ✆ (021) 276411 (*inexpensive*). Takeaway or eat in sandwiches, croissants and cakes.

Co. Cork

Ballymaloe House, Shanagarry, ✆ (021) 652532 (*expensive*). Famed throughout Ireland for its superb food, it never disappoints you.

Longueville House, Mallow, ✆ (022) 47156 (*expensive*). Adventurous and generous cuisine.

Shiro Japanese Dinner House, Ahakista, Durras, ✆ (027) 67030 (*expensive*). If you are staying anywhere near, arrange a meal here, for not only are you guaranteed a superb meal, but the whole atmosphere is magical. The husband-and-wife team have combined all the right elements of Japanese love of beauty and decoration in the rooms in which you eat, and in the preparation of the food. She is Japanese, he is German, and the view outside the window, pure Irish sea beauty. Dinner only; booking essential.

Blairs Cove House, Durras, near Bantry, ✆ (027) 61127 (*expensive*). Situated in the stable building of a Georgian mansion, run by a French couple. Steaks and fish grilled in front of you. Dinner and Sunday lunch only.

The Blue Haven, 3 Pearse Street, Kinsale, ✆ (021) 772209 (*expensive*). Very good restaurant in this cosy hotel. Seafood a speciality, steaks good too.

Max's Wine Bar, Main Street, Kinsale, ✆ (021) 772443 (*moderate*). Attractive old house. Varied menu.

Dunworley Cottage, Butlerstown, Bandon, ✆ (023) 40314 (*moderate*). Very popular locally. Good for vegetarians. *Lunch and dinner.*

The Altar Restaurant, Toormore, Schull, ✆ (028) 35254 (*moderate*). Good pâté and seafood.

Heron's Cove Restaurant and B&B, Goleen, Skibbereen, ✆ (028) 35225 (*moderate*). Harbour-side setting, very good fish and shellfish dishes. *Lunch and dinner.*

Mountain View Hotel, Glengarriff, ✆ (027) 63103 (*moderate*). Family-run hotel, cordon bleu cooking.

Bawnleigh House, Ballinhassig, ✆ (021) 771333 (*moderate*). Décor rather grim but creative, delicious food. (Closer to Half Way Village than Ballinhassig.)

Mill House, Rineen, Skibbereen, ✆ (028) 36299 (*moderate*). Seafood restaurant.

Aherne's Pub and Seafood Bar, North Main Street, Youghal, ✆ (024) 92424/ 92533 (*moderate*). Good atmosphere and delicious seafood.

Lettercollum House, Timoleague, ✆ (023) 46251 (*moderate*). Only 8 tables, booking essential, set menu, delicious.

Annie's, Ballydehob, ✆ (028) 37292 (*moderate*). Good set meals and special portions for children.

Tra Amici, Coomhola Road, near Ballylickey, ✆ (027) 50235 (*moderate*). Excellent Italian cooking.

Larchwood House, Pearson's Bridge, nr Ballylickey, ✆ (027) 66181 (*moderate*). Friendly and informal atmosphere, good home-cooking.

Bushes Bar, Baltimore, ✆ (028) 20125 (*inexpensive*). Bar overlooking the harbour.

5A Café, Banack Street, Bantry (*inexpensive*). Cheap, hippyish vegetarian café.

Achle's Bakery and Restaurant, Main Street, Schull, ✆ (028) 28459 (*inexpensive*).

The Courtyard, Main Street, Schull, ✆ (028) 28209 (*inexpensive*). Bar/restaurant/craftshop/delicatessen.

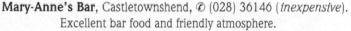

Mary-Anne's Bar, Castletownshend, ✆ (028) 36146 (*inexpensive*). Excellent bar food and friendly atmosphere.

Dillon's Bar, Timoleague, Bandon, ✆ (023) 46390 (*inexpensive*). Continental style bar/café with good snacks.

O'Donovan's Pub, 44 Pearse Street, Clonakilty, ✆ (023) 33250 (*inexpensive*). Plain cooking and pub grub.

Johnny Barry's Bar, Glengarriff (*inexpensive*). Inexpensive bar food.

The Snug, The Quay, Bantry, ✆ (027) 50057 (*inexpensive*). Eccentric bar opposite the harbour with simple home-cooked dishes.

The Tin pub, Ahakista (*inexpensive*). Wacky bar opposite Shiro Japanese dinner house.

Theatre, music and film: check the *Cork Examiner* and *Evening Echo*. In the evenings there is plenty to choose from but try to see a production by the Theatre of the South, at the Cork Opera House. They tend to produce only contemporary Irish writers' work which can be very good. The Theatre of the South is open for about eight weeks every summer. Opera House, Emmett Place, ✆ (021) 270022. Otherwise, go to the Everyman Theatre, McCurtain Street, ✆ (021) 501673, which does not restrict itself in any way—tragedy, farce and comedy, by any author as long as he or she is good. The Triskel Arts Centre, off South Main Street, ✆ (021) 272022/272023, hosts a wide range of events—music, exhibitions, drama, film seasons, poetry readings.

Clubs/pubs: Klub Kaos on Oliver Plunkett Street is currently the 'in' nightspot. Mollies on Tuckey Street is where to go for drinks beforehand; and a new club called Hysteria, near French Church Street augurs well. For music and a pint of Murphy's Stout, Charlie's, the Lobby, and the Phoenix, all on Union Quay often have music whilst An Bodhran, 42 George's Quay or An Spailpin Fanach on South Main Street specialise in traditional Irish.

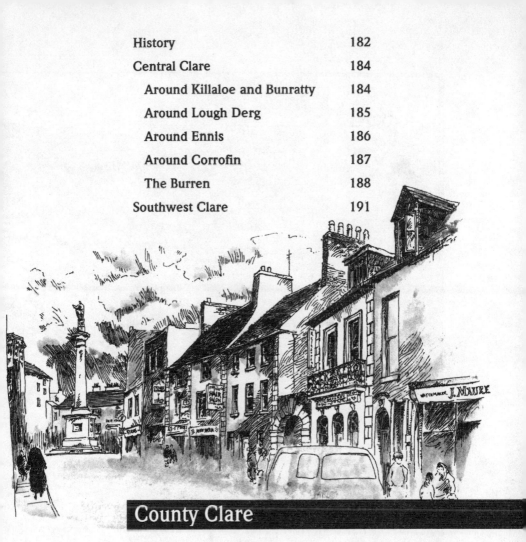

County Clare

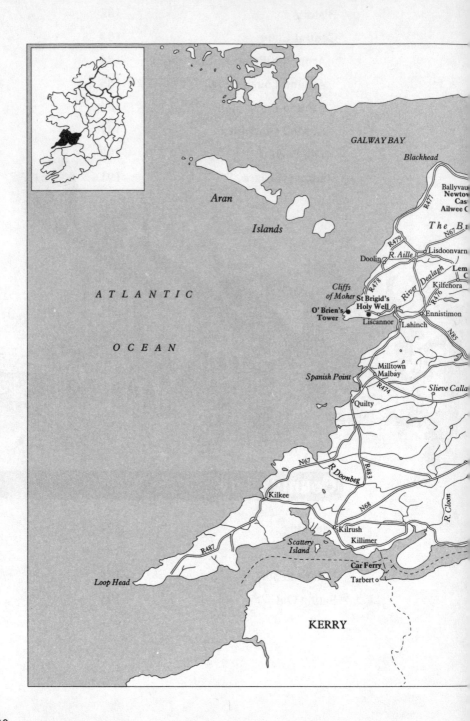

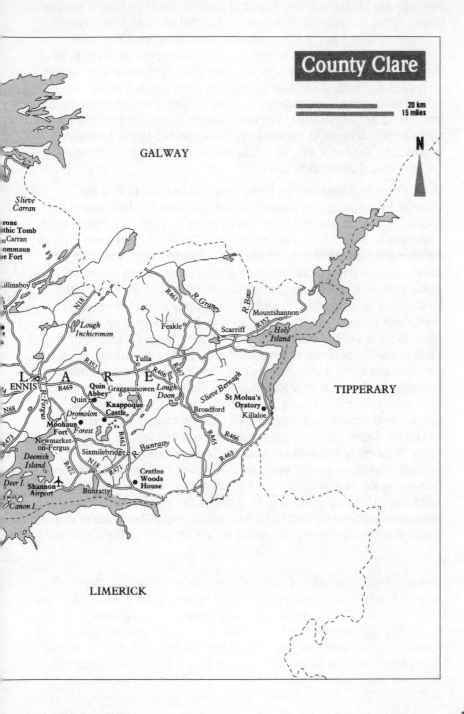

County Clare

20 km
15 miles

N

GALWAY

Slieve
Carran

rone
thic Tomb
Carran
ommaun
e Fort

illinaboy

N18

Lough
Inchicronan

R461

R Graney

R Bow

Mountshannon

Feakle

Scarriff

R352

Holy
Island

Tulla

R352

R466

R461

ENNIS

L   A   R   E

R469

Quin
Abbey

Graggaunowen

Lough
Doon

Slieve Bernagh

TIPPERARY

Quin

Knappoque
Castle

Broadford

St Molua's
Oratory

N68

Dromolon

Killaloe

Moohaun
Fort

Forest

R462

R Bunratty

R465

R466

R473

Newmarket-
on-Fergus

Sixmilebridge

N18

R471

R463

Deenish
Island

R472

Cratloe
Woods
House

Deer I.

Shannon
Airport

Bunratty

Canon I.

LIMERICK

Until the 4th century Clare was part of Connacht, after which it became known as the Kingdom of Thomond. It is a wild and beautiful county, still marked with signs of a tempestuous past: there are 2300 stone forts or 'cahers' dating back to pre-Celtic times. It is unspoilt by tourism, even though it has huge Shannon Airport in the south. The locals earn money from farming, tourism and fishing, and the airport gives a lot of employment to the surrounding area. Nearly three-quarters of the county boundary is formed by water and the Shannon Scheme is the largest hydro-electric scheme in the country. It is separated by the Shannon Estuary from County Kerry, its neighbour in the south, though there is a car ferry from Tarbert to Killimer.

Most people go inland, almost to the centre of Ireland, to find the Limerick bridge, and then only shoot through Clare on their way to the delights of Connemara. But Clare has its plunging cliffs and strange karst landscapes to attract the more adventurous. The west Clare coast ends in the dramatic Cliffs of Moher. To the north, overlooking Galway Bay, the Barony of the Burren looks like some misplaced section of the moon— white, crevassed and barren, but springy turf grows in the earth-filled fissures, and cattle manage to graze quite happily around the cracks that could catch them in a leg-breaking fall. The Burren region extends over some 25 miles (40km) from east to west and 15 miles (24km) from north to south—between Galway Bay on the north, the Atlantic coast on the west, and a line drawn roughly through Doolin, Kilfenora, Gort and Kinvara. The Burren is very rich in antiquities left by Stone Age farmers who cleared the hills of forest. By medieval times, the hills were treeless, and the wide expanses of fissured rock exposed (*see* pp.62–3 and pp.188–9). There are many places to bathe and fish around the coast, whilst the scenery and walks around the lakes and hills of Slieve Bernagh, which rise on the west side of the long stretch of Lough Derg, are some of the best you will ever find. In the last few years a few of the wonderful carved stone heads to be found in the ancient holy sites have been stolen, apparently hacked off and driven away. The Office of Public Works may have to substitute replicas for the originals if this continues.

History

The 12th-century *Book of Invasions*, or *Lebor Gabala*, connects Clare with the Fir Bolgs, but we know little about these shadowy people. Many centuries later, it was a Clare man, Brian Boru of the clan O'Brien, who conducted a vigorous and successful campaign against the Vikings and defeated them at Clontarf in 1014. He became High King of Ireland in 1002, and built the Palace of Kincora as his royal residence in 1012. Sadly, he was killed in his tent after the battle of Clontarf, and the fragile national unity he had managed to create disappeared very fast. There is nothing left of Kincora today.

In the tales of ancient Ireland the countryside was fraught with the battles of the land-owning Celtic clans: O'Briens, O'Deas, McNamaras and MacMahons who, when they were not waging fierce war on foreigners, filled in the time by fighting amongst themselves. In 1172 the incumbent chief of the O'Briens, Donal Mor, enlisted the help of a new group of invaders, a party of Norman mercenaries, in his war against the O'Conors of Connacht. Despite this initial foothold in the country, the Norman-English forces did not make much of a mark in County Clare until the accession of Henry VIII in 1534 and his acknowledgement as King of Ireland. The O'Briens were made Earls of Thomond, and remained more or less loyal to the English crown until the Cromwellian conquest (*see* **History**, pp.73–4). After that time, Clare became a seat of rebellion against English rule. When Cromwell heard that a large part of Clare had no trees to hang a man, nor enough water to drown him, nor enough earth to bury him, he thought it would be just the place to banish the rebellious Irish whom he had thrown off the land in other parts of the country.

Getting There and Around

By air: Shannon International Airport, ✆ (061) 471444.

By boat: Kerry-Clare ferry from Killimer. Single car ticket costs IR£7, return is IR£9. The ferry departs from Killimer on the hour between 7am and 7pm, Mon–Sat (9pm April–Sept).

By rail: Limerick is the nearest main terminal, ✆ (061) 418666. Ennis train station, ✆ (065) 40444.

By bus: Good local services, ✆ (065) 24177.

By car: cars are available for hire at Shannon Airport; Dan King, Shannon Road, Newmarket-on-Fergus, ✆ (061) 368126; Tom Mannion, O'Connell Street, Ennis, ✆ (065) 24211.

By bike: The Raleigh Rent-a-Bike network operates all over Clare, ✆ Dublin (01) 6261333. Your local dealer in Ennis is Michael Tierney, 17 Abbey Street, ✆ (065) 29433.

Tourist Information

Ennis, Limerick Road, ✆ (065) 28366, all year.

Lisdoonvarna, ✆ (065) 74062, June to beginning of October.

Lahinch, ✆ (065) 81474, 15 May to September.

Cliffs of Moher, ✆ (065) 81171, May to December.

Shannon Airport, ✆ (061) 471664, all year.

Festivals

May: The Wildlife Symposium, Ballinalacken Castle, Fanore, ✆ (065) 76105.

Late May: The Fleach Nua, a festival of traditional music, dancing and singing, in Ennis in the last weekend of the month, ✆ (065) 24143/(01) 280 0295.

Early June: Ennistymon Festival of traditional singing.

Early August: Carnival of Music, Lisdoonvarna, ✆ (065) 74042.

August: Feakle Festival of Music, ✆ (061) 924131.

September: Match-Making Festival of Ireland, Lisdoonvarna, ✆ (065) 74042.

Central Clare

Around Killaloe and Bunratty

Killaloe is right on the great Shannon and connected to Ballina in Co. Tipperary by a bridge of 13 arches. Not far from the bridge, on the west bank of the river, is the gem of Killaloe, **St Flannan's Cathedral**, the fine 12th-century building built by Donal O'Brien on the site of an earlier church founded in the 6th century by St Lua. There is a magnificent Hiberno-Romanesque door which is said to be the entrance to the tomb of Murtagh O'Brien, King of Munster, who died in the same century the cathedral was built. The bold and varied carvings of animals and foliage on the shafts and capitals, and the pattern of the chevrons on the arches are not merely decoration: they are modelled to make the entire conception an organic whole. Nearby is **Thorgrim's Stone**, the shaft of a cross bearing a runic and ogham inscription of about the year AD 1000. The view from the top of the square cathedral tower is superb. You can see all the mountains that crowd round the gorge of Killaloe, and the beautiful Lough Derg. In the grounds of the cathedral is **St Flannan's Oratory** with a lovely high stone roof, with its Gothic doorway a splendid contrast to the cruciform cathedral.

The oratory, which dates from the 12th century, has a Romanesque west door but the inside is dark and gloomy. It dates from the 12th century. The Roman Catholic church standing high above the town is believed to be on the site of Kincora, the great palace of Brian Boru where riotous banquets were the order of the day. Inside the church are some fine stained-glass windows by Harry Clarke, who worked upon many church windows in the early decades of this century. His style is fantastical and fairylike in the manner of the English illustrator Aubrey Beardsley (1872–98), and the colours are exceptionally vivid. In the grounds is **St Molua's Oratory**, a very ancient ruin reconstructed here after being removed from an island in the Shannon, before it was flooded by the Shannon hydroelectric scheme in 1929. Killaloe is a centre for fishing and boating. There are facilities for water-skiing and sailing, and a large marina (*see* 'Activities', below).

A mile (1.6km) or so out of Killaloe on the R463 is **Crag Liath**, known locally as the Grianan, overlooking the road northwards to Scarriff. It was written in 1014 in the annals of Loch Ce that this fort was the dwelling place of Aoibhill (also known as Aibell), the celebrated banshee of the Dalcassian Kings of Munster, the O'Briens. (In Irish, *Dal gCais* means sept or tribe of Cas. A banshee (*bean-sidhe*) or fairy woman is a ghost peculiar to people of old Irish stock; her duty is to warn the family she attends of the approaching death of one of its members.) Thus it was that Aoibhill appeared to Brian Boru on the eve of Clontarf and told him that he would be killed the next day, though not in the fury of the battle. This is exactly what happened, for he was murdered in his tent when the battle was over and the victory his. The short climb to the fort is lovely. All around is beauty: woods, water and mountain. (*The fort is always accessible; adm free.*)

If you cross the Shannon at Limerick, you will find yourself heading for **Bunratty Castle** on the Newmarket road (N18). Bunratty is a splendid tower house standing beside a small stone bridge over River Ratty; a perfect, restored example of a Norman-Irish castle keep. The present castle dates from 1460, though it is at least the fourth to have been built on the same spot. It was built by the McNamaras, who were a sept of the O'Briens, and it remained an O'Brien stronghold until 1712. It was then occupied by the parliamentarian Admiral Penn, the father of William Penn who founded Pennsylvania. After years of neglect it was bought by Lord Gort in 1954, who restored it with the help of Bord Failte and the Office of Public Works. They have managed to recreate a 15th-century atmosphere and there is a wonderful collection of 14th- to 17th-century furniture. In the evenings it provides a memorable setting for medieval-style banquets. In the grounds surrounding the castle, a **folk park** (*open daily throughout the year, 9.30–5 (7pm June–Aug); adm; © (061) 361511*) has gradually grown up with examples of houses from every part of the Shannon region; many of them were re-erected after being saved from demolition during the Shannon Airport extension. You can see butter-making, basket-weaving and all the traditional skills which made people self-sufficient in days gone by. There is also a very good collection of agricultural machinery. There is a good craft centre at the Ballycasey Workshops about 3 miles (5km) west on the N18.

It is also worth making an expedition to **Cratloe Woods House** (*open June–mid-Sept, Mon–Sat 2–6; adm; © (061) 87306*), on the main Limerick/Shannon to Ennis Road (N18), about 5 miles (8 km) from Limerick. Cratloe Woods is an ancient O'Brien house, and the only surviving example of an Irish long house that is still lived in as a home. It is packed with interesting history, and there is a good tea and craft shop. The woods themselves have some of the only primeval oak forest left in Ireland, and if you climb the hill you will get a fine view.

Around Lough Derg

Broadford, **Tulla** and **Feakle** are all pleasant villages where you can stay in farms or town and country houses and explore the Clare lakelands. Lough Graney is especially beautiful, with its wooded shores. Most of the loughs are well stocked with bream and pike. Near Feakle the witty and outrageous poet Brian Merriman earned his livelihood as a schoolmaster. Here, also, is the cottage of Biddy Early, the wise woman about whom at the turn of the century Lady Augusta Gregory collected stories for her book *Visions and Beliefs of the West of Ireland*.

From the pretty village of Mountshannon on Lough Derg it is possible to get a boat to Iniscealtra, also known as Holy Island, about ½mile (1km) from the shore. (It is easy to hire a boat at the harbour, which is a main stopping place on the lake for hire-cruisers and sailing boats.) The Christian settlement on the island is attibuted to St Caimin, who lived here in about AD 640. Today there are five ancient churches, a round tower, a saint's graveyard, a hermit's cell and a holy well. St Carmin's Church, beside the incomplete round tower, has a wonderful Hiberno-Romanesque chancel arch, impressive in its simplicity. The festival at the holy well was famous for the Bacchanalian revelry that accompanied it. It was stopped by the priests, sometime in the last century, because the local squireens would steal the girls at it. The memorial stones are still in place in the saint's graveyard for the period covering the 8th to the 12th centuries. Unfortunately the whole effect is rather spoiled by modern tombstones and garish plastic wreaths.

Around Ennis

Newmarket-on-Fergus takes its name from a 19th-century O'Brien, Lord Inchiquin, who was very enthusiastic about horses. In the grounds of his Neo-Gothic mansion, now a luxury hotel, is **Mooghaun Fort** (also spelt Maughaun), one of the largest Iron Age hill-forts in Europe, enclosing 27 acres (11ha) with three concentric walls. Maybe it was people from this fort who buried the enormous hoard of gold ornaments which was discovered nearby in 1854 by workmen digging the way for a railway line. Unfortunately much of it was melted down, probably by dealers, but a few pieces of 'the great Clare gold find' have found their way to the National Museum in Dublin. You can reach the fort through Dromoland Forest. Access is by foot via a forestry car park signposted to the left off the N18 road between Newmarket-on-Fergus and Dromoland.

At **Craggaunowen** off the Quin-Sixmilebridge Road (R469) there is a reconstructed *crannog* or lake dwelling, and a four-storey tower house (*open May–Oct, daily, 10–6, adm;* © *(061) 367178*). This is a fascinating centre which gives a good idea of how our ancestors lived. The valley surrounding it is beautiful, and the teatime scones at the reception cottage delicious. On display is the Brendan, a replica of the original boat used by St Brendan on his voyages. Tim Severin, a modern-day adventurer, sailed it to North America via Iceland and Greenland, with the purpose of demonstrating that St Brendan could have been the first to discover America, in the 6th century. Nearby, at Quin (about 8 miles (13km) northwest of Bunratty), is **Knappoque Castle**, run on the same lines as Bunratty Castle with medieval evening banquets (*open daily, April to end Sept, 9.30–5, adm; medieval banquets twice-nightly at 5.45 and 8.45, May–end Sept;* © *(061) 368103*).

At the next crossroads, to the east of the town, a right-turn leads to **Quin Abbey** (*always accessible; adm free*) which is very well preserved, and therefore subject to countless coach tours. It was founded for the Franciscans in 1402 and incorporated with a great castle built by one of the de Clares. The monastic buildings are grouped around an attractive cloister and there is a graceful tower. Buried here is the famous duellist with the wonderful name of Fireballs MacNamara.

Ennis (*Inis:* river-meadow), the county capital, is sited on a great bend of the River Fergus. The streets are narrow and winding, and in the centre is a hideous monument to the great Daniel O'Connell, who successfully contested the Clare seat in 1828 even though the repressive laws of the time disqualified Catholics. Right in the middle of the town is **Ennis Friary**, a substantial ruin (*open May–Sept, 9.30–6.30; rest of the year key with caretaker, Mary Kearns,* © *(065) 22464*). The friary was founded for the Franciscans by Donchadh O'Brien, King of Thomond, just before his death in 1242. It is rich in sculptures and decorated tombs although the building itself has been rather mucked about, with additions and renovation. On one of the tombs is the sculptured device of a cock crowing. The story goes that, standing on the rim of a pot, he cries in Irish, 'the son of the Virgin is safe', a reference to the Bible story of the cock that rose from the pot in which it was cooking to proclaim that, 'Himself above on the Cross will rise again', to the astonishment of the two Roman soldiers who had questioned the prophecy.

There is a small **museum** (*open Mon–Fri*) in Harmony Row which specializes in objects associated with famous Clare people. Fans of Percy French (1854–1920), the painter and entertainer, can look at the old steam engine immortalized in his song, 'Are you right there, Michael, are you right?' This song about the West Clare Railway, and the engine's habit of stopping at places other than stations, led to a libel action with the directors.

Around Corrofin

On the way to Corrofin (off the N85 to Ennistimon, and 2 miles (2.5km) off the R476), is the famous religious settlement of **Dysert O'Dea**. It was started in the 7th century by St Tola, but he probably lived in a cell of wattle and daub. The present ruin is a much-altered 12th-century Hiberno-Romanesque church with a badly reconstructed west doorway that now stands in the south wall. The door is sumptuously carved, and the arch has a row of stone heads with Mongolian features and proud but rather sad expressions. The idea for the heads came from northern France. (Monks and scholars moving between Ireland and the Continent had much more influence on building and style than was once thought.) Beside the church is the stump of a round tower, and about a hundred yards (91m) east is a high cross from the 12th century. Christ is shown in a pleated robe, and below him is a bishop with a crozier. A decisive battle fought here in 1318 drove the Anglo-Normans out of the surrounding area for several centuries, when the O'Brien chief of the time defeated Richard de Clare of Bunratty and expelled him.

Corrofin village lies between two pretty lakes, the Inchiquin and Atedaun. There is good game and coarse fishing here, and plenty of caves, for this is marginal shale and limestone countryside in which the River Fergus plays some tricks. The **Clare Heritage Centre** (*open all year, daily (exc Sundays in winter) 10–6; adm; © (065) 37955*) in the old Church of Ireland hall offers a 'tracing your ancestor' service, and displays give a very interesting guide to rural Ireland 150 years ago.

About 2 miles (3.2km) further up on the R476 is **Killinaboy**, a small village close to the northern tip of Lough Inchiquin which is spelt Kilnaboy on some maps. The remains of a round tower rest in the graveyard of a ruined church which dates from the 11th century. Over the south door is a *Sheila-na-Gig*, a grotesque and erotic figure of a woman. These *Sheila-na-Gigs* are often carved and fixed to ecclesiastical buildings, probably as a sort of crude warning to the monks and laity of the power of feminine sexuality. There are many gallery graves around here. A mile (1.6km) northwest of Killinaboy at **Roughan**, just over a stile and in a field, is the Tau Cross, shaped like a T with a carved head in each of the arms. Several like this have been found in a Celtic sanctuary at Roquepertuse in France, and it is likely that this is pre-Christian. The original Tau Cross is now in St Catherine's Church, Corrofin, this is a replica as such ancient treasures are so vunerable to theft.

On the main road leading to Kilfenora (R476) is the ruined **Lemaneagh Castle** which belonged to the O'Briens. It is a really lovely old ruin with a tower dating from 1480 and an early-17th century fortified house. Sir Conor O'Brien, who built the four-storey house, had a very strong-minded wife called Red Mary, many of whose exploits have passed into folklore. After Sir Conor died, she married an influential Cromwellian to ensure the inheritance of her son, Donat, and to prevent the expropriation of her lands. The story goes that when one day he made an uncalled-for remark about her first husband, she promptly pushed him out of the window.

The Burren

Kilfenora is a place of ancient importance on the fringe of the Burren. It is worth staying a while, not only to look at the **Burren Display Centre** (*open daily, Mar–Oct 10–5, June 10–6, July and Aug 9–7; adm; ℗ (065) 88030*) which explains the flora, fauna, butterflies and rock formations of the area, but also because it has four 12th-century carved crosses, all of the same excellent standard, which suggests they might have been produced by the same workshop or even by a single carver. The small 12th-century Church of St Fachnan is called 'the Cathedral', and its bishopric is still held by the Pope!

The district is generally called 'the Burren' after the ancient Barony of that name. It extends some 25 miles (40km) from east to west and 15 miles (24km) from north to south, between Galway Bay and the Atlantic Ocean, with the villages of Doolin, Kilfenora, Gort and Kinvarra forming its southeastern border. One of the amazing things about the Burren is that its 50 square miles (130sq km) are dotted with signs of ancient habitation—stone forts and megalithic tombs, which blend perfectly with a landscape strewn with strangely shaped rocks. In late May the place becomes starred with gentians, cranesbill, geraniums and orchids. Arctic alpine mountain avens sprawl lavishly over the rocks and Irish saxifrage tufts cover sea-sprayed boulders. Sheltered in the damp clefts of limestone are shade loving plants such as the Maidenhair fern. The plentiful rainfall disappears into the limestone and into a pot-holers' dream of passages and caverns. Impermanent lakes known as turloughs appear when the ground water floods through the fissures after a lot of rain. No one has yet been able to explain fully how such a profusion of northern and southern plants came to grow together, some of which are unknown in continental Europe. The temperate winter and warm limestone beneath the turf suit the plants, and their colonies have grown up unhindered because the arid land has never been cultivated, only grazed by cattle.

On the R480 to Ballyvaughan, 6 miles (9.7km) past Lemaneagh Castle, is the great dolmen of Poulabrone (the pool of sorrows) with a massive capstone; and nearer Killinaboy in the upland part of the Burren is the great stone fort of Cahercommaun. To get to it, turn left in Carran village and left again at the next junction. Look out for a shrub-lined avenue to the left which leads to a car park. From here you go a short way by foot. The fort is situated on a cliff edge across some ankle-breaking country, but notice the flower life between the stones. A Harvard excavation team reached the conclusion that the fort was occupied during the 8th and 9th centuries by a community that raised cattle, hunted red deer and cultivated some land for growing grain. Also on the road to Ballyvaughan, a mile (1.6km) out of Kilfenora, is one of the finest stone forts in Ireland, known as Ballykinvarga. This has a very effective trap for those trying to launch an attack: chevaux de frise, which are sharp spars of stone set close together in the ground. The great fort of Dun Aengus on the Aran Islands has a similar arrangement.

At Ballyvaughan on the north of the Burren you can rent yourself an Irish cottage and explore Black Head, which looks over the shimmering Galway Bay and gives clear views of the Aran Islands and the Cliffs of Moher. The islands are made of the same grey limestone as the Burren and have the same bright flowers in the springtime. Ballyvaughan village is set in a green wooded vale, an oasis after the bleached plateaux of limestone, mighty terraces and escarpments to the south. The village has good craft shops, and the harbour is the starting point for boat trips to the Aran Islands. There are a couple of tower houses built in the 16th century to explore: Gleninagh, signposted between Ballyvaughan and Lisdoonvarna, was occupied by the O'Loughlins until 1840; Newtown Castle is unusual in that it is round with a square base. It is not signposted; you will find it down a lane, 2 miles (3.2km) south of Ballyvaughan.

The **Aillwee Caves** (open daily, Mar–early Nov 10–6.30, July and Aug 10–7.30; adm; ✆ (065) 77036) are 2 miles (3.2km) southeast of Ballyvaughan on the N67. All over the Burren there are hundreds of caves formed by the underground rivers—great sport for the speleologist. Aillwee Caves date back to 2 million BC. When the river dried up, or changed its course, they became the den of wild bears and other animals. Today the entrance has been tamed to make it easier for the less intrepid, and the caverns are festooned with stalagmites and stalactites.

By taking the corkscrew road to **Lisdoonvarna** (*Lios Duin Bhearna*: the enclosure of the gapped fort), you get a series of lovely views of Galway Bay. Since the decline of Mallow, Lisdoonvarna is the most important spa in Ireland. The waters are said to owe much to their natural radioactivity; there are sulphur, magnesia and iron springs, a pump room and baths for those who come to take the waters. Hotels, guest houses and bed and breakfasts have sprung up everywhere, for the place is very crowded in the summer, and there is much courting, inspired no doubt by the invigorating properties of the water. There are also plenty of dances and concerts during the spa season. Excitement is at its height in September with the **Match-making Festival**. Spinster ladies come all the way from America for the fun. There is a sandy cove at **Doolin**, 3 miles (4.8km) away, good for fishing but dangerous for bathing. This little fishing village is famous for its traditional music, and you can get a boat from here to Innisheer, the smallest of the Aran Islands, a crossing that takes about 40 minutes (*© (065) 74455/74189 for information*).

In the area are curious mineral nodules formed by limestone and shale which look just like tortoise shells. There are three of these built into the wall beside the Imperial Hotel in Lisdoonvarna. From here, the coast road (R478) leads to the **Cliffs of Moher**, which drop down vertically to the foaming sea. Seabirds somehow manage to rest on the steep slopes; guillemots, razorbills, puffins, kittiwakes, various gulls, choughs and sometimes peregrines. The cliffs stretch for nearly 5 miles (8km) and are made of the darkest sandstone and millstone grit. On a clear day there is a magnificent view of the Twelve Bens and the mountains of Connemara. **O'Brien's Tower** was built in 1835 by a notorious landlord as an observation post; behind it is an Information Centre (*open Mar–Oct*).

On the R478 southeast of the cliffs is **Liscannor**, a little fishing village where the fishermen still use curraghs. John P. Holland (1841–1914), who invented the submarine, was born here. However, it is more famous locally for the **Holy Well of St Brigid**, about 2 miles (3km) northwest of Liscannor on the R478, near the cliffs of Moher. The well is an important place of pilgrimage. An aura of faith and devotion lingers in the damp air and amongst the trivial offerings of holy pictures, bleeding hearts and plastic statues of the Pope. You approach by a narrow stone passage, probably still feeling slightly amazed by the life-sized painted plaster model of St Brigid next to the entrance of the well, which is sufficiently naturalistic to be macabre when first glimpsed.

Lahinch, 1 mile (1.6km) south of Liscannor, is a small seaside resort with a pretty arc of golden sand and waves big enough for surfing. The golf course at Lahinch is championship-standard, but as a guest you are most welcome. There is an amusing story of one enthusiast who putted a winner and got the trophy. He remarked with the skill and colour only the Irish can summon, 'I declare to God I was that tense I could hear the bees belchin'. **Ennistymon**, with its colourful shop fronts, is 2½ miles (4km) inland on the N85, in a wooded valley beside the cascading River Cullenagh.

Southwards, following the N67 down the coast from Lahinch, you come to Spanish Point (just off the R482), where a great number of ships from the Spanish Armada were wrecked. Those sailors who struggled ashore were slaughtered by the locals on the orders of the Governor of Connacht. **Milltown Malbay**, opposite Spanish Point on the N67, has a summer school, held as a tribute to Clare's greatest piper, Willie Clancy (1921–73), who was not only a musician, but also a folklorist and master carpenter. He was especially noted for his beautiful rendering of slow Irish airs on the *uileann* pipe. The summer school, held at the beginning of July for 10 days, comprises lectures, recitals, concerts, workshops and traditional music. It is a splendid time to visit for all the fun (*see* 'Festivals').

From Milltown Malbay, you can have a swim at the silver strand of **Freach**, just to the north of the town, or climb **Slieve Callan**, the highest point in west Clare, and on the way rest at the little lake at **Boolynagreana**, which means 'the summer milking place of the sun'. To get there, follow the R474 southwards for 6 miles (9.6km) to the Hand Crossroads, and then walk over rough land for about a mile (1.6km). All round these foothills the ancient agricultural practice of transhumance was pursued. This is known in Ireland as 'booleying' and involves moving livestock to mountain pasture during the summer months. Booleying has fallen into disuse with modern feeding methods.

Back on the coast road (N67) you will find **Quilty**, a strange name for an Irish village which comes from the Irish *coillte*, for woods, but there are no trees on this flat part of the coast. The great lines of stone walls are bestrewn with seaweed being dried for kelp-making. The seaweed is either burnt, and the ash used for the production of iodine, or exported for the production of alginates which produce the rich, creamy head on Guinness. The church here is reminiscent of the Early-Christian churches, but in fact it was built in 1907, with money given by some French sailors who were rescued by the villagers when their ship was wrecked one stormy night.

Southwest Clare

Kilkee to Killimer

Kilkee (*Cill Chaoidhe*: Church of St Caoidhe), about 12 miles (19.2km) south on the N67, is a grand place for a holiday by the sea. It is built along a sandy crescent-shaped beach, and the Duggerna Rocks, acting as a reef, make it safe for bathing at any stage of the tide. The coast lying southwestwards for about 15 miles (24km) from here to Loop

Head is an almost endless succession of caverns, chasms, sea-stacks and weird and wonderfully shaped rocks. The cliff scenery is on a par with the Cliffs of Moher. There is a colourful legend about Ulster's hero Cú Chulainn, who was generally well loved by women, but this time was being pursued relentlessly by a termagant of a woman called Mal. Eventually he came to the edge of the cliffs on Loop Head and leapt on to a great rock about 30ft (9m) out to sea. Mal was not to be outdone and made the same leap with equal agility and success. Cú Chulainn straight away performed the difficult feat of leaping back to the mainland and this time Mal faltered, fell short, and disappeared into the raging ocean below. Out of this legend came the name Loop Head, Leap Head in Irish. As for poor Mal, she must have been a witch, for her blood turned the sea red and she was swept northwards to a point near the Cliffs of Moher called Hag's Head.

Kilrush (*Cill Rois*: the Church of the Promontory) is a busy place overlooking the Shannon Estuary with a newly built marina at **Cappagh**. The **Heritage Centre** (open May to Sept ✆ 065 51047) in the Town Hall has a permanent exhibition about Kilrush in Landlord times. Two miles (3.2km) out into the estuary, **Scattery Island** (Cathach's Island), found by St Senan in the 6th century, has some interesting monastic remains. An island in the broad Shannon was easy meat for the Vikings, who raided it several times. The round tower is very well preserved and has its door at ground level, so the unsuspecting monks must have been surprised by the aggressive Norsemen. The five ruined churches date from medieval times. Boat trips from Cappagh to Scattery Island are available in the summer (*call Atlantic Adventures ✆ (065) 52133 or Stephen Brennan ✆ (065) 52031*). Bottle-nosed dolphins have made their home in this part of the Shannon Estuary. It is possible to see them at close quarters from local ferry boats which will take you along the Loop Head Peninsula. Contact the tourist office for details.

The **Fergus Estuary**, where the mouth of the River Shannon gapes its widest, is a paradise of forgotten isles, untouched and deserted, with names like Deer Isle, Canon Isle and Deenish. You can base yourself near **Killadysert**, on the R473 going north to Ennis, and have great fun exploring them. The McMahon family still farm on Canon Isle, and if you make enquiries they may take you out there in their boat.

Shopping

Crafts: from Knappoque Castle, Cratloe Woods House and the Shannon Airport Duty Free Shop, which you can visit only as you are leaving the country. Woven clothing, candles and prints from Bunratty Folk Park. Crafts, books and Tim Robinson's excellent map of the Burren from the Aillwee Caves Complex, near Ballyvaughan. The Manus Walsh Craft Shop, Ballyvaughan sells paintings, silver, jewellery and enamels. The Design Yard in Lahinch sells designer woollens by Lyn Mar. Close to Shannon Airport on the junction of the N18/N19, The Ballycasey Craft Workshops, Ballycasey, ✆ (061) 364115, have a great selection of tweeds, arans, pottery, woodwork etc.

Delicacies: The Farmshop, Aillwee Cave Co. Ltd, Ballyvaughan, ✆ (065) 77036, sells food for picnics or to take home—all made by the Johnston family. They also bottle the natural spring water from the caves, and Ben makes his own cheese, Burren Gold. Open Sesame wholefood shop, 29 Parnell Street, Ennis, ☎ (091) 31315, sells organic veg and local cheeses. Sausages are made by Gerry Howard, La Verna, Lisdoonvarna town centre. Unglert's Bakery in Ennistymon produces German rye breads and strudels.

Cheese: Annaliese Bartelink Gouda-style cheeses flavoured with herbs in person or by post from Poulcoin, Killinaboy.

Shellfish: Oyster Shell Company, New Quay, The Burren (behind Linnaue's Bar); ☎ (065) 78105.

Mead: The Bunratty Winery, Bunratty (behind Durty Nelly's Bar); ☎ (061) 362222.

Local cartographer Tim Robinson has produced an excellent large-scale map of the Burren. Available locally, IR£3.25.

Activities

Cruising: at Killaloe through Derg Line Cruisers, who also organize water-skiing and day cruises, ☎ (061) 376364. Mount Shannon Harbour across the lough is a great place from which to make boat trips up the lovely River Graney (also known as the Scariff).

Yacht charter: Yachting International, Trident Hotel, Kinsale, ☎ (021) 772301. Shannon Sailing Centre, Dromineer, Co. Tipperary, ☎ (067) 24295. This company charters yachts that can be picked up in Kilrush, and also organizes wind-surfing, canoeing, water-skiing, day cruises and sailing on Lough Derg.

Fishing: for brown trout on the lakes. M. Tierney, 17 Abbey Street, Ennis, ☎ (065) 29433 or Michael Mammon, Lough Derg Angling Centre, Killaloe, ☎ (061) 376329; Tom Burke, Burke's Shop, Main Street, Corrofin, ☎ (065) 37677.

Deep-sea fishing: Atlantic Adventures, Cappa, Kilrush, ☎ (065) 52133; Dermot Collins, Clare Coast Charter, Ballyvaughan, ☎ (065) 21131/77014; William O'Callaghan, Rosslevan, Ennis, ☎ (065) 21374. Kieran O'Driscoll Marine Charter, Fanore, ☎ (065) 76112/088 575163.

Sailing: sailing in traditional Galway Hookers, Ballyvaughan, ☎ (091) 37539.

Swimming: in Lough Graney, and in the sea at Lahinch and around the coast by Spanish Point, Fanore and Doonbeg.

Caving: John MacNamara, Admiral's Restaurant, Fanore, ☎ (065) 76105. Kilshanny Outdoor Centre, Lisdoonvarna, ☎ (065) 730230.

Spa: Sulphur baths at Lisdoonvarna, ☎ (065) 74023. IR£6 for a bath in this little-changed Victorian Spa well.

Golf: At Lahinch, ☎ (065) 81003. At Shannon (between the runways of the airport and the estuary), ☎ (061) 61020; Dromoland Castle, ☎ (061) 368444.

Pony-trekking: Residential Riding Holidays at Clonmore Lodge, Quilty, ✆ (065) 87020. Cliffs of Moher Equestrian Centre, Liscannor, ✆ (065) 81283. Trekking through the Burren with the Yellow Rose Riding Centre, Ballinagaddy, Ennistymon, ✆ (065) 71385.

Hunting: Clare Hunt meets from early November to mid-March, ✆ (061) 364146/368329.

Conducted walks: in the Burren area to look at flora, ✆ (065) 20885 or (065) 74603/74580; Burren Education Centre, ✆ (065) 78066.

Traditional music: Clare is particularly famous for its music sessions. Ennistymon boasts some good venues, as does Doolin. Try McGann's, O'Connors or Vaughans in Kilfenora. For a quiet drink in Ballyvaughan, try O'Lochlain's which is more traditional than the touristy Mark's. For a spot of knee-bending, Lois na h Abhna on the Gort road, outside Ennis organises 'Ceilidhs' (traditional Irish dancing). Set dancing and music, ✆ (065) 20996 for details.

Where to Stay
luxury

Dromoland Castle, Newmarket-on-Fergus, ✆ (061) 368144. Owned by the consortium that also operates Ashford Castle in Co. Mayo, the hotel has beautiful grounds, golf course and delicious food; the atmosphere is a bit impersonal.

Lord Inchiquin, **Thomond House**, Newmarket-on-Fergus, ✆ (061) 368304. Conor O'Brien, the 18th Baron Inchiquin, is the O'Brien of Thomond. The exquisite Georgian-style house overlooks Dromoland Castle and its lake, the original home of the O'Briens which is now a luxury hotel. There is salmon fishing, deer stalking, riding and golf, all of which need to be arranged in advance.

expensive

Gregan's Castle, near Ballyvaughan, ✆ (065) 77005. Not actually a castle, but an old manor house with delicious food and comfortable rooms. Set at the top of Corkscrew Hills, in green gardens which are in fantastic contrast to the Burren moonscape, with wonderful views over Galway Bay.

The **Falls Hotel**, Ennistymon, ✆ (065) 71004. Had a great reputation 50 years ago, and still has a spectacular river view. Full of atmosphere and faded charm.

moderate

Ballinalacken Castle Hotel, Lisdoonvarna, ✆ (065) 74025. Beautifully situated overlooking the beach. Recently upgraded from guesthouse to hotel.

Ballykilty Manor, Quin, ✆ (065) 25627. Set in wooded grounds with fishing on the River Rine.

Keane's Hotel, Lisdoonvarna, ✆ (065) 74011. Small family-run hotel.

Carnelly House, Castlecastle, ✆ (065) 28442. Early Georgian house with wonderful Francini ceiling. Elegant rooms. Only 9m from Shannon Airport.

Sheedy's Spa View Hotel, Lisdoonvarna, ℰ (065) 74026. Friendly, family-run hotel with a popular restaurant.

inexpensive

Fergus View, Kilnaboy, Corrofin, ℰ (065) 27606. Farmhouse with good home-cooking. Mary Kelleher makes all her own yoghurt and museli.

Caherbolane Farm, Corrofin, ℰ (065) 27638. Simple but good cooking.

Ballymarkham House, Quin ℰ (065) 25726. Fine country house.

Kelleher family, **Inchiquin View**, Killinaboy, ℰ (065) 37731. Comfortable modern farmhouse.

Smyths Village, Feakle, ℰ (0619) 24002. Cosy fishing hotel.

Mrs O'Connor, **Clohaunincy House**, Seafield, Quilty, ℰ (065) 87081. Good home-cooking.

Halpin's Hotel, 2 Erin Street, Kilkee, ℰ (065) 56032. Good service and comfort in cosy hotel.

Dilly Griffey and family, **Lahardan House**, Crusheen, Ennis, ℰ (065) 27128. Old family house, comfortable rooms with en suite baths, and delicious home-cooking.

Parochial House, Cooraclare, ℰ (065) 59059. Relaxed, family home in former priest's residence. Good for children and handy for Killimer car ferry.

The **Doolin Hostel**, Doolin, ℰ (065) 74006. Modern with a shop and kitchen facilities.

John and Anne Simms, **Island View**, Doolin, ℰ (065) 74346. Friendly, knowledgeable hosts, very comfortable.

self-catering

Old-style farmhouse. Contact **Mrs O'Callahan**, Blean, Killydysart, ℰ (065) 26594.

Mount Shannon Village: traditional-style cottages, close to the harbour and sailing club. Contact **Bridie Cook**, Gortatleva Bushypark, Galway, ℰ (091) 25295. IR£130–430 a week, depending on the season.

Rent-an-Irish-cottage, Ballyvaughan. Traditional cottages, ℰ (061) 411109.

Bellharbour traditional-style cottages, on the coast between Ballyvaughan and Kinvara. Contact Jacinta Stacey, **Trident Holiday Homes**, Unit 2, Sandymount Village Centre, Dublin 4. ℰ (01) 683534. IR£140–410 per week.

Traditional Irish Cottages, Feakle, in the east Clare lakelands. Contact the Secretary, Mrs B. Purcell, **Irish Cottages**, Feakle, ℰ (061) 924053.

Traditional farm cottage near Mullagh, with sea-view. Contact **Mrs Torpey**, Mullagh, Ennis, ℰ (065) 87031. From IR£150 a week.

5-bedroomed old Georgian house, Corrofin. **Mr Cronin Magle**, Corrofin, ℰ (061) 411773. IR£475–575.

expensive

MacCloskey's Restaurant, Bunratty House Mews, Bunratty, ✆ (061) 364082. In the cellars of an attractive house built in 1846 by a hopeful son waiting to inherit the castle from his father. Décor and atmosphere reflect a vanished leisurely way of life. Exquisite food. *Evenings only.*

moderate

Au Tintean Restaurant, Main Street, Doonbeg, ✆ (065) 55036. Seafood restaurant with Swiss chef. *Evenings only.*

Gregan's Castle, near Ballyvaughan, ✆ (065) 77005. Delicious food all day in the Corkscrew Bar, with its low-beamed ceiling and welcoming fire.

Claire's Restaurant, Ballyvaughan, ✆ (065) 77029. Small and unpretentious with a vegetarian dish as standard, great atmosphere. Very popular locally.

Medieval banquets at Bunratty and Knappoque Castles through Castle Tours, ✆ (061) 61788 (*see* pp.185–6).

The Orchard Restaurant in **Sheedy's Spa View Hotel**, Lisdoonvarna, ✆ (065) 74026. Surprisingly sophisticated food in this family run hotel.

Mr Eamons, Lahinch, ✆ (065) 81050.

Barrtia Seafood Restaurant, Lahinch, ✆ (065) 81280. Simple but good seafood restaurant just outside Lahinch with views of the bay.

Manuel's Seafood Restaurant, Corbally, Kilkee, ✆ (065) 56211. Fabulous views over the bay, the River Shannon and the Kerry Mountains. *Dinner only.*

inexpensive

Lantern House, Ogonnello, Killaloe, ✆ (061) 23034. Home cooking, overlooking Lough Derg.

Aillwee Cave Restaurant, Ballyvaughan, ✆ (065) 77036/77067. Eating in a cave is rather a novel experience. Delicious soups, pies, cakes. Lunch only.

Roadside Tavern, Lisdoonvarna, ✆ (065) 74084. Wood-panelled pub-cum-smoking house. Delicious smoked trout, salmon and chowder.

The Cloister, Abbey Street, Ennis, ✆ (065) 29521. Old World bar. Good soups, local cheeses, bread during the daytime; more formal (and expensive) at night.

Mac's Pub, Mount Shannon. Good atmosphere and bar snacks.

Durty Nelly's, Bunratty, ✆ (065) 364861. Pub and eating house popular with locals as well as visitors.

An Fear Gorta, Pier Road, Ballyvaughan, ✆ (065) 77023. Tea room and restaurant, good cakes and seafood.

Linnane's Bar, New Quay, ✆ (065) 78120. Pub specialising in lobster and oysters.

Monk's Bar, Ballyvaughan. Delicious mussels and brown bread; traditional music.

The Old Gods and Heroes

The first Celts arrived in Ireland before 1000 BC; the last around the 2nd century BC. The Greek chroniclers were the first to name these people, calling them Keltori. Celt means act of concealment, and it has been suggested that they were called 'hidden people' because of their reluctance to commit their great store of scholarship and knowledge to written records. Kilt, the short male skirt of traditional Celtic dress, may also come from this word!

The Celtic civilization was quite sophisticated, and much of the road-building attributed to the Romans has been found to have been started by the Celts. The Romans built on their foundations. In Ireland, ancient roads are quite often discovered when bog is being cleared.

The Irish language, and its ancient and rich epic stories, is predated only by Greek and Latin. But the tradition was strictly oral until the Christian era. Even then, it was well into the 7th century before the bulk of it was written down by scribes, who often added to or changed the story to make some moral Christian interpretation. The reluctance of the Celts to commit their knowledge to writing is directly related to the Druids and their power, for the Druidic religion was the cornerstone of the Celtic world, which stretched from Ireland to the Continent and as far south as Turkey. Irish mythology is therefore concerned with the rest of that Celtic world: there are relationships with the gods and heroes of Wales, Scotland, Spain and middle Europe.

The Book of the Dun Cow and *The Book of Leinster*, the main surviving manuscript sources, date from the late 11th century. Many earlier books were destroyed by the Viking raids and entire libraries lost. The various sagas and romances which survived have been categorized by scholars into four cycles. First, the **mythological cycle**: the stories which tell of the various invasions of Ireland, from Cessair to the Sons of Milesius. These are largely concerned with the activities of the Tuatha dé Danaan, the pagan gods of Ireland. Next there is the **Ulster Cycle**, or deeds of the Red Branch Knights, which include the tales of Cú Chulainn. Then there is the **Cycle of Kings**, mainly stories about semi-mythical rulers, and finally, the **Fenian Cycle** which relates the adventures of Fionn MacCumhail (Finn MacCool) and the warriors of the Fianna. Only qualified story-tellers could relate these sagas and tales under Brehon (Celtic) laws, and they were held in great respect. Several qualities emerge from these sagas and tell us a great deal about the society of Iron Age Ireland, and indeed Europe. The stories are always optimistic, and the Celts had evolved a doctrine of immortality of the soul.

The heroes and gods were interchangeable—there were no hard and fast divisions between gods and mortals. Both had the ability to shape change, and often reappear after the most gruesome deaths. The gods of the dé Danaan were tall, beautiful and fair, although, later, in the popular imagination they became fairies or the 'little people'. They were intellectual as well as beautiful, and as gullible as mortals with all our virtues and vices. They loved pleasure, art, nature, games, feasting and heroic single combat. It is difficult to know whether they are heroes and heroines made into gods by their ancestors. In the 11th century, Cú Chulainn was the most admired hero, particularily by the élite of society. Then Fionn MacCumhail took over. He and his band of warriors became very popular with the ordinary people right up to the early 20th century. The English conquests in the 17th century and the resulting destruction and exile of the Irish intelligentsia meant that much knowledge was lost, though the peasantry kept it alive in folklore recited by the *seanachie* or village story-teller. Then, with the famines and vast immigration of the 19th century, the Irish language came under great threat and, with it, the folklore.

It was anglicized by antiquarians and scholars at the end of the 18th century, and later in the 19th century, who did much to record and translate the Irish epic stories into English, and to preserve the Gaelic; many were Ulster Presbyterians. Other names which should be remembered with honour are William Carleton, Lady Wylde, T. Crofton-Croker, Standish James O'Grady, Lady Gregory and Douglas Hyde. Their writings and records of Irish peasant culture have become standard works.

The question of where Irish myth ends and history begins is impossible to define. Historical accounts are shot through with allegory, supernatural happenings and fantasy. Nothing has changed, for a similar mythical process is applied to modern history.

Directory of the Gods

Amergin: a Son of Milesius. The first Druid of Ireland. There are three poems credited to him in *The Book of Invasions*.

Aonghus Óg: the God of Love. His palace was by the River Boyne at Newgrange.

Ard Rí: the title of High King.

Badb: goddess of battles.

Balor: a god of death, and one of the most formidable Fomorii. His one eye destroyed everything it gazed on. Destroyed by his own grandson, Lugh.

Banba, Fotla and Eire dé Danaan: sister goddesses who represent the spirit of Ireland, particularily in Irish literature and poetry. It is from the goddess Eire that Ireland takes its modern name.

Bilé: god of life and death. He appears as Cymbeline in Shakespeare's play.

Bran: 'Voyage of Bran'. The earliest voyage poem, which describes through beautiful imagery the Island of Joy and the Island of Women. Also, the hound of Fionn MacCumhail.

Brigid: goddess of healing, fertility and poetry. Her festival is one of the four great festivals of the Celtic world. Also a Christian saint who has become confused in popular folklore with the goddess.

Caílte: cousin of Fionn MacCumhail. One of the chief Warriors of the Fianna, and a poet. A Christian addition to his story has returned him from the Otherworld to recount to St Patrick the adventures of the Fianna.

Conall Cearnach: son of Amergin, a warrior of the Red Branch, and foster brother and blood cousin of Cú Chulainn. He avenged Cú Chulainn's death by slaying his killers.

Conchobhar MacNessa: king of Ulster during the Red Branch Cycle. He fell in love with Deidre (*see* below) and died from a magic 'brain ball' which had been lodged in his head seven years before by the Connacht warrior, Cet.

Conn: one of the Sons of Lir, the ocean god, changed into a swan by his jealous stepmother, Aoife. Also, Conn of the hundred battles, High King from AD 177 to 212.

Cormac MacArt: High King from AD 254 to 277 and patron of the Fianna, who reigned during the period of Fionn MacCumhail and his adventures. His daughter was betrothed to Fionn MacCumhail but eloped with one of Fionn's warriors, Diarmuid. His son succeeded him and destroyed the Fianna.

Cú Chulainn: the hound of Culann, also called the Hound of Ulster. He has similarities with the Greek hero, Achilles. He was actually called Sétanta until he killed the hound belonging to Culann, a smith god from the Otherworld. He promised to take its place and guarded his fortress at night. He became a great warrior whose battle frenzy was incredible. Women were always falling in love with him, but Emer, his wife, managed to keep him. He is chiefly famous for his single-handed defence of Ulster during the War of the Tain (Bull of Cuailgne) when Ailill and Medb of Connacht invaded (*see* Medb). He was acknowledged as champion of all Ireland, and forced to slay his best friend, Ferdia, during a combat at a crucial ford. Later Cú Chulainn rejected the love of the goddess of battles, Mórrigan, and his doom was sealed; his enemies finally slew him. During the fatal fight he strapped his body to a pillar stone because he was too weak to stand. But such was his reputation that no one dared to come near him until Mórrigan, in the form of a crow, perched on his shoulder, and finally an otter drank his blood.

Dagha: father of the Gods and patron god of the Druids.

Diarmuid: foster son of the love god, Aonghas Óg, and a member of the Fianna. The goddess of youth put her love spot on him, so that no woman could resist loving him. He eloped with Grainne, who was betrothed to Fionn MacCumhail, and the Fianna pursued them for 16 years. Eventually the couple made an uneasy peace with Fionn, who went out hunting with Diarmuid on Ben Bulben, where Diarmuid was gored by an enchanted boar who was also his own stepbrother. Fionn had the power to heal him with some enchanted water, but he let it slip through his fingers. Aoughas Óg, the god of love, took Diarmuid's body to his palace and, although he did not restore him to life, sent a soul into his body so that he could talk to him each day.

Deidre: Deidre of the Sorrows was the daughter of an Ulster chieftain. When she was born it was forecast by a Druid that she would be the most beautiful woman in the land, but that, because of her, Ulster would suffer great ruin and death. Her father wanted to put her to death at once but Conchobhar, the Ulster King, took pity on her and said he would marry her when she grew up. When the time came she did not want to marry such an old man, particularly as she had fallen in love with Naoise, a hero of the Red Branch. They eloped to Scotland. Conchohbar lured them back with false promises, and Naoise and his brothers were killed by Eoghan MacDuracht. Deidre was forced to become Conchobhar's wife. She did not smile for a year, which infuriated her husband. When he asked her who she hated most in the world, she replied, 'you and Eoghan MacDuracht'. The furious Conchobhar then said she must be Eoghan's wife for a year. When she was put in Eoghan's chariot with her hands bound, she somehow mangaged to fling herself out and dash her head against a rock. A pine tree grew from her grave and touched another pine growing from Naoise's grave, and the two intertwined.

Emain Macha: the capital of the kings of Ulster for six centuries, which attained great glory during the time of King Conchobhar and the Red Branch Knights.

Emer: wife of Cú Chulainn. She had the six gifts of womanhood: beauty, chastity, eloquence, needlework, sweet voice and wisdom.

Female champions: in ancient Irish society women had equal rights with men. They could be elected to any office, inherit wealth and hold full ownership under law. Cú Chulainn was instructed in the martial arts by Scáthach, and there was another female warrior in the Fianna called Creidue. Battlefields were always presided over by goddesses of war. Nessa, Queen of Ulster, and Queen Medb of Connacht were great warriors and leaders. Boadicea of Britain was a Celtic warrior queen who died in AD 62, and this tradition survived with Grace O'Malley of County Mayo into the 16th century.

Ferdia: the best friend of Cú Chulainn, killed by him in a great and tragic combat in the battle over the Brown Bull of Cuailgne (or Cooley).

Fergus MacRoth: Stepfather of Conchobhar, used by him to deceive Deidre and Naoise and his brothers. He went into voluntary exile to Connacht in a great fury with the King, and fought against Conchobhar and the Red Branch. But he refused to fight against Cú Chulainn, which meant the ultimate defeat of Queen Medb and her armies.

The Fianna: known as the Fenians. A band of warriors guarding the high king of Ireland. Said to have been founded in about 300 BC, they were perhaps a caste of the military élite. Fionn MacCumhail was their greatest leader. In the time of Oscar, his grandson, they destroyed themselves through a conflict between the clans Bascna and Morna. In the 19th century the term was revived as a synonym for Irish Republican Brotherhood, and today it is used as the title for one of the main Irish political parties, Fianna Fail, which means 'Soldiers of Destiny'.

Fintan: the husband of Cesair, the first invader of Ireland. He abandoned her and survived the Great Deluge of the Bible story by turning into a salmon. Also, the Salmon of

Knowledge who ate the Nuts of Knowledge before swimming to a pool in the River Boyne, where he was caught by the Druid Finegas. He was given to Fionn MacCumhail to cook. Fionn burnt his finger on the flesh of the fish as he was turning the spit, sucked his thumb, and acquired the knowledge for himself.

Fionn MacCumhail: anglicized as Finn MacCool. He was brought up by two wise women, then sent to study under Finegas, the Druid. After acquiring the Knowledge of the salmon, Fintan, he became known as Fionn, the Fair One. He was appointed head of the Fianna by Cormac MacArt, the High King at the time, in place of Goll MacMorna who had killed his father. His exploits are many and magical. His two famous hunting hounds were Bran and Sceolan, who were actually his own nephews, the children of his bewitched sister. His son, Oísín, was the child of the goddess Sadb, but he suffered unrequited love for Grainne. In the story of the Battle of Ventry, Fionn overcomes Daire Donn, the King of the World. He is said not to be dead, but sleeping in a cave, waiting for the call to help Ireland in her hour of need.

Fionnbharr and Oonagh: gods of the dé Danaan who have degenerated into the King and Queen of the Fairies in folklore.

Fionnuala: the daughter of Lir. She and her brothers were transformed into swans by her jealous stepmother, Aoife. The spell was broken with the coming of Christianity, but they were old and senile by then.

Fir Bolg: 'Bagmen'. A race who came to Ireland before the dé Danaan. They do not take much part in the myths.

Fomorii: a misshapen and violent people, the evil gods of Irish myth. Their headquarters seems to have been Tory Island, off the coast of County Donegal. Their leaders include Balor of the Evil Eye, and their power was broken for ever by the dé Danaan at the second Battle of Moytura, in County Sligo.

Gaul: Celt: Gaulish territory extended over France, Belgium, parts of Switzerland, Bohemia, parts of modern Turkey and parts of Spain.

Geis: a taboo or bond which was usually used by Druids and placed on someone to compel them to obey. Grainne put one on Diarmuid.

Goibhnin: smith god, and god of handicraft and artistry.

Goll MacMorna: leader of the Fianna before Fionn MacCumhail.

Grainne: anglicized as Grania. Daughter of Cormac MacArt, the high king. She was betrothed to Fionn MacCumhail but thought him very old, so she put a *geis* on Diarmuid to compel him to elope with her. Eventually he fell in love with her (see Diarmuid). After Diarmuid's death, although she had sworn vengeance on Fionn, she allowed herself to be wooed by him and became his wife. The Fianna despised her for this.

Laeg: charioteer to Cú Chulainn.

Lir: ocean god.

Lugh: sun god who slew his grandfather, Balor, and the father of Cú Chulainn by a mortal woman. His godly status was diminished into that of a fairy craftsman, Lugh Chromain, a leprechaun.

Macha: a mysterious woman who put a curse called *nioden* on all Ulstermen, so that they would suffer from the pangs of childbirth for five days and four nights in times of Ulster's greatest need. This curse would last nine times nine generations. She did this because her husband boasted to King Conchobhar that she could race and win against the king's horses, even though she was pregnant. She died in agony as a result.

Medb: anglicized as Maeve. Queen of Connacht, and wife of Ailill. She was famous for her role in the epic tale of the cattle raid of Cuailgne (Cooley), which she started when she found that her possessions were not as great as her husband's. She wanted the Brown Bull of Cuailgne which was in Ulster, to outdo her husband's bull, the White-Horned Bull of Connacht. This had actually started off as a calf in her herd, but had declined to stay in the herd of a woman! She persuaded her husband to join her in the great battle that resulted. The men of the Red Branch were hit by the curse of the *noiden* (see Macha), and none could fight except Cú Chulainn, who was free of the weakness the curse induced and single-handedly fought the Connacht champions. Mebh was killed by Forbai, son of Conchobhar, whilst bathing in a lake. The bulls over which the great battle had been fought eventually tore each other to pieces.

Milesians: the last group of invaders of Ireland before the historical period. Milesius was their leader, a Spanish soldier, but his sons actually carried out the Conquest of Ireland.

Nessa: mother of Conchobhar. A strong-minded and powerful woman who secured the throne of Ulster for her son.

Niall of the Nine Hostages: High King from AD 379 to 405, and progenitor of the Uí Neíll dynasty. There is a confusion of myth and history surrounding him.

Niamh: of the golden hair. A daughter of the sea god Manannán Maclir. She asked Oísín to accompany her to the Land of Promise and live there as her lover. After three weeks, he discovered three hundred years had passed.

Nuada of the Silver Hand: the leader of the dé Danaan gods, who had his hand cut off in the great battle with the Fomorii. It was replaced by the god of healing.

Ogma: god of eloquence and literature, from whom Ogham Stones were named. These are upright pillars carved with incised lines which read as an alphabet from the bottom upwards. They probably date from AD 300.

Oísín: son of Fionn and Sadh, the daughter of a god, and leading champion of the Fianna. He refused to help his father exact vengeance on Grainne (to whom Fionn was betrothed) and Diarmuid (with whom Grainne eloped), and went with Niamh of the Golden Hair to the Land of Promise. Oísín longed to go back to Ireland, so Niamh gave him a magic horse on which to return, but warned him not to set foot on land, as three hundred years had passed since he was there. He fell from his horse by accident and turned into an old, blind man. A Christian embellishment is that he met St Patrick, and Oísín told him the stories of the Fianna, and they had long debates about the merits of Christianity. Oísín refused to agree that his Ireland was better off for it. The spirit of his mood comes through in this anonymous verse from a 16th-century poem translated by Frank O'Connor.

> *Patrick you chatter too loud*
> *And lift your crozier too high*
> *Your stick would be kindling soon*
> *If my son Osgar stood by.*

Oscar or Osgar: son of Oísín. He also refused to help Fionn, his grandfather, against Diarmuid and Grainne. The high king of the time wished to weaken the Fianna and allowed the two clans in it, Morna and Bascna, to quarrel. They fought at the battle of Gabhra. Oscar was killed and the Fianna destroyed.

Partholón: the leader of the third mythical invasion of Ireland. He is supposed to have introduced agriculture to Ireland.

Red Branch: a body of warriors who were the guardians of Ulster during the reign of Conchobhar MacNessa. Their headquarters were at Emain Macha. The Red Branch cycle of tales has been compared to the *Iliad* in theme. The main stories are made up of the Tain Bo Cuailgne (the Brown Bull of Cuailgne or Cooley). Scholars accept that the cycle of stories must have been transmitted orally for nearly a thousand years, providing wonderfully accurate descriptions of the remote past.

From Stone Circles to Castles

Ireland is fascinatingly rich in monuments, and you cannot fail to be struck by the number and variety of archaeological remains all over the southwest. They crown the tops of hills or stand out, grey and mysterious, in the green fields. Myths and stories surround them, handed down by word of mouth. Archaeologists too have their theories, and they are as varied and unprovable as the myths!

Man is known to have lived here since Middle Stone Age times (roughly from about 6000 BC). There are no structures left from these times but, after the coming of Neolithic or New Stone Age peoples, some of the most spectacular of the Irish monuments were built.

Here is a brief description of the types to be seen in order of age.

Stone Circles

The stone circles served as prehistoric temples and go back to Early Bronze Age times. Impressive examples may be seen at Lough Gur, County Limerick. Earthen circles probably served a similar purpose. They have been variously interpreted as ritual sites and astronomical calendars. Associated with them are standing stones.

Megalithic Tombs

Neolithic colonisers came with a knowledge of agriculture to Ireland between 3000 and 2000 BC and erected the earliest megalithic chambered tombs. They are called the court cairns, because the tombs are made up of a covered gallery for burial with one or more unroofed courts or forecourts for ritual. Pottery has been found in these tombs. Court cairns are mainly found in the northern part of the country—north of a line between Clew Bay in the west and Dundalk Bay in the east. Linked to the court cairns is the simple and imposing type of megalith —the dolmen or portal dolmen. This consists of a large, sometimes enormous, capstone and three or more supporting uprights. The distribution of the dolmen is more widespread but tends to be eastern.

Another variety of megalith is the wedge-shaped gallery. There are numbers of such tombs in the Burren area in County Clare, where they are built from the limestone slabs so common in the region. Most excavated wedges belong to the Early Bronze Age—2000 to 1500 BC. They are now largely bare of the cairns or mounds which covered them. The people who built them advanced from being hunters to growing crops and keeping domestic animals.

The most spectacular of the great stone tombs are the passage-graves. The graves belong to a great family of structures found from eastern Spain to southern Scandinavia. The decorative carving which covers many of the stones consists of spirals, lozenges and other motifs, and it is thought to have some religious significance. Unchambered burial mounds also occur throughout the country. They date largely from the Bronze Age, but earlier and later examples are known.

Standing Stones

Also known as gallauns. Single pillar stones which also have a ritual significance, and occasionally mark grave sites. Others carry inscriptions in ogham characters.

Ring-forts

The most numerous type of monument to be seen in Ireland is the ring-fort, known also as rath, lios, dun, caher, and cashel. There are about 30,000 in the country. These originated as early as the Bronze Age and continued to be built until the Norman invasion. The circular ramparts, varying in number from one to four, enclosed a homestead with houses of wood, wattle-and-daub or partly stone construction. A well-preserved example of stone forts is that at Staigue, County Kerry.

Hill-forts

Larger and more defensive in purpose are the hill-forts, whose ramparts follow contour lines to encircle hill-tops.

Crannogs

Crannogs, or artificial islands, found in lakes and marshy places, are defensive dwelling sites used by farmers, with even earlier origins than the forts, which continued in use sometimes until the 17th century. The Craggaunowen Centre in county Clare has a very good example.

Early Irish Architecture

Before the Norman invasion most buildings in Ireland were of wood. None of these has survived. In the treeless west, however, tiny corbelled stone buildings shaped like beehives and called **clochans** were constructed. They were used as oratories by holy men. Some, possibly dating from the 7th century, still exist. Clochans are particularly common in County Kerry: there are many in the Dingle Peninsula and some very well preserved examples in the early monastic settlement on the Skellig Rock, off the Kerry coast. Also in Kerry is the best-preserved example of an early boat-shaped oratory, at Gallarus.

Most of the early mortared churches were modelled on wooden prototypes. They were very small, and already were built with stylistic features which are characteristic of Irish buildings: steeply pitched roofs, inclined jambs to door and window-openings. Many of these small churches would have been roofed with wood, tiled or thatched, but some were roofed with stone. The problem of providing a pitched roof of stone over a rectangular structure was solved by inserting a relieving semi-circular arch below the roof. The small space over the arch forms a croft. These buildings lack features by which they can be accurately dated; a conservative dating would be from the beginning of the 9th century onwards.

Round Towers

Contemporary with these early Irish churches and very characteristically Irish, are round towers, of which about 120 are known to have existed in the whole of Ireland. They are tall, gracefully tapering buildings of stone, with conical stone roofs, which were built as monastic belfries, with the door approximately 12ft (3.5m) from the ground. This is a clue to their use as places of refuge or watch towers during the period of Viking raids between the 9th and 11th centuries. Food, precious objects and manuscripts were stored in them. The ladder could then be drawn up. The monk who wrote these beautiful lines expresses the tensions of those days:

> *Bitter the wind tonight,*
> *Combing the sea's hair white:*
> *From the North, no need to fear*
> *the proud sea coursing warrior.*

Version by John Montague

High Crosses

These carved stone crosses, usually in the typical 'Celtic' ringed form, contain a great variety of Biblical scenes and ornament. They are found in most parts of the country in early monastic sites. The earliest type are simple crosses carved on standing stones. They are most common in the west and in the Dingle Peninsula, County Kerry. The development of low-relief carving began in the 7th century, gradually becoming more complex. The ringed high cross first appears at a later date; the earliest group of high crosses, dating from the 8th century.

Sandstone was used again for these crosses in the 10th century; they still grace monastic ruins scattered across the Central Plain. The West Cross and Muiredach's Cross at Monasterboice in County Louth are the best examples. In each case the east and west faces are carved with scriptural scenes while the north and south faces have spirals, vine-scrolls, and other decorations. Favourite subjects for the carver were the Crucifixion; the Last Judgment; Adam and Eve; Cain and Abel; and the arrest of Christ.

By the end of the 11th century the cross was changed; the ring was often left off, and the whole length of the shaft was taken up with a single figure of the crucified Christ. Ecclesiastical figures often appear on the opposite face and on the base, and the decoration of the north and south faces usually consists of animal-interlacing. Crosses of this style were carved up until the mid-12th century.

Romanesque Architecture

Characteristics of this decorative style appear in Irish buildings of the 12th century. While remaining structurally simple, the Irish churches of the period have carved doorways, chancel-arches or windows, with ornament in an Irish variation of the style.

Many of the characteristic features of the early churches, such as antae and sloping jambs, were kept throughout the Romanesque period. The use of the chevron, an ornamental moulding, is common in Irish-Romanesque work, and it is nearly always combined with rows of beading.

Transitional Architecture

At the same time as the Romanesque style was so popular, another plainer type of church building was being introduced by the Cistercian order. They were designed after churches of the Continental type and carved decoration was simple.

Gothic Architecture

With the coming of the Normans and changes they wrought, the native tradition in building declined, and Gothic architecture was introduced in the 13th century. The Irish Gothic cathedrals were on a smaller scale than their English and Continental counterparts and the grouping of lancets in the east window and south choir wall are typical of the Irish buildings. Gothic parish churches in the plain Early-English style were built only in the anglicized parts of the country. Because of the turbulent times during the 14th century there was very little building done in Ireland, but this changed in the 15th and 16th centuries and a native Gothic style began to emerge, particularly in the west. It is best seen in the Franciscan friaries and the rebuilt Cistercian abbeys of the period. A good example of the Franciscan style, with narrow church, a tall tapering tower, carved cloister and small window openings can be seen at the well-preserved ruin at Quin, County Clare. The Cistercian style was a larger church with a huge square tower topped by stepped battlements, and a large carved cloister.

Castles

Although the Normans had built many castles before they came to Ireland, in the first years of the invasion they built fortifications of wood, usually taking over the sites of ancient Irish forts. The remains of these can be seen in the form of mottes and baileys. At the end of the 12th century the construction of stone fortifications on a large scale began. A very attractive feature of the Irish countryside is the ruined 15th- or 16th-century tower house. From about 1420 these buildings became common fortified farms consisting of a tall, square tower which usually had a small walled bawn or courtyard.

Glossary of Archaeological, Architectural and Associated Terms

Anglo-Norman: the name commonly given to the 12th-century invaders of Ireland, who came in the main from southwest Britain, and also their descendants, because they were of Norman origin.

Bailey: the space enclosed by the walls of a castle, or the outer defenses of a motte (*see* Motte-and-bailey).

Barrel-vaulting: simple vaulting of semi-circular form..

Bastion: a projecting feature of the outer parts of a fortification, designed to command the approaches to the main wall.

Battlement: a parapet pierced with gaps to enable the defenders to discharge missiles.

Bawn: a walled enclosure forming the outer defences of a castle or tower-house. Besides being an outer defence it provided a safe enclosure for cattle.

Beehive hut: a prehistoric circular building, of wood or stone, with a dome-shaped roof, called a clochan.

Bronze Age: the earliest metal-using period from the end of the Stone Age until the coming of the Iron Age in Ireland, 2500 BC.

Caher: a stone Fort.

Cairn: a mound of stones over a prehistoric grave; they frequently cover chambered tombs.

Cashel: a stone fort, surrounded by a rampart of dry stone walling, usually of late Iron Age date (*see* Ring-fort).

Chancel or choir: the east end of a church, reserved for the clergy and choir, and containing the high altar.

Chapter house: the chamber in which the chapter, or governing body of a cathedral or monastery met

Chevaux-de-frise: a stone or stake defence work set upright and spaced.

Cist: A box-like grave of stone slabs to contain an inhumed or cremated burial, often accompanied by pottery. Usually Bronze Age or Iron Age in date.

Clochans (I): little groups of cottages, too small to be villages, grouped in straggly clusters according to land tenure and the ties of kinship between families. The land around the clochan forms the district known as a townland. A familiar sight is deserted or ruined clochans in mountain and moorland areas where huge numbers of people left with the sheep-clearances and famine during the 19th century.

Clochan (clochaun) (II): a small stone building, circular in plan, with its roof corbelled inwards in the form of a beehive. There are many examples in the west, especially in County Kerry. The word clochan is from the Irish *cloch*, a stone. The structures were early monks' cells. Nowadays they are used for storing things.

Cloisters: a square or rectangular open space, surrounded by a covered passage, which gives access to the various parts of a monastery. Many medieval cloisters survive in Ireland, e.g. at Quin, County Clare.

Columbarium: a dovecote.

Corbel: a projecting stone in a building, usually intended to carry a beam or other structural member.

Corbelled vault: a 'false dome', constructed by laying horizontal rings of stones which overlap on each course until finally a single stone can close the gap at the centre. It is a feature of prehistoric tombs.

Corinthian: the third order of Greek and Roman architecture, a development of the Ionic. The capital has acanthus-leaf ornamentation.

Court cairn: a variety of megalithic tomb consisting of a covered gallery for burials and one or more open courts or forecourts for ritual purposes.

Crannog: an artificial island constructed in a lake or marsh to provide a dwelling-place in an easily defended position for isolated farming families. They would have been in use until the 17th century.

Curragh or currach: a light canoe consisting of skins, or in more recent times tarred canvas, stretched over a wickerwork frame.

Curtain wall: the high wall constructed around a castle and its bailey, usually provided at intervals with towers.

Demesne: land/estate surrounding a house which the owner has retained for his own use.

Dolmen: the simplest form of megalithic tomb, consisting of a large capstone and three or more supporting uprights. Some appear to have had forecourts.

Doric: the first order of Greek and Roman architecture, simple and robust in style. The column had no base and the capital was quite plain.

Dun: a fort, usually of stone and often with formidable defences.

Early English: the earliest Gothic architecture of England and Ireland, where it flourished in the 13th century. It is characterized by narrow lancet windows, high pointed arches and the use of rib-vaulting.

Esker: a bank or ridge of gravel and sand, formed by sub-glacial streams.

Folly: a structure set up by a landlord to provide work for needy tenants in the 19th century, and to amuse himself.

Fosse: a defensive ditch or moat around a castle or fort.

Gallaun: *see* Standing Stone.

Gallowglass: Scottish mercenary soldier hired by Irish clan leaders to fight their enemies.

Hill-fort: a large fort whose defences follow a contour round a hill to enclose the hilltop. Hill-forts are usually Early Iron Age.

Hospital: in medieval times, an alms-house or house of hospitality with provision for spiritual as well as bodily welfare, usually established to cater for a specific class of people.

Ionic: the second order of Greek and Roman architecture. The fluted column was tall and graceful in proportion and the capital had volutes (spiral scrolls in stone) at the top.

Irish-Romanesque: the Irish variety of the Romanesque style in architecture. (See Romanesque).

Iron Age: the Early Iron Age is the term applied to the earliest iron-using period: in Ireland, from the end of the Bronze Age, *c.* 500 BC, to the coming of Christianity in the 5th century.

Jamb: the side of a doorway, window or fireplace. Early Irish churches have characteristic jambs inclined inwards towards the top. The incline is called the batter.

Keep: the main tower of a castle, serving as the innermost stonghold. Castles with keeps date from the late 12th century until about 1260.

Kerne: an Irish foot-soldier of Tudor times.

Kitchen-midden: a prehistoric refuse-heap, in which articles of bronze, iron, flint and stone have been found; also shellfish debris, which indicate what our ancestors ate.

Lancet: a tall, narrow window ending in a pointed arch, characteristic of the Early-English style. Lancets often occur in groups of three, five or seven.

La Tène: a pre-Christian Irish classic ornamental style, which is linked to ornamental designs found in France.

Lunula: a crescent-shaped, thin, beaten gold ornament, of Early Bronze Age date—an Irish speciality.

Megalithic tomb: a tomb built of large stones for collective burial, Neolithic or Early Bronze Age in date.

Misericord or miserere: a carved projection on the underside of a hinged folding seat which, when the seat was raised, gave support to the infirm during the parts of a church service when they had to stand. Good examples in St Mary's Cathedral, Limerick.

Motte-and-bailey: the first Norman fortresses which were made of earth. The motte was a flat-topped mound, shaped like a truncated cone, surrounded by a fosse and surmounted by a wooden keep. An enclosure, the bailey, bounded by ditch, bank and palisade, adjoined it. The bailey served as a refuge for cattle and in it were the sheds and huts of the retainers. This type of stronghold continued to be built until the early 13th century.

Nave: the main body of the church, sometimes seperated from the choir by a screen.

Neolithic: applied to objects from the New Stone Age which was characterized by the practice of agriculture, in Ireland, between 3000 and 2000 BC.

Ogham stones: early Irish writing, usually cut on stone. The characters consist of strokes above, below or across a stem-line. The key to the alphabet may be seen in the *Book of Ballymote*, now in the library of the Royal Irish Academy, Dublin. Ogham inscriptions occur mainly on standing stones. The inscription is usually commemorative in character. They probably date from AD 300.

Pale: the district around Dublin, of varying extent at different periods, where English rule was effective for some four centuries after the Norman invasion of 1169.

Passage grave: a type of megalithic tomb consisting of a burial-chamber approached by a long passage, and covered by a round mound or cairn.

Pattern: the festival of a saint, held on the traditional day of his death.

Plantation castles: a name given to defensive buildings erected by English and Scottish settlers under the plantation scheme between 1610 and 1620.

Portcullis: a heavy grating in a gateway, sliding up and down in slots in the jambs, which could be used to close the entrance quickly.

Rath: the rampart of an earthen ring-fort. The name is often used for the whole structure.

Rib-vaulting: roofing or ceiling in which the weight of the superstructure is carried on comparatively slender intersecting 'ribs' or arches of stone, the spaces between the ribs being a light stone filling without structural function.

Ring-fort, rath or lis: one or more banks and ditches enclosing an area, usually circular, within which were dwellings. It was the typical homestead of Early-Christian Ireland, but examples are known from *c.* 1000 BC to *c.* AD 1000. The bank sometimes had a timber palisade. Some elaborate examples were defensive in purpose.

Romanesque: the style of architecture, based on late Classical forms, with round arches and vaulting, which prevailed in Europe until the emergence of Gothic in the 12th century. See Irish-Romanesque.

Round towers: slender stone belfries, also used as refuges. Built between the 9th and 12th centuries.

Rundale: a system of holding land in strips or detached portions.

Sedilia: seats recessed in the south wall of the chancel, near the altar, for the use of the clergy.

Sept: in the old Irish system, those ruling families who traced their descent from a common ancestor.

Sheila-na-Gig: a cult symbol or female fertility figure, carved in stone on churches or castles. No one is sure of their origin.

Souterrain: artificial underground chambers of wood, stone, earth, or cut into rock. They served as refuges or stores and in some cases even as dwellings. They occur commonly in ring-forts and, like these, date from the Bronze Age to at least Early-Christian times.

Standing stone: an upright stone set in the ground. These may be of various dates and served various purposes, marking burial places or boundaries, or serving as cult objects.

Stone fort: a ring-fort built of dry-stone walling.

Sweat houses: an ancient form of sauna. Sometimes the mentally ill were incarcerated in them for a while in an attempt to cure them.

Teampull: a church.

Torc: a gold ornament from the Middle to Late Bronze Age, made of a ribbon or bar of gold twisted like a rope and bent around to form a complete loop. They are of Middle to Late Bronze Age date

Tracery: the open-work pattern formed by the stone in the upper part of Middle- or Late-Gothic window.

Transepts: the 'arms' of a church, extending at right-angles to the north and south from the junction of nave and choir.

Tumulus: a mound of earth over a grave; usually the mound over an earth-covered passage grave.

Undertaker: one of the English or Scottish planters who were given confiscated land in Ireland in the 16th century. They 'undertook' certain obligations designed to prevent the dispossessed owners from reacquiring their land.

Vaulting: a roof or ceiling formed by arching over a space. Among the many methods, three main types were used: barrel-vaulting, groin-vaulting and rib-vaulting. Rib-vaulting lent itself to great elaboration of ornament.

Zoomorphic: describing decoration based on the forms of animals.

The Irish Language

The Irish language is the purest of all the Celtic languages, and Ireland is one of the last homes of the oral tradition of prehistoric and medieval Europe. Preserved by the isolated farming communities, there are also many expressions from the dialects of early English settlers. Irish was spoken by the Norman aristocracy and they patronized the Gaelic poets and bards. But with the establishment of an English system of land tenure and an English-speaking nobility Gaelic became scarce, except in the poorer farming areas. The potato famine in the 1840s hit the people who lived in such areas, thousands died and emigrated, and Gaelic speaking was severely reduced.

The Gaelic League, founded in 1870, initiated a new interest and pride in the language and became identified with the rise of nationalism. In 1921 its survival became part of the the new State's policy. It was decided that the only way to preserve Gaelic was to protect and stimulate it where it was still a living language. The areas where it is spoken today are mostly in the west, and around the mountainous coast and islands. They form the Gaeltacht. Here everything is done to promote Irish-speaking in industry and at home. Centres have been set up for students to learn amongst native speakers. There are special grants for people living in Irish-speaking areas but the boundaries are rather arbitrary.

You can appreciate all the reasons for promoting Irish, but it is only in the last few generations that the language has become popular. Before, it was left to Douglas Hyde and Lady Gregory to demonstrate the richness of Irish language and myth, and they had the advantage of being far away from the grim realities of hunger and poverty that the Irish-speakers knew. Gaelic, like certain foods (usually vegetables), had associations with hunger and poverty, and belonged to a hard past. Even now, people prefer to use English rather than stay in the Gaeltacht existing on grants and other government hand-outs. Gaelic is a compulsory subject in schools in the Republic, and there is a certain amount in the newspapers, on television, signposts and street names (with English translations!). But on the whole it is only *just* a living language.

The carrying over of the Irish idiom into English is very attractive and expressive. J. M. Synge captured this in his play *Riders to the Sea*. In fact, English as spoken by the Irish is in a class of its own. Joyce talked of 'the sacred eloquence of Ireland', and it is true that you could hardly find a more articulate people. Their poetry and prose is superb, and the emotions which their songs and ballads can release is legendary. Hardship has not killed the instinctive desire within to explain life away with words. The monks who scribbled in the margin of their psalters wrote with oriental simplicity this poem entitled 'Winter'.

> My tiding for you: The stag bells
> Winter snows, summer is gone.
> Wind is high and cold, low the sun,
> Short his course, sea running high.
> Deep red the bracken, its shape all gone,
> The wild goose has raised his wonted cry.
> Cold has caught the wings of birds;
> season of ice—these are my tidings.

(9th-century, translation by Kuno Meyer)

That hardship brings forth great poetry is a theory strengthened by the school of contemporary Northern Irish poets who have become known all over the world: Seamus Heaney, James Simmons, Derek Mahon, to name a few. The cutting criticisms of Brian O'Nolan (known as Flann O'Brien), the gentle irony of Frank O'Connor and the furious passion of Sean O'Casey, Patrick Kavanagh and Liam O'Flaherty to name only a few, have become part of our perception of the Irish spirit since Independence. The list of recent writers could go on and on. One can only urge you to read them. There is a particularly good anthology of short stories edited by Benedict Kiely and published by Penguin, and an anthology of Irish verse, edited by John Montague and published by Faber & Faber which you could get copies of.

Even though the disciplined cadences of the Gaelic bardic order was broken by the imposition of an English nobility in the 17th and 18th centuries, the Irish skill with words has survived, and is as strong as ever. As a visitor to Ireland you will notice this way with words when you have a conversation in a pub, or ask the way at a crossroads, or simply chat to the owners of the farmhouse where you spend the night.

The Meaning of Irish Place Names

The original Gaelic place names have been complicated by attempts to give them an English spelling. In the following examples, the Gaelic versions of the prefixes come first, followed by the English meaning.

agh, augh, achadh	a field
aglish, eaglais	a church
ah, atha, áth	a ford
all, ail, aill	a cliff
anna, canna, éanarch	a marsh
ard, ar, ard	a height
as, ess, eas	a waterfall
aw, ow, atha	a river
bal, bel, béal	the mouth (of a river or valley)
bal, balli, bally, baile	a town
ballagh, balla bealach	a way or path
bawn, bane, bán	white
barn, bearna	a gap
beg, beag	small
boola, booley, buaile, booleying	the movement of cattle from lowland to high pastures
boy, buidhe	yellow
bun	the foot (of a valley) or the mouth (of a river)
caher, cahir, cathair, carraig	a rock
cashel, caiseal, caislean	a castle
clogh, cloich, cloch	a stone
clon, clun, cluain	a meadow
derg, dearg	red
doo, du, duv, duf, dubh	black
dun, dún	a fort
dysert, disert	hermitage
glas, glen, gleann	a valley
illaun, oileán	an island
knock, cnoc	a hill
ken, kin, can, ceann	a headland
kil, kill, cill	a church

lis, liss, lios	a fort	*ross, ros*	a peninsula, a wood
lough, loch	a lake or sea inlet		
ma, may, moy, magh	a plain	*see, suidhe*	a seat, e.g. Ossian's seat
mone, mona, móna	turf or bog		
monaster, mainistir	a monastery	*shan, shane, sean*	old
more, mór, mor	big or great	*slieve, sliabh*	a mountain
owen, avon, abhainn	a river	*tir, tyr, tír*	country
rath	a ring-fort	*tubber, tobrid, tubbrid, tobar*	a well
rinn, reen	a point		
roe, ruadh	red	*tra, traw, tráigh, trá*	a strand or beach

Proverbs and Sayings

Wise, and beautifully expressed with a delightful wry humour, these sayings and proverbs have passed into the English language. They highlight the usual Irish preoccupations with land, God, love, words and drinking, as well as every other subject under the sun. These are just a few examples; for a comprehensive collection read *Gems of Irish Wisdom*, by Padraic O'Farrell.

On God

It's a blessing to be in the Lord's hand as long as he doesn't close his fist.

Fear of God is the beginning of wisdom.

God never closes the door without opening another.

Man proposes, God disposes.

On the Irish Character

The wrath of God has nothing on the wrath of an Irishman outbid for land, or horse or woman.

The best way to get an Irishman to refuse to do something is by ordering it.

The Irish forgive their great men when they are safely buried.

Advice

No property—no friends, no rearing—no manners, no health—no hope!

Never give cherries to pigs, nor advice to a fool.

Bigots and begrudgers will never bid the part farewell.

When everybody else is running, that's the time for you to walk.

You won't be stepped on if you're a live wire.

Keep away from the fellow that was reared in his bare feet, for they will be hardened from walking on people.

If you get the name of an early riser you can sleep till dinner time.

There are finer fish in the sea than have ever been caught.

You'll never plough a field by turning it over in your mind.

Don't make a bid till you walk the land.

A man with humour will keep ten men working.

Do not visit too often or too long.

If you don't own a mount, don't hunt with the gentry.

You can take a man out of the bog but you cannot take the bog out of the man.

What is got badly, goes badly.

A watched pot never boils.

Enough is as good as plenty.

Beware of the horse's hoof, the bull's horn and the Saxon's smile.

Time is the best story-teller.

On Marriage and Love

Play with a woman that has looks, talk marriage with a woman that has property.

After the settlement comes love.

A lad's best friend is his mother until he's the best friend of a lassie.

A pot was never boiled by beauty.

There is no love sincerer than the love of food. (G.B. Shaw)

It's a great thing to turn up laughing having been turned down crying.

Though the marriage bed be rusty, the death bed is still colder.

On Argument and Fighting

Argument is the worst sort of conversation. (Dean Swift)

There is no war as bitter as a war amongst friends.

Whisper into the glass when ill is spoken.

If we fought temptation the way we fight each other we'd be a nation of saints again.

We fought every nation's battles, and the only ones we did not win were our own.

On Women

It takes a woman to outwit the Devil.

A cranky woman, an infant, or a grievance, should never be nursed.

A women in the house is a treasure, a woman with humour in the house is a blessing.

She who kisses in public, often kicks in private.

If she is mean at the table, she will be mean in bed.

On Drinking

If Holy Water was porter he'd be at Mass every morning.

It's the first drop that destroys you; there's no harm at all in the last.

Thirst is a shameless disease, so here's to a shameless cure.

On the Family

Greed in a family is worse than need.

Poets write about their mothers, undertakers about their fathers.

A son's stool in his father's home is as steady as a gable; a father's in his son's, bad luck, is shaky and unstable.

On Old Age

The older the fiddle, the sweeter the tune.

There is no fool like an old fool.

On Loneliness

The loneliest man is the man who is lonely in a crowd.

On Bravery

A man who is not afraid of the sea will soon be drowned. (J. M. Synge)

On Flattery

Soft words butter no turnips, but they won't harden the heart of a cabbage either.

On Experience

Experience is the name everyone gives to their mistakes. (Oscar Wilde)

c. 8000 BC	Humans arrive in Ireland, travelling across the land bridge with Scotland.
c. 3000 BC	New Stone Age race build Newgrange in County Meath.
c. 2000 BC	Arrival of Beaker people.
c. 100 BC	Arrival of one wave of Gaelic (Celtic) peoples.
AD 200	The Kingdom of Meath is founded, and the high kingship at Tara, County Meath begins.
AD 432	St Patrick starts his Mission.
AD *c.* 7–8	Gaelic Christian Golden Age.
795	Viking raids begin.
1014	Battle of Clontarf and death of Brian Boru, the high king who won this decisive battle over the Vikings.
1170	Anglo-Norman conquest begins with the arrival of Richard, Earl of Pembroke, called 'Strongbow'.
1171	Henry II visits Ireland, and secures the submission of many Irish leaders and that of his own Norman barons.
1314	The Bruce Invasion, which failed, under Edward Bruce.
1366 an	Statutes of Kilkenny which forbade the English settler to speak the Gaelic language, adopt an Irish name, wear Irish apparel, or marry Irishwoman.
1394–99	Irish leaders war with Richard II.
1534–35	Rebellion of Silken Thomas, known as the 'Kildare Rebellion'.
1541	Irish Parliament accepts Henry VIII as King of Ireland.
1558	Accession of Elizabeth I. The Reformation does not succeed in Ireland.
1562 on	Elizabethan Conquest and settlement of various counties.
1569–73	The first Desmond Revolt.
1579–83	Final Desmond Revolt and suppression.
1592–1603	Rebellion of the Northern Lords, known as the Tyrone War.

Chronology

1601	Battle of Kinsale—a defeat for Hugh O'Neill, Earl of Tyrone and his Ulster chiefs.
1607	Flight of the Earls of Tyrone and Tyrconnell to the Continent.

1608	Plantation of Ulster with Scots begins in Derry and Down.
1641	Irish Rising begins. At this time, 59 per cent of land in Ireland is held by Catholics.
1642–49	Catholic Confederation of Kilkenny.
1649	Cromwell arrives in Ireland.
1650	Catholic landowners exiled to Connacht.
1652	Cromwellian Act of Settlement.
1660	Restoration of Charles II.
1680	Accession of James II.
1689	April to July, Siege of Derry.
1690	July, The Battle of the Boyne. A great victory for William of Orange.
1691	September to October, Siege of Limerick.
1691	October, Treaty of Limerick.
1695	Beginning of Penal Laws. Catholics now own 14 per cent of land.
1699	Irish woollen industry destroyed by English trade laws.
1704	Protestant non-conformists excluded from public office by Test Act.
1714	Catholics own 7 per cent of land.
1772	Rise of the Patriot Party in parliament, known as Grattan's parliament.
1778	Organization of Irish Volunteers.
1778	Gardiner's Relief Act for Catholics eases the Penal Laws.
1779	English concessions on trade and the repeal of most of the restrictive laws.
1782	Establishment of Irish Parliamentary independence.
1791	The Society of United Irishmen founded.
1795	Orange Order founded.
1798	Rebellion of '98.
1801	Act of Union.
1829	Catholic Emancipation Bill passed.
1842–48	The Young Ireland Movement.
1845–49	The Great Famine which began with the blight of the potato harvest.
1840s on	Emigration of thousands to the New World.
1848	Abortive rising led by Smith O'Brien.

1867	Fenian Rising.
1869	Disestablishment of the Church of Ireland.
1875	Charles Parnell elected Member of Parliament for County Meath.
1877	Parnell becomes Chairman of the Home Rule Confederation.
1879–82	Land war.
1886	Gladstone's first Home Rule Bill for Ireland defeated.
1890	Parnell cited in divorce case and he loses the leadership of the Irish Party in the House of Commons.
1892	Gladstone's second Home Rule Bill defeated.
1893	Gaelic League founded.
1899	The beginning of the Sinn Fein movement.
1903	Wyndham's Land Act.
1912	The third Home Rule Bill introduced.
1913	Ulster Volunteer Force founded.
1914	The outbreak of the First World War. The third Home Rule Bill receives Royal assent, but is deferred until the end of the war.
1916	The Easter Uprising.
1918–21	The Anglo-Irish War.
1920	Amendment Act to the Home Rule Bill which allows the Six Counties in Ulster to vote themselves out and remain with the rest of Britain.
1920–21	Heavy fighting between the Auxiliaries (the Black and Tans) and the Irish Nationalist forces.
1921	July, King George V officially opens the Stormont Parliament in the Six Counties.
1921	December, the Anglo-Irish treaty signed.
1922	January, the treaty is ratified in Dail Eireann. The start of the Irish Civil War between pro-treaty majority and anti-treaty forces.
1922	November, executions of anti-treaty leaders by Free State in Dublin.
1923	End of Civil War.
1926	De Valera founds Fianna Fail.
1932	General Election. Fianna Fail win.
1937	Constitution of Eire.
1938	Agreement with Britain; economic disputes are ended. Britain gives up tributary and naval rights in 'Treaty' ports.

1939	IRA bombing campaign in Britain. Outbreak of Second World War; Eire is neutral.
1945	End of Second World War.
1948	General Election in Ireland. Defeat of Fianna Fail, and de Valera is out of office for first time in 16 years.
1952	Republic of Ireland declared and accepted by Britain, with a quali-fying guarantee of support to the Six Counties.
1956–62	IRA campaign in the North.
1968	First Civil Rights march.
1969	January, people's democracy march from Belfast to Derry. Marchers attacked at Burntollet Bridge.
1969	August, British troops sent to Derry.
1971 IRA	February, first British soldier killed by IRA. August, internment of suspects. Reforms to the RUC, and electoral system.
1972	30 January. British troops opened fire on marchers of the Derry Civil Rights Association in the Bogside area of Derry. Thirteen were killed in the event which became known as 'Bloody Sunday'.
1972	Direct Rule imposed from Westminster. Stormont Government and Parliament suspended.
1973	The Sunningdale Agreement. An Assembly established with power-sharing between different political leaders.
1974	Ulster Worker's Strike brings down Assembly. Direct Rule reimposed.
1981	Bobby Sands dies after 60-day hunger strike.
1985	Anglo-Irish Agreement.
1993	Downing Street Initiative.
1994	August—IRA Ceasefire.

Brennan, M., *Boyne Valley Vision* (Dolmen).

Craig, Maurice, *Classical Irish Houses of the Middle Size: Lost Demesnes* (Architectural Press).

Craig, Maurice, *Dublin 1660–1860* (Allen Figgis).

Crookshank, Anne and The Knight of Glin, *Painters of Ireland* c. *1660–1920* (Barrie & Jenkins).

De Breffny and Folliott, *Houses of Ireland* (Thames & Hudson).

De Breffny and Mott, *Castles of Ireland* (Thames & Hudson).

Further Reading

De Breffny and Mott, *Churches and Abbeys of Ireland* (Thames & Hudson).

De Paor, Maire, *Early Irish Art* (Aspect of Ireland Series).

Estyn Evans, E., *Prehistoric Ireland* (Batsford).

Harbison, P., Potterton, H. and Sheehy, J., *Irish Art and Architecture* (Thames & Hudson).

Henry, Françoise, *Early Christian Irish Art* (Mercier).

O'Riordain, S. P. O., *Antiquities of the Irish Countryside* (Methuen).

Sheehy, J., *Discovery of Ireland's Past* (Thames & Hudson).

White, *John Butler Yeats and the Irish Renaissance* (Dolmen).

Burkes Guide to Country Houses: Ireland (Burkes).

Guides and Topographical

Craig, Maurice and Knight of Glin, *Ireland Observed* (Mercier Press).

Harbison, Peter, *Guide to the National Monuments of Ireland* (Gill & Macmillan).

Mason, T. H., *The Islands of Ireland*.

Morton, H. V., *In Search of Ireland* (Methuen).

Murphy, Dervla, *A Place Apart* (Penguin).

O'Faolain, Sean, *An Irish Journey*.

Praeger, R., *The Way That I Went* (Figgins).

A Literary Map of Ireland (Wolfhound).

Irish Walk Guides

O'Suilleabhain, Sean, *No. 1 South West* (Gill & Macmillan).

Maps

Historical Map (Bartholomew).

Ireland Map, Bord Fáilte (Ordnance Survey).

Irish Family Names Map (Johnson & Bacon)—divided into North, East, South and West.

Ordnance Survey maps, 25 sheets—1:126720 (Half-Inch). (Sheet 5 covering Belfast is no longer available.)

Folklore, Music and Tradition

Cross, E., *The Tailor and Ansty* (Mercier).

Danaher, *Folktales of the Irish Countryside* (Mercier).

Estyn Evans, E., *Irish Folk Ways* (Routledge).

Flower, R., *The Irish Tradition* (Clarendon Press).

Gaffney, S. and Cashman, S., *Proverbs and Sayings of Ireland* (Wolfhound).

Gregory, Lady Isabella Augusta, *Gods and Fighting Men* (Smythe).

Healy, J. N., *Love Songs of the Irish* (Mercier)

Healy, J. N., *Percy French and his Songs* (Mercier).

Henry, S., *Tales from the West of Ireland* (Mercier).

Hyde, Douglas, *Beside the Fire* (Irish Academic Press).

Hyde, Douglas, *The Stone of Truth and other Irish Folktales* (Irish Academic Press).

O'Boyle, Sean, *The Irish Song Tradition* (Gilbert Dalton).

O'Connell, James, *The Meaning of the Irish Coast* (Blackstaff).

O'Faolain, S., *Short Stories* (Mercier).

O'Farrell, P., *Folktales of the Irish Coast* (Mercier).

O'Flaherty, Gerald, *A Book of Slang, Idiom and Wit* (O'Brien).

O'Keeffe, D. and Healy, J. N., *Book of Irish Ballads* (Mercier).

O'Sullivan, Sean, *Handbook of Irish Folklore*.

Wilde, William, *Irish Popular Superstitions* (Irish Academic Press).

Photography

Turner, B. S. and Estyn Evans, E., *Ireland's Eye: The Photographs of Robert John Welch* (Blackstaff).

Walker, B. M., O'Brien, A. and McMahon, S., *Faces of Ireland* (Appletree Press).

History and Literary History

Beckett, J. C., *The Making of Modern Ireland* (Faber paperback).

Corkery, Daniel, *Hidden Ireland* (Gill & Macmillan).

Cruise O'Brien, M. and C., *Concise History of Ireland* (Thames & Hudson).

Cruise O'Brien, Conor, *States of Ireland*.

Dudley Edwards, R., *A New History of Ireland* (Gill & Macmillan).

Dudley Edwards, R., *An Atlas of Irish History* (Methuen).

Foster, R. F., *Ireland 1600–1672* (Penguin).

Foster, R. F., *Modern Ireland 1600–1972* (OUP).

Foster, R. F. (ed.), *The Oxford History of Ireland* (OUP).

Kavanagh, P., *The Irish Theatre* (The Kerryman).

Kee, Robert, *The Green Flag* (Sphere).

MacLysaght, E., *Surnames of Ireland* (Irish Academic Press).

MacLysaght, E., *Irish Families: Their Names and Origins* (Figgins).

Maxwell, Constancia, *Country and Town under the Georges* (Dundalgan Press).

O'Connor, Frank, *The Backward Look: A Survey of Irish Literature.*

O'Farrell, P., *England and Ireland since 1800.*

O'Farrell, P., *How the Irish Speak English* (Mercier).

Stewart, A. T. O., *The Narrow Ground* (Faber).

Wallace, M., *A Short History of Ireland* (David & Charles).

Burkes Landed Gentry (Burkes).

Burkes Irish Family Records (Burkes).

Biography and Memoirs

Bence Jones, Mark, *Twilight of the Ascendancy* (Constable).

Butler Yeats, John, *Early Memories* (Irish Academic Press).

Chambers, Anne, *Granuaile: The Life and Times of Grace O'Malley* (Wolfhound).

Joyce, James, *Portrait of an Artist as a Young Man* (Longman).

Krause, David, *A Self Portrait of the Artist as a Man (Sean O'Casey through his letters)* (Dolmen).

Lyons, J. S., *Oliver St John Gogarty*, A Biography (Blackwater Press).

Moore, George, *Hail and Farewell* (Smythe).

Murphy, William, *The Yeats Family and the Pollexfens of Sligo* (Dolmen).

[**O'Crohan, Thomas**, The Islandman]

O'Sullivan, Maurice, *Twenty years a growing.*

Shuilleabhain, E. H., *Letters from the Great Blasket* (Mercier).

Somerville Larg, P., *Irish Eccentrics.*

Thomson, David, *Woodbrook* (Penguin).

Yeats, W. B., *Synge and the Ireland of his Time* (Irish Academic Press).

All the *Irish Heritage* Series (Eason).

Fiction

Berry, James, *Tales of the West of Ireland* (ed. Horgan, M. Gertrude) (Dolmen).

Birmingham, George, any novels (Blackstaff, BBC and others).

Bowen, Elizabeth, *Elizabeth Bowen's Irish Stories* (Poolbeg).

Boyle, Patrick, *At Night all Cats are Grey*.

Carleton, William, *The Black Prophet* (Irish University Press).

Crone, Anne, *Bridie Steen* (Blackstaff).

Durcan, Paul, Yeats, W. B., Heaney, Seamus, Simmons, James and Clarke, Austin, *The Faber Book of Irish Verse*.

Edgeworth, Maria, *The Absentee* (Oxford University Press).

Farrell, J. G., *Troubles* (Penguin).

Friel, Brien, Stories and plays (Penguin and others).

Hanna Bell, Sam, any novels (Blackstaff, BBCand others).

Kickham, C., *Knocknagow, Or the Homes of Tipperary* (Mercier).

Lavin, Mary, any stories (Penguin).

O'Brien, Carpenter (ed.) and Fallon, *The Writers, A Sense of Ireland*.

O'Brien, Kate, any novels (Blackstaff, BBC and others).

O'Connor, Frank, *Guests of the Nation* (Poolbeg).

Somerville, Edith and Ross, Martin, novels, especially *The Great House at Inver* (Zodiac Press) and *The Real Charlotte* (Arrow Books).

Synge, J. M., all the plays.

Trevor, William, any novels (Penguin and others).

The Penguin Book of Irish Verse and *The Penguin Book of Irish Short Stories* (Penguin).

Cooking, Crafts, Flora and Fauna

Anything by **Theodora Fitzgibbon** (look out for her recipes in the *Irish Times* on Saturdays).

Heron, Marianne, *The Hidden Gardens of Ireland* (Gill & Macmillan).

Lewis, C. A., *Hunting in Ireland*.

O'Brien, Louise, *Crafts of Ireland* (Gilbert Dillon).

O'Reilly, Peter, *Trout & Salmon Loughs of Ireland* (Harper Collins).

O'Reilly, Peter, *Trout & Salmon Rivers of Ireland* (Merlin Unwin Books).

Reeves-Smyth, Terence, *Irish Gardens* (Appletree Press).

Ruttledge, R. F., *Irish Birds*.

Webb, D. A., *An Irish Flora*.

Ballymaloe Cook Book.

Traditional Irish Recipes (Appletree Press).

Bridgestones Guides to Where to stay and eat in Ireland (Estragon Press).

Gill & Macmillan do a series of fishing guides on Game, Coarse and Sea Angling.

230

Major entries for counties are printed in **bold**. Numbers in *italic* indicate maps.

Index

china 31
Church of Ireland *see* religion
Ciaran of Cape Clear, St 153
Civil Rights Movement 91, 98
Civil War (Irish) 66, 88–9, 153
Clancy, Willie 191
Clan-na-Gael 83
Clare 179–96, *180–81*
    activities 22–3, 193–4
    eating out 196
    entertainment 194
    festivals 64, 183–4
    history 74, 182–3
    shopping 32, 192–3
    tourist information 183
    travel 183
    where to stay 185, 194–5
Clare, Glens of (Limerick) 119
Clare family *see* de Clare
Clarke, Harry 184
Clear *see* Cape Clear
climate 14
clochans 127, 134, 139, 207, 210
Cloghane (Kerry) 140
Clonakilty (Cork) 154, 155, 167, 170–72, 174, 177
Clonkeen (Limerick) 119
Clontarf, battle of 71, 182, 184
Cloon, Lough (Kerry) 134
Cloonee Loughs (Kerry) 129
Cloyne (Cork) 163
coaches *see* bus travel
Cobh (Cork) 154, 155, 160–61, 171–4
Collins, Michael 65–6, 88, 153

Colmcille (or Columba), St 70, 105, 107
Columba, St *see* Colmcille, St
Columban, St 70, 105
Comhaltas Ceoltóirí Eireann 52–3
Connor Pass (Kerry) 140
consulates 15
cookery schools 37, 59
Coppinger's Court (Cork) 167
Cork 149–78, *150–51*
    activities 21–3, 28–9, 59, 171–2
    eating out 163, 166, 176–7
    entertainment 178
    festivals 59, 155
    gardens 59–60
    history 61, 152–3
    shopping 163, 169–71
    tourist information 154
    travel 2–6, 8–10, 153–4
    where to stay 163, 172–5
Cork, Richard Boyle, first Earl of 153, 163, 167
Cork Airport 2–3, 26, 153, 154
Cork City ix–x, 155–61, *156–7*
    activities 21–2, 28–9, 171–2
    architecture 58–9, 156–61
    eating out 158, 175–6
    entertainment 178
    excursions 159–61
    festivals 59, 155
    gardens 59–60
    history 152–3, 155–6

parking 11, 24
shopping 31, 158, 169–70
tourist information 154
travel 153–4
where to stay 172
Cormac MacArt 70, 200
Corrofin (Clare) 187, 195
cottages (rented) 44
country (community) holidays 7
country houses 42–3, 55–7
Courtmacsherry (Cork) 167, 170, 171, 174
craft shops 30–32
craft summer school 37
Crag Cave (Kerry) 141
Craggaunowen (Clare) 186
Crag Liath (Clare) 184–5
crannogs 69, 207
Cratloe Woods House (Clare) 185, 192
Creagh Gardens (Cork) 168
credit cards 19, 26
crime 24, 25
Cromwell, Oliver 74–5, 183
Croom (Limerick) 112, 118
crosses, high 101, 208
Crosshaven (Cork) 28, 162, 171
cruising (inland) 33
    see also sailing
Cú Chulainn 138, 192, 198, 200
curraghs 69, 139–40, 211
Currane, Lough (Kerry) 143
currency 26
customs 7–8, 20–21
cycling 7, 12, 44
    cycle hire 12, 113, 128, 142, 154, 183

folk arts 53
  festivals 53, 155
  folk park 185
folklore *see* fairy people
food 17–19, 32, 60
Fota (Cork) 58, 161, 172
Foynes (Limerick) 118
France 78–80
Francini brothers 58, 159–60, 194
Freach (Clare) 191
French, Percy 187
Fungi (dolphin) 138, 143

Gaelic Athletic Association 35, 86
Gaelic language 86, 198–9, 216–18
Gaelic League 86, 216
Gaelic literature ix, 118, 128, 139, 199, 216–17
Gaels *see* Celts
Gallarus, Oratory of (Kerry) 140, 207
Galway hookers 29
gardens 59–60
Garinish Island (Cork) 169
Garrettstown (Cork) 162
George III, King of England 80
Geraldines 113, 118
Germany 83, 87
Ginkel, General Godert van 75–6, 114–15
Gladstone, W. E. 85
Glandore (Cork) 167, 173
Glanmire (Cork) 58, 159–60, 169
glassware 31
Glenbeigh (Kerry) 21, 136
Glengarriff (Cork) 154, 169, 174, 176, 177

Gleninagh (Clare) 189
Glennagalt Valley (Kerry) 138
Glens of Clare (Limerick) 119
Glenstal, Mansion of (Limerick) 119
Glin (Limerick) 118
Glin, Knight of 118
gods *see* Tuatha Dé Danaan
Goleen (Cork) 168, 176
golf 21–3
  list of clubs 22–3
  see also under counties (activities)
Gougane Barra (Cork) 166
Grainne 136, 200, 202
Graney, Lough (Clare) 185, 193
Grattan, Henry 78
Grattan's Parliament 78, 80
Great Hunger 82
Gregory, Lady Augusta 185, 216
greyhound racing 116
guest houses 42
guides 23, 50
Guinness 19, 191
Gur, Lough (Limerick) 119

Hag of Beare viii–ix
Hag's Head (Clare) 192
hang–gliding 34
Healy, Michael 140
heritage centres 25
hill–walking *see* walking
historic houses 55–7
history 55–7, 67–98, 198–9, 221–4
hitch–hiking 12, 46
Holland, John P. 190

Holy Well of St Brigid (Clare) 190
Home Rule 80, 85–7
horse–drawn caravans 36
horse–racing 34, 36, 131
horse–riding *see* riding
hostels 39, 44–5
hotels 39–42
hovercraft trips 113, 115
Huguenots 101
Hunt Collection 116
hunting 34–5, 120, 172, 194
hurley 35, 86
Hyde, Douglas 86, 164, 216

Ightermurragh Castle (Cork) 163
Imbolc 104
Inacullin (Cork) 169
Inch, Strand of (Kerry) 138
Inchiquin, Barons 186, 194
Inchiquin, Lough (Clare) 187
Ine, Lough (Cork) 168
Iniscealtra (Holy Island; Clare) 185–6
Innisfallen Island and Abbey (Kerry) 132
insects 23
insurance 25
  emergencies 24
interpretative centres 25
IRA *see* Irish Republican Army
Irish coffee 20
Irish language *see* Gaelic language
Irish people 48–9, 53, 68, 102–3, 217
Irish Republic
  Constitution 89, 94, 96

'Cadogan Guides have a reputation as the outstanding series for the independent traveller who doesn't want to follow the crowd...'

Daily Telegraph

'The quality of writing in this British series is exceptional... The Cadogan Guides can be counted on for interesting detail and informed recommendations.'

Going Places

'The characteristic of all these guides is a heady mix of the eminently practical, a stimulating description of the potentially already familiar, and an astonishing quantity of things we'd never thought of, let alone seen.'

The Art Quarterly

'Cadogan Guides are entertaining... They go a little deeper than most guides, and the balance of infectious enthusiasm and solid practicality should appeal to first-timers and experienced travellers alike.'

Michael Palin

'...the guidebooks that are widely acclaimed for their wit, originality and revealing insights.'

Sunday Telegraph

'...proper companions...amusingly written with fascinating snippets on history and culture.'

Woman magazine

'Perhaps the nicest thing about these Cadogan Guides is that they are very informal and relaxed. They strike a happy balance between background and sightseeing information, plus lots of helpful historical notes and amusing anecdotes.'

The Good Book Guide

'Acceptably enthusiastic, never gushing, firmly factual yet as absorbing as a really good novel.'

The Art Quarterly

Country Guides

THE CARIBBEAN & THE BAHAMAS
CENTRAL AMERICA
CENTRAL ASIA
ECUADOR, THE GALAPAGOS & COLOMBIA
EGYPT
FRANCE: THE SOUTH OF FRANCE
FRANCE: SOUTHWEST FRANCE; Dordogne, Lot & Bordeaux
GERMANY
GERMANY: BAVARIA
GUATEMALA & BELIZE
INDIA
IRELAND
ITALY
ITALY: NORTHWEST ITALY
ITALY: SOUTH ITALY
ITALY: THE BAY OF NAPLES & THE AMALFI COAST

ITALY: LOMBARDY, Milan & the Italian Lakes
ITALY: TUSCANY, UMBRIA & THE MARCHES
JAPAN
MEXICO
MOROCCO
PORTUGAL
SCOTLAND
SCOTLAND'S HIGHLANDS & ISLANDS
SOUTH AFRICA
SPAIN
SPAIN: SOUTHERN SPAIN
SYRIA & LEBANON
TUNISIA
TURKEY
TURKEY: WESTERN TURKEY

City Guides

AMSTERDAM
BERLIN
BRUSSELS, BRUGES, GHENT & ANTWERP
FLORENCE, SIENA, PISA & LUCCA
LONDON
MOSCOW & ST PETERSBURG

NEW YORK
PARIS
PRAGUE
ROME
VENICE & THE VENETO

Island Guides

BALI
THE CARIBBEAN: N. E. CARIBBEAN The Leeward Islands
THE CARIBBEAN: S. E. CARIBBEAN The Windward Islands
CYPRUS
GREEK ISLANDS

GREECE: THE CYCLADES
GREECE: THE DODECANESE
GREECE: THE IONIAN ISLANDS
MADEIRA
MALTA, COMINO & GOZO
SICILY

Also Available

HEALTHY TRAVEL: BUGS BITES & BOWELS

TRAVEL BY CARGO SHIP